Islamic Upbringing of Children

I0568141

al-Burāq Publications

AL-BURĀQ
Heighten The Mind

Copyright

ISBN: 978-1-956276-15-2

Published by al-Burāq Publications.

Ordering Information

We offer discounts and promotions for wholesale purchases, non-profit organizations, and other educational institutions. Contact us at the email below for further information.

www.al-Buraq.org
publications@al-Buraq.org

First printed edition | April 2022

Dedication

The publication of this book was made possible through the generous support of our donors.

Please recite *Sūrah al-Fātiha* and ask God for the Divine reward (*thawāb*) to be conferred upon the donors and also the souls of all the deceased in whose memory their loved ones have contributed graciously towards the publication of *Islamic Upbringing of Children*.

We begin by giving all praise and thanks to God for giving us the tawfiq to translate this book. He has guided us and without Him, we would not have been guided to the straight path embodied by the Prophet Muḥammad and the Ahl al-Bayt.

This book is dedicated to all the scholars, martyrs and believers who worked tirelessly to promote the pure Muḥammadan path.

We want to also give our thanks and appreciation to all believers from around the world and acknowledge the team which helped al-Burāq Publications complete this work, spending countless hours to make its publication possible. Please recite Sūrah al-Fātiḥah on behalf of them and their marḥūmīn.

This book is dedicated in honor of Imām al-Ḥusayn and the following individuals. Please remember them in your prayers and may God have mercy on them and their loved ones.

Afifeh Awad
Agha Akber Hussain
Al-Sayed Sobh Hamid Sobh
Ali Ahmed Ftouni
Ali Haider
Alya Yazback
Athar Shigri
Band-e-Khuda
Basima Awad
Ghassan Kassem
Gulamabbas Rattansi
Haji Sobhia Aoun
Haji Wafa Fakih-Hijazi
Hajj Ali Hammoud
Hajj Ali Hijazi
Hajj Farid Hamka
Hajj Hassan Sobh
Hajj Mahdi Ali Hijazi
Hajj Mohamad Baydoun
Hajj Mohammad Hussaini
Hajj Sami Ftouni
Hajji Amneh Sobh-Ftouni
Hajji Fawzieh Dabaja
Hajji Hiam Hojeije
Hajji Iman Elsaghir
Hajji Latifa Dabaja
Hajji Naziha Shukr
Hajji Samira Ghamlouche
Hajji Zakiya Khalifeh
Ibrahim Mazeh
Ibtisam Hammoud
Lawahez Chahine
Mahmoud Hijazi
Mahmoud Tiba
Majeda Nasserdine
Makarem Awad
Mohamed Ali Hijazi
Munawwar Jehan
Shahīd Ibrāhīm Hadi
Shaker Fawzi Khayat
Shandar Fatima
Shuhada e Millat e Jaffaria
Surraya Hamdani
Syed Abbas Kazmi
Syed Mehdi Rizvi
Syed Nawab Kazmi
Syed Nurul jafri
Syed Tasleem Fatima
Syed Tehmaaz Kazmi
Syeda Khursheed Najafi
Turfah Sobh
Yasmin Abbas
Zeinab Abdullah

Terms of Respect

The following Arabic phrases have been used throughout this book in their respective places to show the reverence which the noble personalities deserve.

عزّ وجلّ

Used for God, meaning:
Exalted and Sublime (Perfect) is He

صلى الله عليه وآله

Used for Prophet Muḥammad, meaning:
Blessings from God be upon him and his family

عليه السلام

Used for a man (singular) of a high status, meaning:
Peace be upon him

عليها السلام

Used for a woman (singular) of a high status, meaning:
Peace be upon her

عليهما السلام

Used for men/women (dual) of a high status, meaning:
Peace be upon them both

عليهم السلام

Used for men and/or women (plural) of a high status, meaning:
Peace be upon them all

قدس سره

Used for a deceased scholar, meaning:
May his resting [burial] place remain pure

عجل الله تعالى فرجه الشريف

Used for Imām Muḥammad al-Mahdī, meaning:
May God hasten his return

Duaa al-Hujja

اللهم كن لوليك الحجة بن الحسن صلواتك

عليه وعلى آبائه في هذه الساعة وفي كل

ساعة وليا وحافظا وقائدا وناصرا ودليلا

وعينا حتى تسكنه أرضك طوعا وتمتعه فيها طويلا

O God, be, for Your representative, the Hujjat (proof), son of al-Hasan, Your blessings be upon him and his forefathers, in this hour and in every hour: a guardian, a protector, a leader, a helper, a proof, and an eye - until You make him live on the Earth, in obedience (to You), and cause him to live in it for a long time.

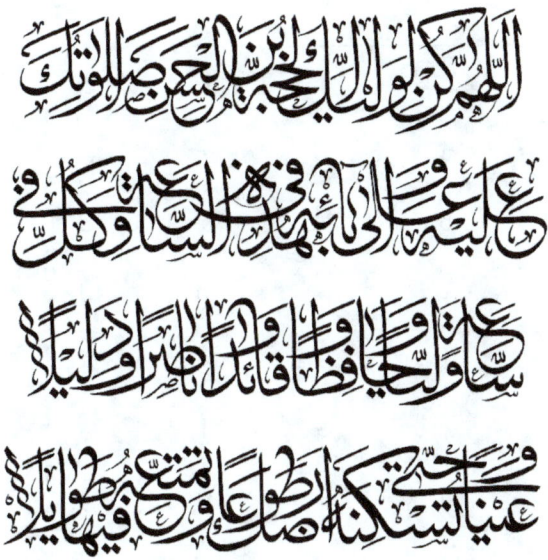

Transliteration Table

The method of transliteration of Islamic terminology from the Arabic language has been carried out according to the standard transliteration table below.

ء	ʾ	ر	r	ف	f
ا	a	ز	z	ق	q
ب	b	س	s	ك	k
ت	t	ش	sh	ل	l
ث	th	ص	ṣ	م	m
ج	j	ض	ḍ	ن	n
ح	ḥ	ط	ṭ	و	w
خ	kh	ظ	ẓ	ه	h
د	d	ع	ʿ	ي	y
ذ	dh	غ	gh		
Long Vowels					
ا	ā	و	ū	ي	ī
Short Violets					
ـَ	a	ـُ	u	ـِ	i

Table of Contents

Publisher's Preface

بسم الله الرحمن الرحيم

In the Name of God, the Most Gracious,
the Most Merciful

Praise be to God ﷻ, Lord of the worlds. And may the peace and blessings of God be upon our master Muḥammad ﷺ and his pure family عليهم السلام.

Educational scholars have attempted, lately and in the past, to find a comprehensive educational approach for identifying the methods, values and criteria that are necessary to study what is appropriate for the different phases of childhood. And they had exerted great, hard and constant efforts before they managed to reach hypotheses, suggestions and recommendations that are considered – from a scientific viewpoint – valuable and beneficial. However, despite these efforts, they were not able to identify an accurate approach that can be relied upon in resolving the complicated problems that surround that sensitive phase within the human timeline. Moreover, they didn't manage to overcome the difficulties that kept increasing day after day, and which were encountered by educational institutions, fathers, mothers and educators in this field.

It is rather unfortunate that many Muslims, especially those who work in the educational field, turn to western educational schools so they can adopt their educational approaches, and yet remain oblivious to the fact that the Islamic Sharia includes an integrated educational approach that resolves and provides effective premises and methods for all the issues which they couldn't unravel, in addition to the fact that the biography of the great Prophet ﷺ and that of his pure household ﵈ are an inexhaustible source of commandments, instructions, teachings and guidance which – if used in the education field and implemented in its various areas – are sufficient to establish the most superb values and ideals within the child.

The Islamic approach whose features and grounds can be identified by referring to the Noble Qur'ān, the pure Prophetic Sunnah and what was narrated on behalf of the infallible Imāms ﵈, aims at achieving a balanced education for the child which starts before he becomes a fetus in his mother's womb and continues until he reaches the age of independence, while passing through the phases of pregnancy, birth giving and breastfeeding, and early childhood.

And this book – child education in Islam – is concerned with child education and his preparation on a psychological, intellectual and behavioral level, in a concise and simple way, while referring to the verses of the Noble Qur'ān, the narrations on behalf of the great Messenger, our Prophet Muḥammad ﷺ and the pure Ahl al-Bayt ﵈, and benefitting from recent scientific studies in this field. Given the fact that we elaborated on the educational foundations that are specific to child education in a focused scientific study that was materialized in a book of two parts entitled: "the new approach in child education", our center is glad to provide this enjoyable and beneficial study by which it can contribute to the service of educational institutions, fathers, mothers and workers within the field of child education. For, every father or mother desperately wants to be proud of their children and feel like they have accomplished their hopes and dreams. And every father or mother loves to see the lights of goodness, prosperity and success shining in their children's life; for, this is one of the reasons behind a person's happiness. It's narrated that the Messenger of God ﷺ said: "It is of a man's happiness to have a virtuous child."[1] The narrations focused a lot on the term "virtuous child", one of which was narrated on behalf of Abi Abdillah ؑ where he said: "the Messenger of God ﷺ said: a virtuous child is a sweet basil flower[2] that is granted from God and distributed amongst his servants."[3]

Moreover, a person becomes sorrowful, sad and distressed if his child wasn't virtuous – or was rather an immoral child. The narrations referred to him as "the immoral child". For, in the same way a child can be an adornment to his parents, an immoral child can be a disgrace to his parents so much that they can be shamed and blamed by the people in the community for his behavior, morality and conduct. It was narrated that Imām

---

[1] al-Kulaynī, Shaykh Muḥammad ibn Yaʿqūb, Al-Kāfī, the commentary of ʿAlī Akbar Ghafāri, Tehran, Dar al Kutub al Islāmiyyah, 1365 AH, 4th edition, Vol. 6, p. 3

[2] A sweet basil flower (*Rayhana*): it is a type of plant that has a beautiful scent.

[3] Ibid., Vol. 6, p. 2

'Alī   had said: "An immoral child destroys one's honor and disgraces the ancestors."[4]

Finally, we ask God to grant everyone success in benefitting from this book and other books that we have in the field of Islamic family education.

And Praise be to God, Lord of the Worlds.

al-Burāq Publications

---

[4] al-Mirzā al-Nūrī, Mustadrak al-Wasā'il, the institute of Ahl al-Bayt   for the revival of the legacy, Qom, 1409 AH, 1st edition, Vol. 15, p. 215, ḥadīth 18039

Lesson One

Islamic Upbringing and its Objectives

Lesson Objectives

By the end of this lesson, the student should:

1. Be acquainted with the linguistic and terminological meanings of upbringing.
2. Be able to distinguish between upbringing and teaching.
3. Get introduced to the purpose of child upbringing in Islam.

Preamble

The upbringing process is the most honorable responsibility shouldered by man. How else, when it's the mission granted by God ﷻ to the Prophets عليهم السلام and His friends عليهم السلام. And upbringing has its fundamental role in the life of nations. Opinions have varied in regards to the concept of upbringing and its objectives; so, what is the meaning of upbringing? And what are its objectives?

The Meaning of Upbringing

There are plenty of definitions, in the Arabic language, for the term "upbringing", of which we will mention that which is adopted by many linguistic scholars: Ibn Sida says – in the meaning of Rabb (*Lord*): "It's originally derived from the word tarbiya (*upbringing*), which is nurturing... And the owner is referred to as Rabb (*Lord*) because he owns the right to nurture the – nurtured – thing. And the same goes to the captain of the ship who is referred to as Rabbān because he manages it and is based on it..."[5]

And some linguistic scholars considered that the origin of the term Rabb (*Lord*) is: Reforming something and being based on it.[6]

---

[5] Ibn Sida, Abu al-Ḥasan ibn Ismail, the Andalusian linguistic, Al Mukhassas, examined by the committee of the revival of the Arabian heritage, Beirut-Lebanon, Dar Ihyaā al Turāth al-'Arabi, L.T, L.T, Vol. 5, chapter 2, p. 154-155

[6] Ibn Zakariyyā, Ahmad ibn Fares, the dictionary of Maqayees al Lugha, examined by Abdul Salam Muḥammad Harun, Qom, the Office of Islamic Media, 1404 AH, L.T, Vol. 2, p. 482-484

And some Islamic educators defined it as: "... the gradual upbringing of the human being in all his aspects, in accordance with the Islamic approach, in pursuit of gaining happiness in both abodes."[7]

And we can define upbringing as the process through which the child's guardian - or he who has the latter's permission to do so – creates the child's identity (personality), through speech and action, in all its sides (body, heart and mind), and in all its aspects (social, economic, political ...) in pursuit of leading him to his perfection... in a gradual and sustainable manner, by adopting a set of procedures, methods and techniques that are extracted or compatible with Islamic resources.

As for upbringing according to the terminology adopted by some western scientists and philosophers, it is: "... everything we do for ourselves, and everything that others do for us, with the purpose of bringing us closer to our primordial nature."[8]

And the term "upbringing" is used in contemporary sciences in one of two meanings:

First: Upbringing in its general context: and it includes the upbringing of a human being in the different aspects of his personality and life, and "it involves every process that helps in shaping the individual's mind, morality and body."

---

[7] Al-Hazimi, Khāled ibn Hāmed, Osul al-Tarbiya al-Islāmiyya, Medina, Dar 'ālam al Kutub, 1420 AH- 2000 AD, 1st edition, p. 19

[8] Al-Rashdān, Abdullah, Educational Sociology, Amman, Dar al-Shuruq, 2008 AD, L.T, p. 25

Second: Upbringing in its specific context: and "it means instilling information and cognitive skills through specific institutions that are established for this purpose."[9]

Synonyms for Upbringing in the Noble Qur'ān and Religious Texts

The Noble Qur'ān and the Sunnah of Ahl al-Bayt ﷺ are considered the two fundamental sources from which the finest upbringing curriculum is derived within the upbringing process. And there are synonyms that are mentioned in the Qur'ānic and narrated texts in relation to the upbringing process, which we will mention briefly:

1. Purification (*Tazkiyah*): ﴾*God certainly favored the faithful when He raised up among them an apostle from among themselves to recite to them His signs and to purify them, and to teach them the Book and wisdom*﴿[10]

And purification is when a person does all that makes him or others virtuous, pure and righteous.[11]

---

[9] Mursi, Muḥammad Munir, Osul al-Tarbiya, Cairo, Alam Al Kotob, 2009 AH, L.T, p. 8

[10] Sūrah Al Imran, verse 164

[11] al-Ṭūsī, Shaykh Muḥammad ibn al-Ḥasan, Al-Tibyān fī Tafsīr al-Qur'ān, revised and edited by Ahmad Habīb Kassīr, Qom, Islamic media office, 1409 AH, Vol. 1, p. 467 and al-Ṭabrisī, Shaykh al-Faḍl ibn al-Ḥasan, Majmaʿ al-bayān fī Tafsīr al-Qur'ān, Tehran, Intisharat Nasser Khasrou, Dar al-Ma'rifah, 1406 AH-1986 AD, 1st edition, Vol. 10, p. 6

2. Cleansing (*Tatheer*): like when He ﷻ says: ﴾*Take charity from their possessions to cleanse them and purify them thereby*﴿[12]

And purity, linguistically, comes in the context of wholesomeness and absence of impurities.[13]

3. Guidance: His saying ﷻ: ﴾*And indeed you guide to a straight path*﴿[14]

The Prophet ﷺ said: "By God, to have one man guided by you is better for you than red camels."[15]

And guidance, linguistically, means direction. It implies direction towards the path of maturity and leading one to his desired destination.[16]

---

[12] Sūrah Tawba, verse 103

[13] Ibn Zakariyya, the dictionary of Maqayīs al-Lugha, Vol. 3, p. 428

[14] Sūrah Al-Shoura, verse 52

[15] al-Suyūṭī, ʿAbd al-Raḥmān ibn Abī Bakr, al-Jāmi' al-Saghīr, Dar al-Fikr, Beirut, 1401 AH – 1981 AD, 1st edition, Vol. 2, p. 714, ḥadīth 9606

[16] al-ʿAskarī, Abu Hilal, the dictionary of al-Furouq al Lughawiyyah, organized by Shaykh Bayt God Bayat, Qom, the institute of Islamic publishing which is linked to the group of teachers in Qom, 1412 AH, 1st edition, Vol. 42, and Al Ragheb al-Asfahanī, al-Ḥusayn ibn Muḥammad, Mufradata Alfath Al-Qur'ān, Beirut, al-Amīra for printing and publishing, 1431 AH-2010 AD, 1st edition, p. 705

4. Refinement: Imām 'Alī ﷺ said: "Being busy with self-refinement is more virtuous."[17]

5. Discipline: Imām 'Alī ﷺ said: "The purpose of moral purification is good discipline."[18]

Upbringing and Teaching

There's a difference between the upbringing process on one hand, and teaching on the other hand. For, teaching represents part of upbringing - and it's an introduction to it; whereas upbringing in its larger scale includes teaching and other processes...

1. Teaching (*ta'līm*) in the Arabic language corresponds to the balance taf'īl of the term knowledge (*'ilm*), which means the perception of a thing in its truth.[19]

And teaching (*ta'līm*) means to give and impart knowledge to others, by which they can rid themselves of ignorance. And it is a process that is directed towards one's mind and intellectual side.

2. As for upbringing: it is an integrated developmental process that addresses all a person's powers and faculties, and aims at causing change in his behavior for the better.

---

[17] Al-Wasity, 'Alī ibn Muḥammad, 'Uyun al-Hikam w al-Mawae'dh, examined by Ḥusayn al-Ḥusaynī al-Berjandī, LM, Dar al-Hadīth, LT,1st edition, p. 47

[18] Ibid., p. 281

[19] Al-Ragheb al-Asfahanī, Mufradat Alfadh al-Qur'ān, p. 475

And so, it has become a common misunderstanding amongst some people that upbringing and teaching are the same process. For, teaching is one of the introductions to upbringing; and even if it has a fundamental and dynamic role in shaping a child's personality, nonetheless, this doesn't mean that every upbringing process is preceded by teaching. For example, nourishing and taking care of a child is – in itself – nurturing; however, it doesn't include any teaching position.

Likewise, the school in which a child spends a long period of time remains one of the many influential factors in the upbringing process, and a part of it.

And Islamic upbringing includes, both, teaching and self-purification; and this is manifested in the tolerant Sharia where the Almighty addresses the most perfect educator by saying:

﴾As We sent to you an Apostle from among yourselves, who recites to you Our signs, and purifies you, and teaches you the Book and wisdom, and teaches you what you did not know﴿[20]

Upbringing and Socialization

Some educational researchers have gotten confused between the terms 'upbringing' and 'socialization'; and so, it became necessary to distinguish the two.

For example, some define upbringing, according to the social dimension, as: "the intentional or unintentional process created by society for the sake of raising new generations therein, in a

[20] Sūrah al-Baqarah, verse 151

way that makes them aware of their duties and roles within society."[21]

And this interpretation is closer to socialization than upbringing; for, the former involves enabling the child to adapt to the social environment he lives in, in regards to the habits, traditions, behaviors, attitudes, values and others.

And if we compare upbringing to socialization, the latter will comprise a part of the upbringing process which aims at leading the child to his perfection in all the aspects of his personality, not only the social one.

Moreover, socialization is a reflection of the culture of a given community; whereas the upbringing process aims to make the child adhere to the belief and value-based system of Islam which may oppose the prevailing culture of the community in which the child lives.

Upbringing and Ethics (Moral Science)

Now that the meaning of upbringing has been established, it becomes clear that there's a difference between the latter and ethics. For, the purpose of ethics is to build the internal spiritual content of a person. Therefore, all its focus is directed towards this aspect of a child's personality, and it disregards the other aspects.

Whereas upbringing is more comprehensive than ethics, in a way that it addresses all the aspects of a child's personality.

---

[21] Fahmy, Muḥammad Saif al-Dīn, lectures on the principles on upbringing, Cairo, faculty of education in the university of al-Azhar, 1978 AD, L.T, p. 17

The Purpose of Child Upbringing in Islam

It is a crucial need for the nurturer and the nurtured person to know the purpose of the upbringing process. And this knowledge will support the nurturer in leading the nurtured person towards this purpose, which will make the latter aware of what is needed from him and trigger his motivation towards upbringing.[22]

And 'purpose', linguistically, is a name for every high thing...[23], as for terminology, it was defined as: "the aim or result which is achieved after exerting a certain effort."[24]

And the primary purpose of child upbringing in Islam is: "leading the - nurtured– child to the perfection for which he is prepared." And accordingly, the educator must comprehend the purpose of the upbringing process so that he may take the hand of the child and lead him towards his true perfection.

And since the topic of upbringing rotates around "Man and Child", then the objectives of the upbringing process can be divided - according to the internal factors of which the human personality is composed - into the following objectives:

---

22 Nashawaty, Abdul Majīd, Educational Psychology, Amman, Dar al-Furqan, 1423 AH – 2003 AD, 4th edition, p. 106-195-196

23 Al-Jawhary, Ismail ibn Hamad, al-Sihah Taj al-Lugha wa Sihah al-Arabiyya, examined by Ahmad Abd al-Ghafour Attar, Beirut, Dar al-'Ilm lil Malayīn, 1407 AH-1987 AD, 4th edition, Vol. 4, p. 1442

24 Al-Zaghoul, Imad Abdul Rahīm, Introduction of Educational Psychology, Amman, Dar al Shurouq, 2012 AD, 1st edition, p. 42

1. The intellectual – ideological objectives: It is related to the intellectual and cognitive side of a child's personality. It focuses on all that a child believes in in regards to any topic and on how he views things around him.

2. The heart-related and spiritual objectives: It's associated with the heart-related aspect of a child's personality. Its purpose is to create tendencies and emotions, establish spiritual motivation and direct the child's tendencies and desires towards positive things; and from another side, to create repulsion and repugnance towards negative things.

3. The physical-behavioral objectives: It is related to the physical side of a child's personality. And it aims at developing his bodily side and training it on the movement skills needed to achieve the required goals in this respect.

Moreover, an objective has three formal divisions, which are:

1. The final objective: It is the highest goal sought by the nurturer which doesn't have a goal superior to it. And reaching the final objective – which is true perfection – is not limited within a period of time; and it is the responsibility of the nurturer, in this regard, to provide the child with preparations and actualize the potentials that will turn him into a Godly human being who is close to God ﷻ by the time he reaches the age of duty.

2. The intermediate objective: It is the objective that acts as an intermediary through which a person can reach another

higher goal.[25] And this objective focuses on the supplementary excellences through which a child can reach true perfection, such as creating –for the child – the habit of acting according to common manners with his parents, which include obedience and respect... And these excellences are a liaison that leads the child – through constant practice - to true perfection.

3. The behavioral objective: It is the objective through which the nurtured person accomplishes partial work within a specific time frame.[26]

And the realization of the final objective is not required, intellectually or religiously, within a specific period of time. For, upbringing is a long and gradual process; and it provides the child with capacities and actualizes his potentials to make him a Godly human being by the time he reaches the age of obligation.

True and Supplementary Perfection

Perfection – which is the realization of the desired goal and aimed objective - is divided into two parts:

1. True perfection: And it means the attainment of the position of divine proximity in its different levels.

---

[25] Al-ʿAjami, Muḥammad al-Ḥasanein, Educational Management and Strategy Theory and Practice, Amman, Dar al-Masīrah, 1434 AH – 2013 AD, 3rd edition, p. 60

[26] Al-Zaghoul, An Introduction to Educational Psychology, p. 44

2. Supplementary perfection: And it means the attainment of a thing's perfection according to its nature, such as a child's attainment of a healthy and disease-free life. This, in itself, is considered a supplementary perfection for the child according to the demands of his disposition and primordial nature.

Therefore, every process that provides a child with correct information and creates for him good habits and beneficial movement and intellectual skills... is considered to be partial and true upbringing along the path that leads to the fulfillment of the Islamic upbringing.

Main Concepts

The opinion which was adopted by many linguistic scholars in regards to the definition of upbringing is that it means: upbringing.

Upbringing, according to the scholars' terminology, is: leading the pupil to the perfection - which he's prepared for - in all the aspects of his life.

The chosen opinion in defining upbringing is: the process through which the child's guardian - or he who has the latter's permission to do so – creates[27] the child's identity (personality), or develops his aptitudes and specific potentials, through speech and action, in all the aspects of his life.

---

[27] The term creates is borrowed from His ﷻ saying: ﴾*And you will be created in my image*﴿, Sūrah Taha, verse 39

The Noble Qur'ān and the Sunnah of Ahl al-Bayt 🕮 are considered the two fundamental sources from which the finest upbringing curriculum is derived within the upbringing process. And the Qur'ān and narrations spoke of upbringing using different expressions, such as purification, cleansing, guidance, teaching...

Upbringing and teaching are two different processes. Teaching represents only part of upbringing, and it's an introduction for it. Whereas, upbringing, in its larger scale, encompasses teaching and other processes...

Socialization is a reflection of society's culture; whereas the upbringing process is a belief and value-based system which aims at adhering the child to this system irrespective of the nature of the society he lives in.

And the main purpose of child upbringing in Islam is: "leading the child – who is undergoing upbringing – to the perfection for which he is prepared."

Lesson Two

The Prenatal Stage

Lesson Objectives

By the end of this lesson, the student should:

1. Realize that the child has the right to the "legitimacy and purity of birth".
2. Know the rights of the fetus before he is born.
3. Be acquainted with the etiquettes of the private relationship between the spouses.

Preamble

God ﷻ says: *﴾He produced you from the earth, and since you were fetuses in the bellies of your mothers﴿*[28] A mother's womb is the primary environment in which a child starts paving his way towards the light of life; for, he spends nine months therein. And one of the stations that stand on the path of child education, even before the establishment of his life-germ (*Nutfah*), is the sexual relationship between the spouses. Islam has taken care of all the stages that affect the shaping of the child's identity whether they are prenatal or post-natal. Sayyid al-Khumaynī says in this regard: "The observance of the etiquettes of marriage, intercourse and pregnancy, in addition to the conditions of breastfeeding, the wellbeing of the husband and wife's temperament and the purity of their souls, has a special effect on the serenity and distress of the soul (the child's soul)."[29]

We will dedicate this lesson to the etiquettes that are emphasized in Islam, and which are specific to the prenatal stage.

The Purity of Birth

The child has a series of rights against his parents. And these rights begin before the formation of his life-germ; whereby he has the right to have his life-germ formed out of a legitimate relationship, which was referred to by narrations as the

---

[28] Sūrah al-Najm, verse 32

[29] Subḥānī, Ayatullāh Ja'far, Lubb al-Athar fee al-Jabr w al-Qadar a report on the lectures of Sayyid al-Khumaynī, Qom, Imām al-Ṣādiq Institute, 1418 AH, 1st edition, p. 115

"goodness of birth" and by scholars –terminologically – as the "purity of birth".

The goodness of birth creates a special spiritual tendency within the child, in contrast to having the sperm-drop mixture established from an illegitimate relationship which is referred to as "fornication". For, it will lead to the elimination of the spirit of faith and will cause the illegitimate child to yearn towards the forbidden (*al-haram*), as expressed in the narration by Imām al-Ṣādiq ﷺ where he said: "The child of fornication has signs..." the second of which is: "that he yearns to the forbidden from which he was created..."[30]

This is additional to many negative consequences that befall the child of fornication from the jurisprudential point of view, based on several narrations; some of them are: the unacceptance of his testimony, the invalidity of him leading the prayer, the illegitimacy of taking the position of a judge, the impermissibility of giving him from the alms-money when he is young[31]... etc.

One of the most important reasons behind the strictness in narrations is to instill fear in people to keep them away – as much as possible – from committing such a great sin.

On another hand, narrations have encouraged the goodness of birth, where they praised the chastity of the woman, as narrated

---

30 al-Ṣadūq, Shaykh Muḥammad ibn 'Alī, Man La Yaḥdaruhu al-Faqih, corrected and commented on by 'Alī Akbar al-Khafari, Qom, published by the group of teachers in the sacred city of Qom, L.T, 2nd edition, Vol. 4, p. 417

31 al-Khumaynī, Sayyid Rūhullāh al-Mūsawī, Taḥrīr al-Wasīlah, al-Najaf al-Ashraf, Matba'at al-Adab, 1390 AH, 2nd edition, Vol. 1, p. 339

by Imām al-Ṣādiq ﵇ where he said: "Blessed is he whose mother is chaste."[32] For, the chastity of the mother and goodness of the birth have great positive spiritual effects on the child, and they have an impact on the actualization of his potentials and strengthening of his capacities.

Moreover, it is the right of the child against his parents to have them preserve his spiritual purity in all the stages through which the life-germ passes. The Noble Qur'ān points out to these stages in His ﷻ saying: ﴿*Certainly We created man from an extract of clay. Then We made him a drop of [seminal] fluid [lodged] in a secure abode. Then We created the drop of fluid as a clinging mass. Then We created the clinging mass as a fleshy tissue. Then We created the fleshy tissue as bones. Then We clothed the bones with flesh. Then We produced him as [yet] another creature. So blessed is God, the best of creators!*﴾[33]

In the same context, Islam takes special care of the private relationship between the spouses. It establishes – for this relationship – etiquettes that must be taken into consideration by the parents, given the fact that these etiquettes play a major role in building the child's personality.

The Etiquettes of the Private Relationship between the Spouses

Many religious texts were mentioned in regards to the private relationship between the spouses. And since our discussion

---

[32] al-Ṣadūq, Shaykh Muḥammad ibn 'Alī, 'Ilal al-Sharae', introduced by Muḥammad Ṣādiq Bahr al-'Ulum, L.M, Dar al-Balagha, L.T, L.T', Vol. 2, p. 564

[33] Sūrah Al-Mu'minun, verses 12-14

rotates around the child, we will highlight the etiquettes that impact the formation of his identity. For, there are some etiquettes that must be observed by the spouses before copulation due to its impact on the development of certain potentials within the child, and accordingly on his physical, moral and intellectual wellbeing. And there are others that hinder his attainment of this desired growth. The texts are diverse in this regard, and they are of three types:

First: Pre-Copulation Etiquettes

1. Ablution:

It is narrated that the Messenger of God ﷺ said: "If your wife is pregnant, do not have intercourse with her unless you have performed ablution. For if you have intercourse with her without performing ablution, and a child was conceived, he will have a blind heart and stingy hands."[34]

Ablution before copulation, especially for a pregnant woman, has positive effects on the child and protects him from negative issues such as a blind heart and stingy hand.

2. Performing Ghusl after Copulation:

It is narrated that Imām Abu al-Ḥasan al-Ridā ؑ said: "Having intercourse after another, without performing Ghusl in between them, bequeaths insanity to the child." [35]

---

[34] al-Ṣadūq, Shaykh Muḥammad ibn ʻAlī, Man Lā Yaḥḍuruh al-Faqīh, Vol. 3, p. 553

[35] Burūjirdī, Ayatullāh Sayyid Ḥusayn, Jāmiʿ Aḥādīth al-Shīʻa, Qom, Al Matba'a Al ʻIlmiyyah, 1399 AH, L.T, Vol. 20, p. 201

We learn from this narration that performing Ghusl after intercourse protects the child from negative effects.

3. Remembrance of God:

It is narrated that Abi Abdillah al-Ṣādiq 🌸 said: "If any person from amongst you approaches his wife, let him remember God. For, he who doesn't remember God during copulation - from which a child is conceived –the devil will have a share in his child..."[36] This remembrance is fulfilled through *Basmala* (saying: In the name of God, the most Compassionate, the most Merciful).

4. Supplication:

It is narrated that Imām ʿAlī 🌸 said: "If any of you wanted to have intercourse with his wife, then let him say: (If a man intends to have intercourse with his wife, he should say: 'O' God! I made her private part lawful [for myself] by Your command and I accepted her as a trust from you. So, if You have destined a child from her for me, make him a healthy son; and do not allow Satan to have a share in him nor any partnership.)[37]

God 🌸 pointed out to the satanic partnership in his Gracious Book: *And share with them in wealth and children, and make*

----

[36] al-Ṣadūq, Shaykh Muḥammad ibn ʿAlī, Man Lā Yaḥduruh al-Faqīh, Vol. 3, p. 405

[37] al-Ṣadūq, Shaykh Muḥammad ibn ʿAlī, Al-Khiṣāl, corrected by ʿAlī Akbar Al Ghafari, Qom, the group of teachers in the sacred city of Qom, 1403 AH, L.T, p. 637, ḥadīth 400

promises to them!' But Satan promises them nothing but delusion❳[38]

This partnership between Satan and Man is not mandatory, but rather optional. One of these partnerships is that related to the sexual life from which a child is conceived. If a relationship involves the remembrance of God then Satan has no effect on it. Whereas if it was based on the negligence of God ﷻ then Satan will have a share in it.

Secondly: Etiquettes During Copulation

There is a series of etiquettes that are specific to the time of copulation. The narrations have referred to them; some of which are:

1. Observing the Time of Copulation:

The tolerant Sharia specified the time during which the spouses should not engage in intercourse. And it is of two types:

a. Times during which it is prohibited to engage in sexual intercourse with the wife: such as during her menstrual period, for, it is prohibited to engage in intercourse in this situation due to its prohibition, on one hand, and due to the negative effects it has on the child, on another hand. It is narrated that the Messenger of God ﷺ said: "He who engages in intercourse with his wife during her menses, and

[38] Sūrah Israa, verse 64

whose conceived child turns out to be a leper, he has only himself to blame."[39]

b. Times during which it is disapproved (detestable) to engage in sexual intercourse with the wife: It is understood from religious texts that there are times during which it is disapproved for a person to engage in sexual intercourse with his wife due to her role in educating the child. These periods are either related to time itself or to the actions and specifications associated with this period of time such as traveling and others. And there are many; some of which are: it is narrated that Imām ʿAlī ﷷ said: "If someone wanted to approach his wife, he must be cautious of new moons and the half-months; for, Satan requests a child during these two periods of time. And devils request a share in them; so they come and get pregnant."[40]

2. Calmness and Tranquility:

It is narrated that Imām al-Ḥasan al-Mujtaba ﷷ said: "...if a man approaches his wife and copulates with her with a still heart, calm veins and an undisturbed body, and the life-germ settles inside the womb, then the child will come out resembling his father and mother..."[41]

---

[39] al-Ṣadūq, Shaykh Muḥammad ibn ʿAlī, Man Lā Yaḥḍuruh al-Faqīh, Vol. 1, p. 96

[40] al-Ṣadūq, Shaykh Muḥammad ibn ʿAlī, Al-Khiṣāl, p. 637

[41] al-Ṣadūq, Shaykh Muḥammad ibn ʿAlī, ʿUyūn Akhbār al-Riḍā, commented on by Ḥusayn al-A'lami, Beirut, Al A'lami Publishing Institute, 1404 AH – 1984 AD, 1st edition, Vol. 1, p. 69

And this, according to the implications of the narration, falls under man's choice – to copulate with his wife with a still heart and calm physical state.

3. Lack of Speech:

It is narrated that the Messenger of God ﷺ said: "Do not speak much during copulation. For, if a child is conceived thereof, it is not guaranteed that he won't be mute."[42]

However, it must be pointed out that before copulation, the husband must speak to his wife in words that provide her the feeling of affability and reassurance. As the Messenger of God ﷺ said: "One must not approach his wife like an animal would; let there be a messenger between them. He was asked: And what is the messenger? He ﷺ said: kissing and talking."[43]

4. Refraining from having Intercourse while Standing:

It is narrated that the Messenger of God ﷺ said: "Do not have intercourse with your wife while standing up, for, this is the behavior of donkeys. And if a child is conceived thus, he would frequently pee in his bed like donkeys do everywhere."[44]

---

[42] al-Ṣadūq, Shaykh Muḥammad ibn 'Alī, 'Ilal al-Shara'e, Vol. 2, p. 515, chapter 789, 'Ilal Nawader al-Nikah, ḥadīth 5

[43] al-Fayḍ al-Kāshānī, Muḥammad ibn al-Murtaḍā, Al Mahajja al-Baydaa fi Tahthib al-Ahyaa, corrected and commented on by 'Alī Akbar Al Ghafari, Beirut, published by Al A'lami Publishing Institute, 1403 AH – 1983 AD, 2nd edition, Vol. 3, p. 110

[44] al-Ṣadūq, Shaykh Muḥammad ibn 'Alī, Man Lā Yaḥḍuruh al-Faqīh, Vol. 3, p. 552, Chapter of divorce, Bab al Nawader, ḥadīth 4899

5. Refraining from having Intercourse during Travel:

It is narrated that the Messenger of God ﷺ said: "Do not have intercourse with your wife if you travel for three days and nights; for, if a child is conceived thus he will be a supporter for every oppressor."[45]

The Embryonic Stage

The fetus passes through different stages and numerous phases before he paves his way outside his mother's womb and sees the light of worldly life. The Noble Qur'ān pointed out to these embryonic stages in His ﷻ saying: ﴿*Certainly We created man from an extract of clay. Then We made him a drop of [seminal] fluid [lodged] in a secure abode. Then We created the drop of fluid as a clinging mass. Then We created the clinging mass as a fleshy tissue. Then We created the fleshy tissue as bones. Then We clothed the bones with flesh. Then We produced him as [yet] another creature. So blessed is God, the best of creators!*﴾[46]

This noble verse shows that the fetus develops gradually from a life-germ to a clot, then to a lump (of flesh), and then to bones, and eventually the bones are covered with flesh until God ﷻ inserts the soul into him and develops him into another creation. So, He creates him in the best of forms.

---

[45] Ibid., Vol. 3, p. 553

[46] Sūrah Al Mu'minoun, verses 12-14

The Rights of the Fetus

The fetus has many rights against his parents; and they must preserve these rights and observe them. The most important ones are:

1. Physical and Medical Wellbeing:

This is achieved through doing the necessary check-ups before and during pregnancy, to be able to identify the mother and fetus's needs in terms of medical care at this stage.

2. Intellectual, Psychological and Spiritual Well Being:

This is achieved by preparing the internal hosting environment – and by that we mean the mother. For, she must maintain a high faithful and spiritual energy by performing duties and refraining from prohibitions, due to the great impact this has on the child's identity, in addition to securing a calm external environment in terms of the place she lives in and its surroundings.

3. The Fetus's Right to Life:

It is the right of the fetus that his parents preserve his life. Two issues stem out of this right:

a. Refraining from intentional abortion: Any act that leads to abortion is prohibited. Sayyid al-Khāmina'ī says: "It is impermissible to abort the life-germ after it settles in the womb, nor to abort the fetus in any of its later stages."[47] The prohibition of abortion is a form of strict respect for the right of the human being to life in the primary stages of his creation.[48]

b. Securing the factors that provide him with a healthy development, which is achieved through preparing internal and external environments that are wholesome and healthy for a child.

The mother represents the internal environment for the child; accordingly, the states she passes through on a physical, intellectual and psychological level, be it positive such as the feelings of reassurance, joy and happiness, or negative such as the feelings of anger and sadness, has its special impact on the child. And this is one of the interpretations of the Ḥadīth narrated by the Messenger of God ﷺ: "The miserable person is he who was miserable in his mother's womb; and the happy person is he who was happy in his mother's womb"[49], in addition to the medical condition in terms of well-being or sickness which will be reflected negatively or positively in the wellbeing of her fetus. Therefore, she must take care of her physical and mental health.

---

[47] Refer to: Sayyid 'Alī Ḥusaynī Khāmeni'ī, Jurisprudential Answers, Beirut, Dal al-Mustapha Al 'Alamiyyah, 1431 AH – 2010 AD, 10th edition, Vol. 2, chapter of abortion, excerpt from p. 66, issue 183

[48] Al Jawahiry, Ḥasan, studies in contemporary jurisprudence, L.M, Mujamma' al-Dhakha'er al-Islamiyya, 1429 AH, 1st edition, Vol. 6, p. 392

[49] Al-Aḥsā'ī, Muḥammad ibn 'Alī ibn Ibrāhīm, 'Awāli Al-La'āli' al-'Aziziyyah fi al-Ahādith al-Diniyyah, examined by Mujtaba al-Iraqi, Qom, Sayyid al-Shuhada Publishing, 1403 AH – 1983 AD, 1st edition, Vol. 1, p. 35

As for the external environment: it includes the place and geographical surroundings in which the mother is present. For, the external calm or noisy sounds have a positive or negative impact on the child. Accordingly, it is the fetus's right to have an external environment that is appropriate for him.

4.   Giving him a Good Name:

Some narrations point out to the desirability of naming the fetus while he is in his mother's womb, and before he leaves it to the worldly life. It is narrated that Abi Abdillah ☙ said: My father told me, on behalf of my grandfather, that he said: Imām 'Alī ☙ said: "Name your children before they are born; and if you do not know whether they are males or females, give them names that are fit for both males and females..."[50]

5.   Permissible (*Halāl*) Food:

The mother's food, in terms of permissibility and prohibition, plays a major role in shaping the child's identity; and this is one of the most important rights of the child. It is mandatory for the father to provide his wife with food that is bought from permissible (*halāl*) earnings. For, it is narrated that the Messenger of God ☙ said: "It is the right of the child against his father to only sustain him with what is good."[51]

Narrations have pointed out some kinds of food that play a fundamental role in shaping the child's identity and structure.

---

[50] al-Kulaynī, Shaykh Muḥammad ibn Yaʿqūb, Al-Kāfī, Vol. 6, p. 18

[51] Rayshahrī, Ayatullāh Muḥammad, Mīzān al-Ḥikmah, L.M, Dar al-Ḥadīth, 1416 AH, 1st edition, Vol. 4, p. 3679

And since the life-germ is created from nutritious substances, then one must be attentive to the fact that there are certain nutritious substances that play a role in shaping the child's physical identity. And the father should take into account that the food from which the life-germ is established is permissible, pure and comes from good earning. And narrations have mentioned types of food that have an impact in this regard, and it is plenty, such as: the two narrations on dandelion and quince.

For, it is narrated that Imām al-Ṣādiq ؑ said: "You should eat dandelion; for it increases a man's semen and beautifies the child."[52]

And it is narrated that Abi Abdillah ؑ said: "He who eats quince on an empty stomach will have good semen and a beautiful child."[53]

The Reward of the Pregnant Woman according to the Narrations of Ahl al-Bayt ؑ

A pregnant wife's awareness of the reward prepared for her by God ﷻ has a major role in giving her the strength and determination to endure the hardships of pregnancy; so much that the months will turn into a state of reassurance and calmness away from anxiety and nervousness. These are some of the noble narrations that are relevant to this context:

---

[52] al-Kulaynī, Shaykh Muḥammad ibn Yaʿqūb, Al-Kāfī, Vol. 6, p. 363

[53] Ibid., p. 357

It is narrated that Abi Abdillah al-Ṣādiq ﷺ said: "The Messenger of God ﷺ said: ... If a woman gets pregnant, she earns the status of the person who fasts, prays through the night and struggles with himself and through his money for the sake of God. And once she gives birth, she will be granted a reward that is unknown to her due its greatness..."[54]

And it is narrated that the Prophet ﷺ said to a woman called Hawlaa: "O' Hawlaa, I swear by He who sent me with the truth as a prophet, messenger, missionary and warner, that there is no woman who bears a child from her husband except that she remains in the shade of God (the Mighty and Majestic) until she goes into labor. With every contraction, she receives the reward of someone who frees a faithful slave..."[55]

Main Concepts

A mother's womb is the primary environment in which a child starts paving his way towards the light of life; therefore this stage must be well taken care of.

The purity of birth creates a special spiritual potential within the child, in contrast to the case of having the life-germ born from an illegitimate relationship, referred to as "fornication", which will lead to the elimination of the spirit of faith and to having the child of fornication yearn for the forbidden.

---

[54] al-Ṣadūq, Shaykh Muḥammad ibn 'Alī, Al-Amālī, examined by the department of Islamic studies, Tehran, Ba'tha Institute, 1417 AH, 1st edition, p. 497

[55] al-Mirzā al-Nūrī, Mustadrak al-Wasā'il, Vol. 14, p. 245

The spouses must observe the special etiquettes of the sexual relationship due to its impact on the wellbeing of the child on a physical, moral and intellectual level.

The fetus develops gradually from a life-germ to a clot, then to a lump of flesh and then to bones; and finally the bones get covered with flesh until God ﷻ inserts the soul inside him and develops him into another creation, such that he creates him in the best of forms.

The fetus has a series of rights. Its most important ones are: the right to life, having a virtuous internal and external environment and being given a good name.

A pregnant wife's awareness of the reward prepared for her by God ﷻ has a major role in giving her the strength and determination to endure the hardships of pregnancy.

Lesson Three

Recommended Acts During Childbirth

Lesson Objectives

By the end of this lesson, the student should:

1. Know the importance of the ceremonies carried out on the day of child birth.
2. Realize that a child is a blessing for which one must thank God ﷻ.
3. Get acquainted with the particularity of the seventh day of the child (since childbirth).

Preamble

Islam took care of man and nurtured him in all his life stages extending from cradle to grave, particularly during the first stage of his life which was given special importance due to the feebleness of the child at this stage and his need for special care and attention from the parents. Islam has stipulated etiquettes and recommended acts that are specific to newborns; they comprise some of the child's rights upon his parents. Noble narrations pointed out the positive effects of these recommended acts on the child, whether from the physical or spiritual point of view.

First: Welcoming the Newborn with Joy, Congratulations and Thankfulness to God ﷻ

The annunciation of a newborn is a blessing from God ﷻ for which the parents should thank He who bestowed this blessing upon them. Moreover, it is the newborn's right upon his parents to be well received with joy and pleasure. The Noble Qur'ān mentioned these expressions in several verses, amongst which is this: ﴾*O Zechariah! Indeed We give you the good news of a son, whose name is "John." Never before have We made anyone his namesake*﴿[56] And good tidings (*Bishara*) is derived from the word (*Bishr*) which means the good news that eases the

[56] Sūrah Mariam, verse 7

complexion of the face (of the person who receives the good news) and inserts joy into his heart.[57]

One of the most prominent manifestations of the parents' gratitude for their newborn would be to raise him properly in a way that would lead them to God ﷻ.

Moreover, congratulating one another on the newborn is considered a form of giving thanks to God ﷻ. It was mentioned amongst the narrations of Ahl al-Bayt ﵈ that – in the presence of Imām ʿAlī ﵇ – a man congratulated another man on his newborn son, so he said to him: Let the stallion congratulate you; to which Imām ʿAlī ﵇ responded: "Do not say that. Rather say: I have thanked the Donor, may you be blessed with this donation, and may he reach his peak, and may you be granted his reverence."[58] This narration points out the thankfulness to God ﷻ for the blessing of the newborn. And Islam emphasized on being as joyous about the newborn girl as one is about the newborn boy. For, the Prophet ﷺ received good tidings about having a newborn girl; so he looked at his companions' faces

---

57 Some scholars saw that the origin of the word Bishara contextually doesn't imply joy as it is suggested linguistically. Bishr rather refers to any sort of news be it joyful or sad; due to the fact that just as joy causes a change in the complexion of the face, so does sadness. Accordingly, the term Bishara includes both cases; however it is customarily interpreted as good news because it is more frequently used in this context. Refer to: al-Khumaynī, Sayyid Mustapha, Tafseer al-Qur'ān al-Kareem Ahsan al-Khaza'en al-Ilahiyya, L.M, Institute of organizing and publishing the works of Sayyid al-Khumaynī, 1418 AH, 1st edition, Vol. 5, p. 8

58 al-Sharīf al-Raḍī, Muḥammad b. al-Ḥusayn, Nahj Al-Balāgha, the collection of speeches by Imām ʿAlī ibn Abī Ṭālib ﵇, explained by Muḥammad Abdo, Takhrīj Al Masadir by Ḥusayn Al A'lami, Beirut, Al A'lami Publishing Institute, 1413 AH – 1993 AD, 1st edition, Vol. 4, p. 82, chapter of the chosen words of wisdom by Imām ʿAlī, number 354

and saw them filled with abhorrence. So, he told them: "What's the matter with you! She's a flower I get to smell, whose sustenance is provided by God."[59]

Second: Performing Ghusl to the Newborn

It is popular amongst the scholars that this ghusl is recommended; while others consider it mandatory.[60]

Third: Wrapping the Newborn with a White Piece of Cloth, and Reciting the Adhān and Iqāmah (call to prayer) in his Ears

It is recommended, at the moment of birth, that the newborn is wrapped with a white piece of cloth[61], and that the *Adhān* is recited in his right ear and the *Iqāmah* in his left, as mentioned in several narrations, amongst which is the following:

It was narrated on behalf of 'Alī ibn Maytham, on behalf of his father, that he said: I heard my mother say: I heart Najma the mother of al-Riḍā ﷺ say: "When I was pregnant with my son, I didn't feel any heaviness in the pregnancy..., and when I gave birth to him... his father Mūsā ibn Ja'far ﷺ entered and I gave

[59] al-Ṣadūq, Shaykh Muḥammad ibn 'Alī, Man Lā Yaḥḍuruh al-Faqīh, Vol. 3, p. 481

[60] al-Ḥillī, al-'Allāma al-Ḥasan ibn Yousef, Tathkirat al-Fuqahā', Qom, Institute of Al al-Bayt li- 'Ihyā al-Turāth, 1414 AH, 1st edition, Vol. 2, p. 144

[61] Al-Jawahiry, Shaykh Muḥammad Ḥasan, Jawaher al-Kalām fi Sharh Shara'e al-Islām, examined and commented on by al-Qawjāni, Tehran, Dar al-Kutub al-Islamiyya, 1365 AH, 2nd edition, Vol. 31, p. 251

him (the newborn) wrapped in a white piece of cloth, so he recited the *Adhān* in his right ear and the *Iqāmah* in his left..."[62]

Fourth: Giving the Newborn Something Sweet to Chew

It is recommended that the child is given something sweet to chew on by placing the material in the upper part of his mouth[63]; and usually this material is either fresh (*furāt*) water[64] Ḥusaynī soil, honey, dates or sky water... as mentioned in the narrations, such as the following:

It is narrated that Abi Ja'far ﷺ said: "Give your children fresh water and soil from the shrine of al-Ḥusayn ﷺ to chew on; and if there wasn't any, then give them sky water."[65]

The Particularity of the Seventh Day

If we trace the honorable Prophetic Sunnah, we will find that there's a particularity for the seventh day in regards to dealing with the newborn; whereby narrations specialized many

---

[62] al-Ṣadūq, Shaykh Muḥammad ibn ʿAlī, ʿUyūn Akhbār al-Riḍā, Vol. 2, p. 30

[63] Al-Hindy, al-Fadel Muḥammad ibn al-Ḥasan, Kashf al-Lithām ʿan Qawā'id al-Ahkam, Qom, examined by the Islamic publishing institute which is related to the group of teachers in the honorable city of Qom, 1424 AH, 1st edition, Vol. 7, p. 526

[64] Furāt water means fresh water. The Noble Qur'ān called the water of the rivers, the water that's preserved underground and that which we drink in the name of "Furāt water", which means that which tastes well. God ﷻ says: "And (haven't we) given you agreeable water to drink?" (Sūrah Al Mursalat, verse 27)

[65] al-Kulaynī, Shaykh Muḥammad ibn Yaʿqūb, Al-Kāfī, Vol. 6, p. 24

recommended acts for this day. It's narrated on behalf of Abi Baseer, on behalf of Abi Abdillah ![]: in regards to the newborn:

He said: "He is given a name on the seventh day, a 'aqīqah is performed on his behalf, his head is shaved, silver that is equivalent to the weight of his hair is given as alms, and the midwife receives the leg and hip (of the 'aqīqah), and it is fed upon and given as alms."[66]

First: The 'Aqīqah

The linguistic origin of al-'aqīqah is from 'Aqq, which means to slash and cut.[67]

As for its contextual meaning: it is the sacrifice of one of the four animals[68] on behalf of the newborn (boy or girl) on the seventh day of his birth.

The sacrificed animal is called 'aqīqah because it is sacrificed whereby its throat, esophagus and mouth are cut into pieces.[69]

---

[66] Ibid., p. 29

[67] Ibn Zakariah, Dictionary of Maqayees al-Lugha, Vol. 4, p. 3

[68] The four animals are the lamb, goat, cow and camel.

[69] Al Tareehi, Shaykh Fakhruddine, Majma' al-Bahrein, reestablished upon the first letter of the word by Mahmoud Adel, verified by Ahmad al-Ḥusaynī, L.M, the publishing office of the Islamic culture, 1408 AH, 2nd edition, Vol. 5, p.215, and al-Bahrani, Yousef, Al Hadā'eq al-Naḍira fi Ahkām al-'Itra al-Tāhira, Qom, the institute of Islamic publishing that's related to the group of teachers in the honorable city of Qom, l.t., l.ṭ, Vol. 25, p. 56

And it is of the definite recommended acts that were mentioned in the narrations. It is narrated that Imām ʿAlī said: "Perform 'aqīqah (*sacrifice*) on behalf of your children on the seventh day."[70] And it is narrated that Imām al-Ṣādiq said: "Perform 'aqīqah on his behalf on the seventh day, and give away silver equivalent to his hair as alms, and cut the 'aqīqah (sacrificed animal) into pieces (*Jathawa*)[71], cook it and invite a group of Muslims over for its feast."[72]

The 'aqīqah, as the narrations confirm, provides protection and security for the child; it also saves him from diseases that might befall him in his life. And it is the child's right upon his guardian to receive good guardianship, care and protection.

The Recommendation of having Multiple Sacrifices ('Aqīqah):

It is recommended to make multiple sacrifices ('aqīqah) for one newborn child. For, Imām al-ʿAskarī sacrificed two rams - and in some narrations four – on behalf of Imām Al Mahdi.

In the narration of Abi Harun, the freed slave of Ja'da family, he said: "I used to sit with Abi Abdillah in Medina, then I was absent for days; then I came to him, so he said to me: O' Aba Harun, I haven't seen you for days, so I said: I had a newborn child... then he said to me: Did you sacrifice a 'aqīqah on his behalf? He (Abi Harun) said: I held back. He said: He saw me

70 al-Ṣadūq, Shaykh Muḥammad ibn ʿAlī, Al-Khiṣāl, p. 619

71 Jadhawa is the plural form of Jadhwa, which means piece. According to al-Tahdhīb and al-Wāfī, the term al-jadawel comes from al-jadwal, which means the organ.

72 al-Kulaynī, Shaykh Muḥammad ibn Yaʿqūb, Al-Kāfī, Vol. 6, p. 27

holding back and assumed that I hadn't. So he (the Imām) said: O' Musadif, come close to me. I swear, I didn't know what he told him, but I thought that he ordered him to do something for my benefit. So, I gathered myself to leave, when he said to me: As you are, O' Aba Harun. Then, Musadif came to me with three dinars and placed them in my hand. Then he (the Imām) said: O' Aba Harun, go and purchase two rams, let them be fat; sacrifice them, and eat and feed others from them."[73]

Moreover, it is recommended to multiply the sacrifices when there are multiple newborns; that is, it is recommended for the person who has just had twins to sacrifice a separate 'aqīqah for each child, rather than sacrificing one 'aqīqah for both.

In the narration of Muḥammad ibn Muslim, he said: "Abu Ja'far ﷺ had two newborn sons, so he asked Zaid ibn 'Alī to buy him two sacrifical animals (*Jazour*)[74] to sacrifice as 'aqīqah..."[75]

The recommended 'aqīqah is (recommended) for whoever is capable of carrying it out. As for the poor person, he is exempted from it – as indicated in the noble narrations. For, in the narration of Isḥaq ibn Ammar, he said: "I asked Aba al-Ḥasan ﷺ about whether the 'aqīqah is (recommended) for (both) the financially capable and incapable. He ﷺ said: "It is

[73] al-Kulaynī, Shaykh Muḥammad ibn Ya'qūb, Al-Kāfī, p. 40

[74] Jazour is a term which refers to the sacrificial animal at the moment of its slaughter.

[75] Ibid., Vol. 6, p. 25

not for the person who doesn't find anything (to sacrifice with)."[76]

Yes, the recommendation doesn't become invalid when it is delayed until after the seventh day. For, if money becomes available later on, it is recommended to perform the 'aqīqah then.

Second: Feeding People and having a Feast

It is recommended to feed people after sacrificing the 'aqīqah; as it is recommended that the newborn's household members eat from the 'aqīqah themselves, give from it to the neighbors and distribute its meat – raw or cooked – to the needy and poor faithful people who believe in the Guardianship, or they can cook it and invite some believers over to a feast.

This was confirmed by several narrations - some of which were mentioned earlier – such as:

In the narration of Abdillah ibn Bakir, he said: "I was at Abi Abdillah's ﵇ when his uncle's messenger, Abdullah ibn 'Alī, came to him and said: your uncle says to you: we wanted to perform the 'aqīqah but we didn't find one, what do you think about giving alms with its price money? So he ﵇ said: no, God loves feeding people (food) and shedding blood."[77]

[76] Ibid., p. 27

[77] Ibid., p. 25

Third: Shaving the Head and Giving Alms Money that is Equivalent to its Weight in Silver

One of the recommended acts that are narrated in regards to the seventh day is shaving the newborn's head. According to the narrations, it seems that it (the shaving) must precede the 'aqīqah. It is narrated that Imām al-Ṣādiq ﷺ said: "In Mina, you start with the sacrifice before shaving (the head); and in (performing) the 'aqīqah you start with the shaving before the sacrifice."[78]

The intended meaning is to shave the entire head and give alms money equivalent to the hair's weight in silver, as per the tradition of Ahl al-Bayt ﷺ. It is narrated that Abi Abdillah ﷺ said: "Fatima ﷺ shaved the head of her two sons and gave alms money equivalent to their hair's weight in silver."[79]

Fourth: Smearing his head with perfume (*Khalouq* or saffron...)

One of the recommended *sunnahs* on the seventh day of the newborn child is smearing his head and greasing it with perfume. Those that are mentioned in narrations are: Al Khalouq (an Arabian perfume for women) and saffron. It seems as though they are listed as examples, and not exhaustively.

It is narrated that Abi Abdillah ﷺ said: "... and the fifth: his head is smeared with saffron..."[80]

---

[78] Ibid., Vol. 4, p. 498

[79] Ibid., Vol. 6, p. 26

[80] al-Ṭabrisī, Shaykh al-Faḍl ibn al-Ḥasan, Makārim al-Akhlāq, L.M, Publishings of al-Sahrif al-Radi, 1392 AH – 1972 AD, 6th edition, p. 228

Fifth: Piercing the newborn's ear

Scholars have mentioned this recommended act based on the actual Sunnah of the Prophet ﷺ and what was mentioned in some narrations, such as the saying of Imām al-Ṣādiq عليه السلام: "A 'aqīqah is to be performed on behalf of the newborn, and his ear is to be pierced..."[81]

Sixth: Circumcision

Circumcision, in its linguistic origin, means cutting. And contextually, it means to cut the foreskin i.e. the skin that covers the glans, in such a way that the latter is revealed and what was hidden from it appears.[82]

This was implemented by the Messenger of God with al-Ḥasanain عليهما السلام (Imām al-Ḥasan and Imām al-Ḥusayn عليهما السلام). It is narrated on the behalf of Imām Ja'far al-Ṣādiq, on behalf of his father عليهما السلام, that he said: "The Messenger of God named al-Ḥasan and al-Ḥusayn on the seventh day, and performed the 'aqīqah on their behalf on the seventh day, and circumcised them on the seventh day..."[83]

Moreover, it is recommended to have a feast when the circumcision is executed.

---

[81] al-Mirzā al-Nūrī, Mustadrak al-Wasā'il, Vol. 15, p. 154

[82] al-Ṭūsī, Shaykh Muḥammad ibn al-Ḥasan, Al Mabsout fi Foqh al-Imāmiyya, corrected and commented on by Muḥammad al-Bāqir al-Bahboudi, Beirut, Dar Al Kitab Al Islami, l.t., l.ṭ., Vol. 8, p. 67

[83] Al Himeeri Al Qommi, Shaykh Abdullah ibn Ja'far, Qorb al-Isnad, Qom, Institute of Al al-Bayt li-'Ihya' al-Turāth, 1413 AH, 1st edition, p. 122

Main Concepts

Islam took care of man and nurtured him in all his life stages extending from cradle to grave; for, it stipulated etiquettes and recommended acts specific to the newborn child.

Receiving good tidings about having a newborn is a blessing from God ﷻ for which the parents should thank the Donor. It is the child's right upon his parents to receive him with joy and pleasure.

There are several recommended acts during child birth which were mentioned in the narrations of Ahl al-Bayt عليهم السلام, some of which are: thanking God ﷻ for the newborn child, wrapping him in a white piece of cloth, giving him something sweet to chew, reciting the Adhān and Iqāmah,etc.

Lesson Four

The Child's Right to a Good Name and Breastfeeding

Lesson Objectives

By the end of this lesson, the student should:

1. Know that it's the child's right upon his parents to have a good name chosen for him.
2. Know that breastfeeding is a natural right for a child.
3. Get introduced to the physical and moral benefits of natural breastfeeding.

Preamble

For the sake of containing the negative phenomenon that has begun to pave its way within the Islamic community in regards to giving western or foreign names to (newborn) sons and daughters, influenced by western culture and as an attempt to imitate it, - especially celebrity names-, and due to the fact that names are one of the elements of the cultural identity of any nation, it becomes crucial from an educational point of view – and worth dwelling on in detail - to talk about the criteria of choosing a name for the child.

And for the sake of containing the widespread usage of artificial breastfeeding and denying the child's right to natural breastfeeding – knowing its role in shaping the child's identity – we will highlight the topic of breastfeeding and its impact on the child from the physical and moral perspectives.

The Child's Right to a Good Name

Naming is the process of giving a name to a noun in a way that it becomes corresponding to it; it is launching a particular specific name such as Muḥammad for males and Fāṭima for females in regards to the newborn child.

The object to this inquiry here is the name in its specific context, which is the proper noun that indicates a specific character. Its benefit is to identify the selves and distinguish people; for, an individual is set apart from others through his name.

And it goes undoubted that names cannot be stripped completely – positively or negatively – from two things:

First: the garment of its linguistic meanings; for, it sometimes raises its linguistic concepts in a person's mind.

Second: the garment of some famous historical people, such that the resemblance in the names may lead one's mind to the circle of resemblance amongst the personalities.

And if we take these two points into consideration, it becomes crucial to choose the good name from two perspectives:

a. In terms of pronunciation and combination of letters, such that the pronunciation (of the name) isn't strange, complex or alien...

b. In terms of meaning, such that it has positive connotations and doesn't hold signs to negative meanings. The Islamic educational viewpoint emphasizes and encourages the grant of good names. It considers that it is the child's right upon his guardian to choose for him a good name, due to its positive and social impact on the child. Following is some of that which is mentioned in this regard:

It is narrated that Imām 'Alī ﷺ said: The Messenger of God ﷺ said: The first thing one gifts (*yanhal*)[84] his child is a good name. Let each of you choose a good name for his child."[85]

---

[84] Yanhal means to give or gift.

[85] Al-Rawundi, Fadl-God ibn 'Alī,al-Nawader, verified by Sa'eed Riḍā 'Alī 'Askarī, Qom, Dar al-Ḥadīth, 1377 AH, 1st edition, p. 96, and al-Mirzā al-Nūrī, Mustadrak al-Wasā'il, Vol. 15, p. 127

When is it Recommended to Start Naming?

The narrations that mention the beginning of naming are divided into four groups upon induction:

The first group of narrations: it includes the recommendation of naming (a child) irrespective of specific timing. It is narrated that the first Imām Abi al-Ḥasan al-Kāẓim ﷺ said: "The first honor bestowed by a man on his child is a good name. Therefore, let each of you choose a good name for his child."[86]

The second group: it encouraged the naming of children before birth which was mentioned earlier.[87]

The third group: it speaks of naming (the child) during birth.

It is narrated that Imām al-Kāẓim ﷺ said: "...If he liked to name him on the day of his birth, he could."[88]

The fourth group: it encourages naming (child) on the seventh day of his birth. It is narrated that Abi Abdillah ﷺ said: "The child is named on his seventh day."[89]

We can combine these narrations; for, they are all mentioned to clarify the status of naming in terms of recommendation. And

---

[86] al-Kulaynī, Shaykh Muḥammad ibn Yaʿqūb, Al-Kāfī, Vol. 6, p. 18

[87] Refer to: the lesson of the prenatal stage

[88] al-Kulaynī, Shaykh Muḥammad ibn Yaʿqūb, Al-Kāfī, Vol. 6, p. 24

[89] Al-Maghrebi, Al-Nu'man ibn Muḥammad, Da'aem al-Islam wa Zikr al-Halal wa al-Haram wa al-Qadaya wa al-Ahkām ʻan Ahl al-Bayt ﷺ, verified by Asaf ibn ʻAlī Asghar Faydi, Cairo, Dar al-Ma'aref 1383 AH – 1963 AD, L.T, Vol. 2, p. 188

it can all be performed with the intention of (performing) a recommended act and following the Prophet ﷺ and Ahl al-Bayt ؑ; such that if a person names a fetus he is considered to have performed a recommended act in submission to the saying of Imām ʿAlī ؑ: "Name your children before they are born"[90]; and if he doesn't name him and rather delays it until birth, then he is considered to have performed a recommended act in keeping with the actions of the Messenger of God, Imām ʿAlī and the saying of Imām al-Kāẓim ؑ. And if he delays the naming until the seventh day, as per the previous narrations, then he has performed a recommended act, or it can be considered the most favorable; for, it is best done on the seventh day.

The Narrations that Mention the Recommendation of Some Names

There are some narrations that include certain criteria for determining good names that are recommended to be given to the child and according to which he is named; and it is threefold:

First: it is recommended to name the child with any of the Prophets' ؑ names. Imām ʿAlī ؑ said: The Messenger of God said: "There is no household that includes the name of a

[90] al-Kulaynī, Shaykh Muḥammad ibn Yaʿqūb, Al-Kāfī, Vol. 6, p. 18

prophet except that God ﷻ sends them an angel that sanctifies them day and night."[91]

Second: it is recommended to name the child with every name that manifests worship to God ﷻ. It is narrated that Abi Ja'far al-Bāqir ؏ said: "The most honest of names is that which is named in worship; and the best of it are the names of Prophets ؏."[92]

Third: it is recommended to name the child with any of the names of the Prophet ﷺ and his progeny ؏. It is narrated that Rab'i ibn Abdillah said: Abi Abdillah ؏ was told: "May I be sacrificed for you, we name (our children) with your names and the names of your fathers, does that benefit us? He said: Yes, by God; for, is religion anything else but love?! God ﷻ said: *Say, 'If you love God, then follow me; God will love you and forgive you your sins, and God is all-forgiving, all-merciful'*[93]"[94]

---

[91] al-Ṭūsī, Shaykh Muḥammad ibn al-Ḥasan, Al-Amālī, verified by the department of Islamic studies, Qom, Institute of Al-Ba'tha, 1414 AH, 1st edition, page 454, hafith 1012, narrated in Al-Baghdadi, Ahmad ibn 'Alī, the History of Baghdad or the City of Peace, verified by Mustapha Abdul Qader 'Ata, Beirut, Dar al-Kutub al-'Ilmiyya, 1417 AH – 1997 AD, 1st edition, Vol. 14, p. 244

[92] al-Kulaynī, Shaykh Muḥammad ibn Ya'qūb, Al-Kāfī, Vol. 6, p. 18

[93] Sūrah al-Imrān, verse 31

[94] al-'Ayyāshī, Muḥammad ibn Mas'ūd, Tafsīr al-'Ayyāshī, verified by Hashem al-Rasouli al-Mahallati, Tehran, the Islamic scientific library, 1380 AH, 1st edition, Vol. 1, p. 167-168

The Particularity of Some Names

There are some names that were given particularities in the noble narrations, some of which – for males – are:

1. The name Muḥammad: it is narrated that Abi Abdillah ﷷ said: the Prophet ﷺ said: "He who has four sons and doesn't name either of them by my name, then he has mistreated me."[95]

2. The name ʿAlī: it is narrated that ʿAlī ﷷ said: "He who has four sons and doesn't name either of them by my name, then he has mistreated me."[96]

3. The name Hamza: it is narrated that Abu Abdillah ﷷ said: "A man came to the Prophet ﷺ and said: O' Messenger of God, I have just had a son, what do I name him? He ﷺ said: Name him by the most loved name to me: Hamza."[97]

4. The names of Ahl al-Bayt ﷷ: Imām al-Riḍā ﷷ said: "Poverty doesn't enter a house that has the name: Muḥammad, Aḥmad, ʿAlī, al-Ḥasan, al-Ḥusayn, Jaʿfar, Ṭālib, Abdullah, or Fātima for the women."[98]

---

[95] al-Kulaynī, Shaykh Muḥammad ibn Yaʿqūb, Al-Kāfī, Vol. 6, p. 19

[96] Al-Daylami, Sheruweh ibn Shahradar, Firdaws al-Akhbār bi Ma'thour al-Khitab al-Mukhraj ʿala Kitab al-Shehab, verified by Fawwaz Ahmad Al-Zamali and Muḥammad Al-Mu'tasim bi-llah Al-Baghdadi, L.M, Dar Al-Kitab Al-ʿArabi, 1407 AH – 1987 AD, L.T, Vol. 3, p. 632, ḥadīth 5981

[97] al-Kulaynī, Shaykh Muḥammad ibn Yaʿqūb, Al-Kāfī, Vol. 6, p. 19

[98] Ibid., p. 19

5. The name Fātima: As for females, a particularity was mentioned in regards to this name. Imām al-Ṣādiq said: "Whereas if you name her Fātima, don't cuss, curse or hit her."[99]

On the other hand, it is disapproved (*makrūh*) to give a child unpleasant names. Narrations also provided general criteria in regards to names that shouldn't be given to a child. They are the names of the enemies of Ahl al-Bayt because it pleases the devil. Imām al-Bāqir said: "...If the devil hears someone calling: O' Muḥammad, O' 'Alī, he melts away like bullets. And if he hears someone calling a name of our enemies, he shakes and boasts."[100]

The Recommendation of Giving a Nickname (*kunya*)

Narrations gave emphasis to the recommendation of nicknaming, that is, to give a certain nickname to the boy or girl such that he/she is called "Aba X" or "Um X'. Imām Ridā said: When Imām al-Ḥasan ibn 'Alī was born, Gabriel came down to the Messenger of God to congratulate him on the seventh day, and ordered him to give him a name and a nickname..."[101]

[99] Ibid., p. 19

[100] Ibid., p. 20

[101] Ibid., p. 34

The Child's Right to Breastfeeding

Islam gave attention and special care to the issue of breastfeeding, since it has a fundamental role in the physical, psychological, behavioral and intellectual buildup of the child.

The Definition of Breastfeeding

Breastfeeding, linguistically, means "drinking milk from the udder of the breast."[102]

"Breastfeeding: the suckling of the breast, drinking milk from it."[103] He who drinks milk from a source other than the breast is not said to have breastfed.

The concept of breastfeeding, linguistically, is realized once the child suckles on the breast, even if it's done only once – in addition to breastfeeding for two years.

As for the jurisprudential terminology: Breastfeeding is "the nourishment of someone who is younger than two years old, on the milk of a living human being whose milk sprung out of a legitimate or suspicious marriage, whether she is pregnant or breastfeeding, according to the legitimate quantity, from her breasts while remaining pure."[104] This woman can be the mother, as it can be someone else.

---

102 Ibn Zakariyya, Dictionary of Maqayees al-Lugha, Vol. 2, p. 400

103 al-Ṭabrisī, Shaykh al-Faḍl ibn al-Ḥasan, Majmaʿ al-bayān fī Tafsīr al-Qurʾān, Vol. 2, p. 111

104 Masālik al-Afhām, Vol. 7, p. 234

As for the case where the mother's milk is placed in a bottle, such that the child doesn't suck directly from the breast, it is not called breastfeeding according to religious terminology.

Narrative texts: they perceive breastfeeding as the continuous relationship that lasts for a period of time that is considered as such (continuous) customarily and is inclusive of all the emotional, psychological, health, intellectual and other effects thereof, and which is set by the Noble Qur'ān for two complete years.[105]

For, breastfeeding is one of the most important child's rights in Islam. The Prophet ﷺ attributed the causes of his eloquence, rhetoric, clarity of speech and sweetness of his tongue to: breastfeeding –amongst other causes – where he ﷺ said: "I am the most eloquent from amongst you; I am a Qurashi and I breastfed from Bani Sa'd ibn Bakr."[106]

---

[105] Al-Bajnawardi, Sayyid Ḥasan, Jurisprudential Rules, verified by Mahdī Al-Mahreezi and Muḥammad Ḥusayn Al-Darayti, Qom, al-Hādī publishing, 1419 AH, 1st edition, Vol. 8, p. 332

[106] Al-Hameeri, Abdul Malek ibn Hisham, Al-Sīrah Al-Nabawiyya, verified and commented on by Muḥammad Muhyiddine Abdul Hameed, Cariro, Al-Madani publishing, 1383 AH – 1963 AD, L.T, Vol. 1, p. 107. And it was narrated that he ﷺ said: "I am the most eloquent person from amongst the Arabs; for, I am from Quraysh, I grew up in Bani Sa'd, and I breastfed from Bani Zahra." Al-Nawāwi, Yehya ibn Sharaf, Al-Majmou' Sharḥ al-Muhadhab, L.M, Dar al-Fikr, L.T, L.T', Vol. 18, p. 227, and Al-'Amili, Zeineddine ibn 'Alī, Masālik Al-Afhām ila Tanqīḥ Shara'ea al-Islam, Iran, Institute of Al-Ma'aref al-Islamiyya, 1414 AH, 1st edition, Vol. 7, p. 241

The Child's Right to Having a Well-Chosen Breastfeeding Woman

Narrations emphasized on the importance of choosing a breastfeeding woman accurately, due to its moral, spiritual and physical effects on the child. Therefore, it is mentioned that it's the child's right upon his parents – if they want to choose a woman to breastfeed him – to choose wisely, based on a fundamental narration which has the following gist: "Milk is contagious and changes the character of the child." Accordingly, prohibitions were mentioned against allowing one's child to be breastfed by a woman who carries negative qualities due to its negative effects on the child's personality. Some of these qualities are:

1. The idiot: it is narrated that the Messenger of God ﷺ said: "Do not have your child breastfed by an idiot; for, a child grows upon this quality."[107] And it is narrated that Abi Abdillah ؑ said: Imām 'Alī ؑ used to say: "Do not have your child breastfed by an idiot; for, milk prevails over one's temperament."[108]

2. The fornicator and the daughter of a fornicator: narrations warned of having one's child breastfed by the daughter of a fornicator. For, it is narrated that 'Alī ibn Jaafar said, speaking of his brother Abi al-Ḥasan ؑ: I asked him about a woman who gave birth out of fornication, and whether it is good to have one's child breastfeed from her milk. He said:

---

[107] al-Kulaynī, Shaykh Muḥammad ibn Ya'qūb, Al-Kāfī, Vol. 6, p. 43

[108] Ibid., p. 43

"It is not good, nor from the milk of her daughter who was born out of fornication."[109]

3. Prostitution and Insanity: it is narrated that Imām ʿAlī ﷺ said: "Keep your children away from the milk of the fornicator (*Al-Baghiy*)[110] from amongst women, and the insane one; for, milk is contagious."[111]

And at the same time, narrations emphasized on choosing the woman who has good qualities (for breastfeeding). It is narrated that Muḥammad ibn Marwān said: Abu Ja'far ﷺ said: "Let your child breastfeed from the milk of goodness, and never from the milk of badness; for, milk is contagious."[112]

Who is the Best Woman to Breastfeed a Child?

The mother is the best woman to breastfeed a child; and she has a fundamental role in shaping his educational personality. The Qur'ān addressed her directly when God ﷻ said: ﴿Mothers shall suckle their children for two full years, — that for such a desire to complete the suckling.﴾[113] Moreover, narrations have indicated that the mother's milk is the best milk for the child; for, it is narrated that the Messenger of God ﷺ said: "There isn't

---

[109] Ibid., p. 44

[110] Al-Baghiy means the fornicator, whereby God ﷻ says: ﴿*Do not compel your female slaves to prostitution*﴾ Sūrah Al-Nūr, verse 33.

[111] al-Ṣadūq, Shaykh Muḥammad ibn ʿAlī, Al-Khiṣāl, p. 615

[112] al-Kulaynī, Shaykh Muḥammad ibn Yaʿqūb, Al-Kāfī, Vol. 6, p. 43

[113] Sūrah al-Baqarah, verse 233

any milk that is better for the boy[114] than his mother's milk."[115] Based on this premise, scholars have mentioned in this regard that: "The best milk from which a child has breastfed is his mother's."[116]

Furthermore, narrations gave attention to the nutrition of the nursing woman; whereby they emphasized on eating *Rutab* (wet and moist dates) and ripe dates due to the educational effects they have on the child's identity and the praiseworthy qualities they give him such as patience, intelligence...etc.

Imām 'Alī ﷺ said: the Messenger of God ﷺ said: "Let the first food eaten by a woman who has just given birth be dates; for, God ﷻ told Mariam: ﴾*Shake the trunk of the palm tree, freshly picked dates will drop upon you*﴿[117]"[118] And the Messenger of

---

[114] This includes both, male and female children. However, the term "boy" is usually used in narrations due to the dominant usage of the masculine terms in the Arabic language. Nonetheless, the intended meaning is the general one which includes the male and female, unless there's specific evidence that implies otherwise.

[115] al-Ṣadūq, Shaykh Muḥammad ibn 'Alī, 'Uyūn Akhbār al-Riḍā, Vol. 2, p. 38

[116] Sayyid Muḥammad al-'Amily commented on this expression by saying: "And this is more harmonious with his mood, and more appropriate for his temperament, due to having been nourished from it in his mother's womb." Al-'Amily, Muḥammad ibn 'Alī, Nihayat al-Maram fi Sharh Mukhtasar Shara'e al-Islam, corrected and commented on by Mujtaba Al-Iraqi and 'Alī Al-'Ishtihari and Ḥusayn Al-Yazadi, Qom, Institute of Islamic Publishing, 1413 AH, 1st edition, Vol. 1, p. 460

[117] Sūrah Mariam, verse 25

[118] al-Kulaynī, Shaykh Muḥammad ibn Ya'qūb, Al-Kāfī, Vol. 6, p. 22

God ﷻ said: "Feed the woman during the month in which she gives birth dates; for, her child will thus be patient and pure."[119]

Artificial Breastfeeding Versus Natural Breastfeeding

The main problem that we suffer from in our current community is that mothers have distanced themselves from natural breastfeeding, which is encouraged by noble narrations, and replaced it with feeding the child artificial milk through bottles made specifically for this purpose. This is considered a violation of the child's right, in regards to his well being, since breastfeeding allows him to enjoy good physical health. And at the same time, it is considered a deprivation of emotional and sentimental charges from the psychological point of view, especially that natural breastfeeding has a role in unfolding the child's aptitudes and capacities, which makes replacing it with artificial breastfeeding – in itself – an act of depriving the child from all those things.

Moreover, natural breastfeeding contributes to mothers' health and wellbeing; and it is considered one of the safe and environment-friendly nutritional approaches.[120]

The Reward of the Nursing Mother

It is important that a mother checks out the narrations that speak of the reward of the nursing mother; for, this will encourage her towards the reward that awaits her in this

---

119 Shaykh Al-Tabradi, Makarem al-Akhlaq, page 169

120 Review what is mentioned by the World Health Organization (WHO) using the following link: www.who.int/ar

position and support her in overcoming all the hardships of breastfeeding with delight. It is narrated on behalf of Abi Abdillah ☙ that the Messenger of God ☙ said: "… For, if she breastfeeds, she will gain with every suck the reward of freeing a slave from amongst Ismaīl's sons; and when she finishes from breastfeeding him, a kind angel taps her on her back and says: proceed; for, you have been forgiven."[121]

Refraining from breastfeeding is considered a form of denying the child his right. And some narrations referred to it as oppression. For, it is narrated that Imām al-Ṣādiq ☙ said: "Breastfeeding lasts for twenty one months, the absence of which is considered an oppression against the child."[122]

Is the Child's Right to Breastfeeding Mandatory or Recommended?

It has been mentioned earlier that the child's right to natural breastfeeding is one of his innate rights. However, the question that is raised here tackles the legislative aspect; is it mandatory for a mother to breastfeed her child or is it only recommended? And if it is mandatory, does the obligation lie on the shoulders of the mother herself or is it mandatory for the father to provide the child with a breastfeeding woman? Two opinions were mentioned by scholars in this regard:

The first opinion: the obligation of breastfeeding for two complete years: And they supported their opinion with the noble verse where God ☙ said: *Mothers shall suckle their*

---

[121] al-Ṣadūq, Shaykh Muḥammad ibn ʿAlī, Al-Amālī, p. 497

[122] al-Kulaynī, Shaykh Muḥammad ibn Yaʿqūb, Al-Kāfī, Vol. 6, p. 40

children for two full years, —that for such as desire to complete the suckling﴿[123], such that it was understood that this verse implied mandatory breastfeeding for two years.[124]

The second opinion: the recommendation of having the mother as the breastfeeding woman: And it is the popular opinion amongst the Shia scholars that breastfeeding is recommended for the mother – and not mandatory – for, it is more blessed than others...[125], based on His ﷻ saying: ﴾*Then, if they suckle [the baby] for you, give them their wages and consult together honorably; but if you make things difficult for each other, then another woman will suckle [the baby] for him*﴿[126], which left the decision of the matter up to the mother's will.

Main Concepts

There is emphasis and encouragement in the Islamic educational vision towards choosing good names; and it considers it one of the child's right upon his guardian to choose for him a good name. For, it is narrated that Imām 'Alī ؑ said: "...It is the child's right upon his father to give him a good name..."[127]

---

[123] Sūrah al-Baqarah, verse 233

[124] Al-Ardabīlī, Ahmad ibn Muḥammad, Zubdat al-Bayan fi Ahkām al-Qur'ān, verified by Muḥammad Bāqir al-Bahboudī, Tehran, al-Maktaba al-Mutadawiyyah li 'Ihya' al-'Athar al-Ja'fariyyah, L.T, L.T', p. 556

[125] al-Khumaynī, Sayyid Rūhullāh al-Mūsawī, Taḥrīr al-Wasīlah, Vol. 2, p. 312

[126] Sūrah Al-Talaq, verse 6

[127] Nahj al-Balāgha, Saying 399

There are some narrations that include certain criteria regarding the recommendation of determining good names - which are recommended to be given to the child – some of which are: the recommendation of giving the child the name of the Prophets ﷺ and Ahl al-Bayt ؏, in addition to giving him a name which implies the worshiping of God ﷻ.

Names cannot be stripped completely – positively or negatively – from two things:

First: the garment of its linguistic meanings; for, it sometimes raises its linguistic concepts in a person's mind.

Second: the garment of some famous historical people, such that the resemblance in the names may lead one's mind to the circle of resemblance amongst the personalities.

Breastfeeding, linguistically, means "drinking milk from udder or breast."[128]

"Breastfeeding: the sucking of the breast, drinking milk from it."[129] He who drinks milk from a source other than the breast is not said to have breastfed. Narrations have emphasized on the importance of choosing the breastfeeding woman accurately due to its moral, spiritual and physical effects on the child.

The mother is the best person to breastfeed the child; and has a fundamental role in shaping the educational personality of the child during his first years.

---

[128] Ibn Zakariyya, Dictionary of Maqayīs al-Lugha, Vol. 2, p. 400

[129] al-Ṭabrisī, Shaykh al-Faḍl ibn al-Ḥasan, Majmaʿ al-bayān fī Tafsīr al-Qurʾān, part 2, page 111

The main problem that we suffer from in our current community is that mothers have distanced themselves from natural breastfeeding, which is encouraged by noble narrations, and replaced it with feeding the child artificial milk through bottles made specifically for this purpose. This is considered a violation of the child's right, in regards to his well being.

Lesson Five

The Encouragement to Raise, Teach and Discipline Children

Lesson Objectives

By the end of this lesson, the student should:

1. Get acquainted with the parents' role in raising a virtuous child.
2. Understand the religious texts that encourage a good upbringing of children.
3. Know the child's right to education and be dedicated to it.

Preamble

Narrations focused a lot on the term "virtuous child", some of which was mentioned by the Messenger of God ﷺ where he said: "A virtuous child is a sweet basil flower from God which He divided amongst his servants."[130]

It is also narrated that the Messenger of God ﷺ said: "If the son of Adam dies, his deeds get suspended except from three: a virtuous child who prays for him..."[131] A virtuous child was considered one of the causes of happiness by the parents. It is narrated that the Messenger of God ﷺ said: "It is of a man's happiness to have a virtuous child."[132]

Moreover, a virtuous child requires intercession for his parents even after their death. It is narrated that the Messenger of God ﷺ said: "Isa, son of Mary, ؑ passed by a grave whose owner was suffering. Then, he passed by it at a later time (*qābil*) [133] to find that he is no longer suffering. So he ؑ said: My Lord, I passed by this grave during one year and he was suffering; then I passed by him this year and he was not suffering?! God ﷻ revealed to him: O' Spirit of God, he had raised a virtuous son

---

[130] al-Kulaynī, Shaykh Muḥammad ibn Ya'qūb, Al-Kāfī, Vol. 6, p. 2

[131] Al-Aḥsā'ī, Shaykh Aḥmad, 'Awali al-La'ali, Vol. 1, p. 97. Review: al-Nisa'ee, Ahmad ibn Shu'ayb, Sunan al-Nisa'ee explained by al-Suyūṭī, 'Abd al-Raḥmān ibn Abī Bakr, Beirut, Dar al-Fikr, 1348 AH – 1930 AD, 1st edition, Vol. 6, p. 251

[132] al-Kulaynī, Shaykh Muḥammad ibn Ya'qūb, Al-Kāfī, Vol. 6, p. 3

[133] Qabil قابل means at a later time.

who fixed a road and sheltered an orphan; so I have forgiven him due to his son's deeds..."[134]

On the other hand, narrations condemned the wicked child and considered him a reason for blaming his parents by the people in the community for his behavior, morality and conduct. It is narrated that Imām al-Ṣādiq ﷺ said: "... A father is reproached for the deeds committed by his wicked child..."[135]

The Parents' Responsibility for the Upbringing (of the Child)

A child is attributed, in his goodness and wickedness, to his parents in the first place. Therefore, when a misbehavior appears from his side, the parents shouldn't put the blame on him; they should rather point the blaming finger at themselves. Perhaps, they didn't bear their educational responsibility as they should, or perhaps they had shortcomings in the educational process by which they didn't bear the fruit of a virtuous child after years of nurturing.

A child's undesired behavior is not innate nor originated in his creation; it is rather acquired and learned throughout his interaction with the family environment in which he grew up, and which has a huge role in shaping his identity negatively or positively. For, his contact with this environment will make him imitate his parents' actions and manifest them in speech and action.

---

[134] al-Kulaynī, Shaykh Muḥammad ibn Yaʿqūb, Al-Kāfī, Vol. 6, p. 4

[135] Ibid., Vol. 2, p. 219

Islam created a series of children's right upon their parents, some of which are: what is narrated by Imām ʿAlī al-Ḥusayn Zayn al-ʿĀbidīn ☙: "As for your child's right, it is to know that he comes from you and is added to you in this world with his goodness and evil, and that you are responsible for what you have given him of good manners and the sign of his Lord ☙ and his support in obeying Him, therefore, act in his affair as would a person who knows that he is rewarded for his benevolence towards him and punished for mistreating him."[136]

Therefore, one of the most important responsibilities of the parents towards their children is good upbringing according to the Islamic approach. It isn't sufficient to pray for virtuous offspring without work; for, a child is a trust that should be safely kept by his parents. And his heart which is void of any contamination has the ability to receive anything that is given to him. Imām ʿAlī ☙ told his son al-Ḥasan ☙: "The heart of a child is like an empty land, whatever is placed therein it accepts;

---

[136]al-Ṣadūq, Shaykh Muḥammad ibn ʿAlī, Man Lā Yahḍuruh al-Faqīh, Vol. 2, p. 622; and in another text: "As for your child's right, it is to know that he comes from you and is added to you in this world with his goodness and evil, and that you responsible for what you have given him of good manners and the sign of his Lord ☙ and his support to obey Him in you and himself, and thus are rewarded and punished for that. So, act in his affair as would a person who is adorned by his benevolence towards him in this rushing world and asks forgiveness from his Lord for what goes on between you and him by guarding him – and carrying his actions to Him - well and there no power except in God." al-Harani, ibn Shaʾba al-Ḥasan ibn ʿAlī, Tuhaf al-ʿOqoul, commented on by ʿAlī Akbar al-Ghafari, Baneed al-Qar, Kuweit, Maktabat al-Ameen, 1425 AH – 2004 AD, 1st edition, p. 293

therefore I initiated you with manners before your heart hardens and your core starts working."[137]

Henceforth, parents should bear their nurturing responsibilities; for, it is the child's right upon them to receive a good upbringing. It is narrated that the Messenger of God ﷺ said: "Your child has a right upon you."[138]

Therefore, parents don't have the right to use extra-familial reasons as excuses to avoid this responsibility, such that they sometimes blame the school, and other time friends, or relatives, or the scouts...etc.; for, it is the responsibility of the parents to choose the appropriate school, proper friends and a suitable scouts association, so they can all become a nurturing environment for the wholesome development of their children.

Ayatullāh Muḥammad Riḍā al-Gulpāygānī says: "The parents' job is to discipline their children, raise them upon noble ethics and good manners, train and adapt them to noble habits and good deeds, and prevent them from every action that harms them or others. And the children's guardian must perfect their souls[139] and lead them to what holds their goodness and success."[140]

---

137 Nahj al-Balāghah, from his will to his son al-Ḥasan which he wrote in Hadireen as he was leaving Siffin, number 269, p. 526

138 al-Naysabouri, Muslim ibn al-Hajjaj, al-Jame' al-Saheeh (Saheeh Muslim),Beirut, Dar al-Fikr, L.T, L.T', Vol. 3, p. 163

139 We mentioned the evidence for this in previous chapters.

140 Al-Jahrami, 'Alī Al-Karmi, Al-Durr al-Mandoud fi Ahkām al-Hudoud, Research reports of Ayatullāh Muḥammad Riḍā al-Gulpāyigānī, Qom, Dar al-Qur'ān Al-Kareem, 1414 AH, 1st edition, Vol. 2, p. 282

That's why Islam urged parents to raise, teach and discipline their children properly, whether they are males or females.

Education is the Child's Right upon his Parents

The encouragement towards disciplining and teaching children was mentioned in narrations, of which we will mention the following:

It is narrated that the Prophet ※ said: "May God have mercy on the servant who supports his child in honoring him by being kind to him, making himself familiar to him, and teaching and disciplining him."[141]

It is also narrated that he ※ said: "O' 'Alī, it is the child's right upon his father to give him a good name and good manners, and to put him in a virtuous place."[142]

It is narrated that Imām 'Alī ※ said: "It is the child's right upon his father: ... and to teach him the Qur'ān."[143]

It is narrated that Imām al-Ṣādiq ※ said: "Imām 'Alī used to like to have the poetry of Abi Taleb recited and written down, and he said: learn it and teach it to your children; for, it is aligned

---

[141] al-Mirzā al-Nūrī, Mustadrak al-Wasāʾil, Vol. 15, p. 169

[142] al-Ṣadūq, Shaykh Muḥammad ibn ʿAlī, Man Lā Yaḥḍuruh al-Faqīh, Vol. 4, p. 372

[143] Nahj Al-Balāghah, a chapter that includes his speeches that require explanation, ḥadīth 399

with the religion of God and encompasses a lot of knowledge."[144]

This was not differentiated between males and females; for, it is narrated that the Messenger of God ﷺ said: "He who supports three girls, disciplines them, treats them with mercy and is kind to them, gains Heaven."[145]

Other narrations that urge the education and discipline of children in different areas in pursuit of shaping the child's identity in a way that the result and fruit of the upbringing process is "a virtuous child."

Based on the aforementioned narrations, it seems that it is the child's right upon his parents to educate him. And Islam encouraged this right before any declaration or international children's rights agreement. For instance, article 26 of the Universal Declaration of Human Rights of 1948 stipulates that: "Every child has the right to education; and education must be provided free of charge...", meanwhile, Imām Zayn al-Abidin ؑ mentioned this (year 95 AH -713 AD) in his Treatise on Rights (*Risalat Al-Huquq*) hundreds of years in advance where he said: "As for the right of the young person, it is to treat him with mercy, to educate him and to teach him..."[146]

---

[144]al-Ḥurr al-ʿĀmilī, Shaykh Muḥammad ibn al-Ḥasan (Saḥib al-Wasā'il), Tafseel Wasa'el al-Shia ila Tahsil Masa'il al-Shia, Qom, the institute of al-al-Bayt li-'ihya' al-Turath, 1414 AH, 2nd edition, Vol. 17, p. 331, ḥadīth 22691

[145] Ibn Hanbal, Ahmad, Musnad Ahmad, Beirut, Dar Sader, L.T, L.T', Vol. 3, p. 97

[146] Ibn Sha'ba al-Harāni, Tuhaf al-'Oqoul, page 270

Therefore, parents should also choose the suitable educational place for the child (like the school). It is narrated that the Messenger of God ﷺ said: "It is the child's right upon his father ... to put him in a virtuous place."[147]

Moreover, they should bear responsibility – alongside the school – due to the parents' important role in shaping the child's identity as well; and this requires from the parents to raise their educational level by seeking knowledge and educating themselves due to its impact on motivating the children towards the pursuit and love of knowledge.

And it seems, from the general tone of narrations especially those which include the three 'sevens', that child education - in the sense of entering him into a school – starts from the second age-stage of the educational process, i.e. at the age of seven. It is narrated that Imām Ja'far al-Ṣādiq ؑ said: "A boy plays for seven years, learns the book for seven years and learns what's permissible and forbidden (*halal and haram*) for seven years."[148]

Main Concepts

Narrations focused a lot on the term "virtuous child", some of which was mentioned by the Messenger of God ﷺ where he said: "A virtuous child is a sweet basil flower from God which He divided amongst his servants."

---

[147] al-Ṣadūq, Shaykh Muḥammad ibn 'Alī, Man Lā Yaḥḍuruh al-Faqīh, Vol. 4, p. 372

[148] al-Kulaynī, Shaykh Muḥammad ibn Ya'qūb, Al-Kāfī, Vol. 6, p. 47

Narrations condemned the wicked child and considered him a reason for blaming his parents by the people in the community for his behavior, morality and conduct. It is narrated that Imām al-Ṣādiq said: "... A father is reproached for the deeds committed by his wicked child..."

A child is attributed, in his goodness and wickedness, to his parents in the first place. Therefore, when a misbehavior appears from his side, the parents shouldn't put the blame on him; they should rather point the blaming finger at themselves. Perhaps, they didn't bear their educational responsibility as they should, or perhaps they had shortcomings in the educational process by which they didn't bear the fruit of a virtuous child after years of nurturing.

The encouragement towards disciplining and teaching children was mentioned in several narrations, of which we will mention the following:

It is narrated that the Prophet said: "May God have mercy on the servant who supports his child in honoring him by being kind to him, making himself familiar to him, and teaching and disciplining him.

It's the child's right upon his parents to educate him. And Islam encouraged this right before any declaration or international children's rights agreement.

Parents should bear responsibility – alongside the school – due to the parents' important role in shaping the child's identity as well; and this requires from the parents to raise their educational level by seeking knowledge and educating themselves due to its impact on motivating the children towards the pursuit and love of knowledge.

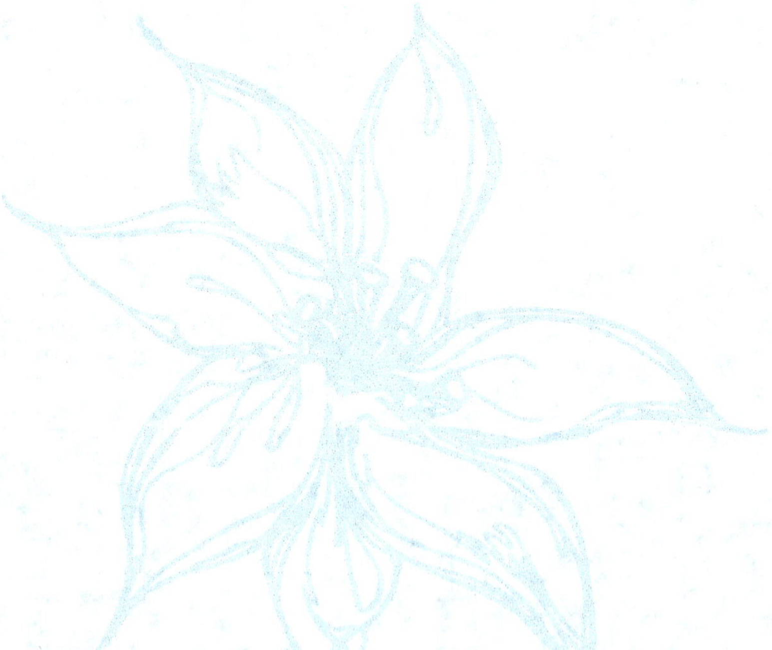

Lesson Six

The Influential Factors in a Child's Personality

Lesson Objectives

By the end of this lesson, the student should:

1. Get acquainted with the concept of environment and its types.
2. Get acquainted with the extent to which the human environment influences the shaping of a child's identity.
3. Understand the role of genetics in transferring qualities to the child.

Preamble

Environment and genetics are considered two of the basic influential factors in shaping a child's personality and his intellectual and spiritual buildup.

So what is the definition of environment and genetics? And to what extent do they affect the shaping of a child's identity?

The Definition of Environment

Environment, in the Arabic language, comes from the verb *bawa'* which means to inhabit a place, live in it and take it as a residence.[149] As for its terminological meaning, it is the surrounding or geographical-social space in which a child lives, receives – based on the resources it contains – the basic elements of his life and carries out all his activities and relationships with the various objects and living beings that surround him.

Types of Environments

Environments are of many types, such as the geographical, cultural, social, and industrial environments...etc. We will highlight its most important types; they are:

The natural environment: the external surrounding which is created by God ﷻ and contains the planets, beings, plants, animals...

---

[149] Review: Ibn Manzour, Muḥammad ibn Mukarram, Lisan al-'Arab, corrected by Amin Muḥammad Abdul Wahhāb and Muḥammad al-Ṣādiq al-'Obeidi, Beirut, Dar 'Ihya' al-Turāth al-'Arabi wa Mu'assasāt al-Tāreekh al-'Arabi, 1417 AH – 1997 AD, 2nd edition, Vol. 1, p. 39, title bawa' بوأ

The human environment: which was built by the human being and formed by his hands so he can live in it. And it includes the material, cultural and social environments.

In other words, the human environment includes four things:

1. Individuals – as individuals;
2. The compositional perception of individuals where they need to live together in one geographical space... such that a community is created with its different circles;
3. The human heritage that has been accumulated throughout history in different areas of knowledge, such as philosophy, arts, law, medicine, mathematics..., and behavior as well, such as customs, traditions and lifestyles;
4. The material accomplishments of human civilization and man's inventions, such as buildings, bridges, factories, institutions...etc.

The Role of the Human Environment in Shaping a Child's Identity

A child leaves his mother's womb as an empty land. It is narrated that Imām 'Alī ﷺ said: "The heart of a child is like an empty land which accepts all that is placed in it."[150] A child's sense of acceptance is strong to the extent that he resembles a

[150] Nahj al-Balāghah, from his will to his son al-Ḥasan ﷺ

photography lens[151] which reflects the image of the community he lives in.

The social environment in which a child grows up - including all its institutions: the family, neighborhood, neighbors, relatives, school and friends, in addition to a special element which has become strongly present in our age which is the virtual world such as the internet, Facebook pages and television shows...- plays a prominent role in determining a child's intellectual, psychological, value-based, behavioral and sentimental identity. For, a child doesn't acquire his perceptions, ideologies, orientations, values, behaviors and skills by himself; rather, he does so through his interaction with the external surroundings upon which the canvas of his personality is formed due to the reaction and influence of the social environment.

Even the pure monotheistic primordial nature which was deposited in the origins of creation within the child's soul doesn't stand a chance in the midst of the influential spirit of the familial and social environments. It is narrated that Imām al-Ṣādiq ﷺ said: "No child is born except that he has within him the (monotheistic) primordial nature. Then, his parents turn him into a Jew, a Christian and Zoroastrians (*Majus*) ..."[152]

This narration provides a clear indicator to the role of the family environment and its influence on shaping the general features of

---

[151] Review: Falsafi, Muḥammad Taqi, The Child Between Genetics and Upbringing, translated to Arabic by Fadel al-Ḥusaynī al-Milani, al-'Awhad Library, 1426 AH – 2005 AD, 1st edition, Vol. 1, p. 196

[152] al-Ṣadūq, Shaykh Muḥammad ibn 'Alī, Man La Yahdaruhu al-Faqih, part 2, page 49, ḥadīth 1668

a child's personality; and the same case applies to the general social environment. A narration was mentioned, in this context, by Imām al-Ṣādiq ☙, where he said: "Initiate your children with narrations before the Murjites[153] get to them first."[154]

In a nutshell: "No one can deny the origin of the influence and power held by the social environment on shaping the personality of each individual human being, and that this influence and power are deep and comprehensive for the vast majority of the people. For, there is no doubt that an individual is often submissive (to) and governed by the will of society."[155]

Nonetheless, it should be noted that despite society's influence in shaping a child's personality, this doesn't mean that it reaches the extent of social determinism which robs a person from his free will and choice.

The Educational Responsibility of the Parents

The aforementioned puts great educational responsibility on the parents' shoulders which manifest in four things:

First: Raising the child upon critical thinking and free inference in order to establish within him a faculty that enables him to distinguish between right and wrong, good and ugly...

---

153 Murji'ites were an early Islamic sect. Murji'ah held the opinion that God alone has the right to judge whether or not a Muslim has become an apostate.

154 al-Kulaynī, Shaykh Muḥammad ibn Yaʿqūb, Al-Kāfī, Vol. 6, p. 47

155 Yazdī, Ayatullāh Muḥammad Taqī Miṣbāḥ, al-Nazra al-Qurʾraniyya lil Mujtamaʾ w al-Tareekh, translated to Arabic by Muḥammad Abdul Munʾim al-Khaqānī, Beirut, Dar al-Rawda, 1416 AH – 1996 AD, 1st edition, p. 49

Second: Strengthening and solidifying the will within the child's personality in order to equip him with the strength and power to confront and resist what society is experiencing – nay the power to change and influence as well.

Third: Creating a suitable family environment that supports the development of the child, since the child perceives his parents as a role model to follow. This requires that the relationship between the father and mother – as well as the siblings – be based on Islamic values such as mutual respect. Therefore, they should not display any negative behavior in front of the child; as this will affect the child's personality in two ways:

a. Imitating them; for, if a child lives in the midst of a broken family, and the relationships amongst its members are based on screaming, anger, quarrels and bad manners, then he will build his relationships with the material and human things around him using the same negative methods that exist within the family.

b. The negative or positive energy at home projects itself onto the rest of the members negatively or positively. And a person feels this thing in his core as a result of accumulated cases and personal experiences.

Fourth: Searching for a good place and suitable environment for the child which will provide him with the appropriate climate and conditions for the formation and sublimation of his identity in a good and proper way.

It is narrated that the Messenger of God ﷺ said: "O' 'Alī, it is the right of the child upon his father to give him a good name, to discipline him and to put him in a good place."[156]

The Natural Environment and its Effect on a Child

The impact of the natural environment on the physical aspect of a child is one of the obvious matters that has been proved by experiential science. A child is a component of the natural ecosystem; for example, no one can deny the impact of the climate factors – such as warmth or coldness ...etc. – on human life, or deny the negative impact of water or air pollution on a child's food security. In addition, the natural environment plays an essential role in the intellectual, temperamental and psychological aspects of a child; for, it plays a prominent role in helping a child explore things around him, which contributes to the development of his capacities, in addition to the intellectual, psychological and skills-based faculties. However, this doesn't mean that the environment constitutes the features of a child's personality in a way that renders him merely receptive and excitable.

The environment has its effects on a child, yet not in a way that makes it the only factor that shapes a child's identity in a deterministic way. Islam doesn't acknowledge the certain influence of only one element; it rather adopts the holistic view which – as a whole – contributes to shaping the personal identity of a child. Sayyid Muḥammad Bāqir al-Sadr states that the perceptions that adopted only one factor in understanding the human being have failed miserably, and he says that: "all

[156]al-Ṣadūq, Shaykh Muḥammad ibn 'Alī, Man Lā Yaḥḍuruh al-Faqīh, p. 784, Chapter of al-Fara'ed, section al-Nawader, ḥadīth 5764, paragraph 14

these attempts do not align with reality and are not acknowledged by Islam, because each and every one of them tried to comprehend – using one factor – the interpretation of the human life in its entirety."[157]

The Influence of the Genetic Factor on a Child's Identity

Amongst the factors which have the most prominent role in determining the child's identity is the genetic factor. And it is considered one of the main elements that are being studied in regards to its influence on creating a child's personality by educators, psychologists, sociologists and biologists. So, what is genetics? And what is its role in designing the child's identity?

The Definition of Genetics

Genetics, linguistically, is the transference of something – wholly or partially – from one person or subject to another whether materially or morally.[158]

The contextual meaning of the word doesn't differ in content from its linguistic meaning.

The topic of genetics has become, today, an independent focus of a specific science from the branches of biology which was called by William Patson: 'the science of genetics'. And its role is

---

[157] al-Ṣadr, Ayatullāh Shahīd Sayyid Muḥammad Bāqir, Iqtiṣādunā, Beirut, Dar al-ta'arof, 1411 AH – 1991 AD, p. 55

[158] Al-Mustafawi, Ḥasan, al-Tahqiq fi Kalimat al-Qur'ān al-Karim, L.M, Institute of publishing and printing in the ministry of education and Islamic guidance, 1417 AH, 1st edition, Vol. 13, p. 77

to study the qualities that are transferred from the parents to the children, the modality of this transference and the explanation of the reasons behind the similarities and differences between relatives.

The Law of Genetics

1. The Law of Genetics from a Biological Point of View:

One of the constants in biological research is that the natural law of genetics which is related to the transference of characteristics and physical qualities from the parents and grandparents to the children and grandchildren is undeniably valid and axiomatic. Narrations by Ahl al-Bayt mentioned this issue, especially those which included the term "ethnicity" and encouraged the proper selection of a wife, such as the following saying by the Prophet : "Choose well for your sperms; for, ethnicity is discreetly intrusive (*dassas*)."[159] Some scholars considered this narration to be a clear indicator which highlights the law of genetics – considering the synonymy between ethnicity and genetics.[160] The meaning of ethnicity is well-known; and linguistically, it also means the origin of

---

[159] Al-Hilli, Muḥammad ibn Mansour, al-Sara'er, Qom, Institute of Islamic Publishing related to the group of teachers in the honorable city of Qom, 1410 AH, 2nd edition, Vol. 2, p. 559, and Al-Fayd al-Kashāni, Muḥammad ibn al-Murtada, al-Mahajja al-Bayda' fi Tahdheeb al-Ahya', corrected and commented on by ʿAlī Akbar al-Ghafari, Beirut, Al-Aʿlami Institute for Printing and Publishing, 1403 AH – 1983 AD, 2nd edition, Vol. 3, p. 93

[160] Falsafi, Muḥammad Taqi, al-Tifl bayn al-Wirātha wal Tarbiya, part 1, page 61, and al-Jawāhiri, Ḥasan, Buhouth fi al-Fiqh al-Muʿāser, Vol. 3, p. 162

everything and its foundation[161]. And *'dassas'* (discreetly intrusive) comes from the word *'dass'* which means to enter something into another thing discreetly. The point of this *ḥadīth* is that there are certain characteristics that are transferred through kinship from the predecessor to the offspring.

2. The Law of Genetics from the Intellectual, Psychological and Behavioral Point of View:

It became clear from the above that the genetic factor has a biological impact on the child's personality. However, the remaining question is: Does genetics include the transference of non-physical characteristics to the offspring, such as intellectual characteristics and psychological and behavioral qualities...etc.? And assuming that they are transferable, is the person capable with his free will and choice to revoke the natural law of genetics?

To answer this question, we must point out an essential issue which is the existence of a unity between man's spirit and body, in the sense that each of them is influenced by the other. And this consequently means that physical qualities and characteristics will influence the intellectual qualities as well.

Shaykh Ja'far Subḥāni says: "Just as children inherit their parents' money and wealth, they inherit their external and internal qualities, where you can see a child resembling his father or paternal uncle, or his mother or maternal uncle... Accordingly, good or bad moral qualities are transferred

---

161 Al-Zubeidi, Muḥammad Murtada, Taj al-'Arous min Jawāher al-Qāmous, verified by 'Alī Sheeri, Beirut, Dal al-Fikr, 1414 AH – 1994 AD, L.T', Vol. 13, p. 324

genetically to the children, where we can see that the son of a brave man is brave, and the son of a coward a coward, in addition to many other physical and moral qualities."[162] One of their proofs of this is what was narrated by the Prophet ﷺ: "Look at the place you put your child in; for, ethnicity is discreetly intrusive."[163] And Sayyid al-Khumaynī ؒ commented on this ḥadīth by saying: "The intended meaning behind using the term '*dassās*' is that parents' morals extend to the children."[164]

The Distinction between the Inheritance of Potentials and Faculties

It seems, from the above, that some physical characteristics and bodily diseases play a role in the mental states and psychological traits of a human being. This has been proven by scientific experiments. Moreover, there is no doubt that the fathers' and mothers' traits play an influential role in forming special potentials in the child which make him closer to some traits rather than others.[165] This has also been mentioned in the narrations of Ahl al-Bayt عليهم السلام.

---

162 Subḥānī, Ayatullāh Jaʿfar, 'Ismat al-'Anbiya' fi al-Qur'ān al-Karim, Qom, The Institute of Imām al-Ṣādiq, 1420 AH, 2nd edition, p. 33

163 Al-Hindi, 'Alī al-Muttaqi, Kanz al-'Ummāl, explained by Bakri Hayani, corrected by Safwat al-Saqam Beirut, The Institute of Al-Risālah, 1409 AH – 1989 AD, Vol. 15, p. 855

164 Subḥānī, Ayatullāh Jaʿfar, Lubb al-Athar fi al-Jabr wal Qadar from the reported lectures of Sayyid al-Khumaynī, p. 120

165 Ibid., p. 114

It is important to point out the difference between saying that these traits play a role in forming special potentials in the child, and saying that they – themselves – transfer to the child. For, the legacy here is the special potential rather than the traits themselves. And this special potential doesn't grow automatically; it rather unfolds gradually through upbringing and a nurturing environment.

That's why some scientists believe in the absence of proof for the transference of acquired traits from the fathers and mothers to the children – nay they believe in the proof of the non-transferability of acquired traits through genetics.[166]

In reality, there are two directions in this regard: the first was adopted by sociologists who believed that genetic traits transfer – as they are – to the children. Meanwhile those who adopted the second direction denied any role of genetics in building the child's identity.

The truth is there isn't any scientific, Qur'ānic or narrative proof for the transference of traits – as it is such as faculties – through genetics. Moreover, one cannot deny the influence of the genetic factor on a child's personality. Therefore, we can choose a third moderate opinion which is that genetics, environment and upbringing – each – has a specific role in shaping a child's personality.

---

166 al-Ṣadr, Ayatullāh Sayyid Muḥammad Bāqir, Falsafatuna, Beirut, Dar Al-Ta'āruf lil Matbou'āt, 1400 AH – 1980 AD, 10th edition, p. 312-315

The Role of Genetics, Environment and Upbringing

Genetics, as pointed out in the noble narrations, has a specific role in this regard whereby the father or mother's traits create a particular potential within the child – which is called genetic potential. Nonetheless, it doesn't rob them of their will and choice; for, one can – through upbringing – guide a child towards a direction that is different from that which the child acquired genetically.

A child's personality isn't formed from only one factor, but rather from a group of factors that intertwine to shape a child's identity, the most important of which is the factor of upbringing. "For, there are some believers who are born from non-believers, and others who are corrupt and evil yet are born from good and pious parents, thus revoking the law of genetics with their own will and choice."[167]

Inherited Potentials

We can divide inherited potentials into two parts:

The first: potentials that have a biological nature which is reflected in the mental traits such as idiocy and mental retardation. These can be cured with the advancement of experimental science and medicine. However, due to the fact that this advancement doesn't cover certain areas, then the potentials thereof will remain unchangeable.

---

167 Shīrāzī, Ayatullāh Nāṣir Makārim, al-Amthāl fī Tafsīr Kitāb God al-Munzal, Qom, School of Imām ʿAlī ibn Abī Ṭālib, 1426 AH, 1st edition, Vol. 4, p. 396

The second: potentials that are capable of change whether easily or with difficulty.

However, what is transferred from fathers and mothers in this regard is divided into two types:

a. The traits that are imposed on children in a way that cannot be eliminated such idiocy, laziness, reason and intelligence... which most likely cannot be eliminated through educational and reformative efforts.

b. The groundwork that is inherited by children which can be eliminated through upbringing means and scientific ways such as genetic diseases (e.g. AIDS) and other psychological states such as rebellion and aggression. For, not all that is inherited by children from fathers and mothers is a necessary destiny and a certain fate. There still remains the human will and choice and other upbringing factors which can change the groundwork of genetics.[168]

Main Concepts

There are many factors that have an influential role in the upbringing of a child and his growth, the most prominent of which is the environment. The environment consists of the external factors that influence the human being; and it includes all the factors that surround him such as material appearances and living, social and cultural patterns.

---

168 Al-Malaki, Ḥasan Muḥammad, al-Ilahiyyat ‘ala Daw’ al-Kitāb wa ‘Alsinat al-‘Aql (lectures of Subḥānī, Ayatullāh Ja‘far), Beirut, al-Dar al-Islamiyyah, 1410 AH – 1990 AD, 1st edition, Vol. 1, p. 662

Environment, in the Arabic language, comes from the verb bawa' which means to inhabit a place, live in it and take it as a residence.[169] As for its terminological meaning, it is the surrounding or geographical-social space in which a child lives, receives – based on the resources it contains – the basic elements of his life.

The social environment in which a child grows up - including all its institutions: the family, neighborhood, neighbors, relatives, school and friends – plays a prominent role in determining a child's intellectual, psychological, value-based, behavioral and sentimental identity.

The impact of the natural environment on the physical aspect of a child is one of the obvious matters that has been proved by experiential science. And a child is a component of the natural ecosystem.

Genetics, linguistically, is the transference of something – wholly or partially – from one person or subject to another whether materially or morally.[170]

The contextual meaning of the word doesn't differ in content from its linguistic meaning.

---

[169] Review: Ibn Manzour, Muḥammad ibn Mukarram, Lisān al-'Arab, corrected by Amin Muḥammad Abdul Wahhāb and Muḥammad al-Ṣādiq al-'Obeidi, Beirut, Dar 'Ihya' al-Turath al-'Arabi wa Mu'assasat al-Tareekh al-'Arabi, 1417 AH – 1997 AD, 2nd edition, Vol. 1, p. 39, title bawa' بوأ

[170] Al-Mustafawi, Ḥasan, al-Taḥqīq fi Kalimat al-Qur'ān al-Karīm, L.M, Institute of publishing and printing in the ministry of education and Islamic guidance, 1417 AH, 1st edition, Vol. 13, p. 77

The truth is there isn't any scientific or Qur'ānic or narrative proof for the transference of traits – as it is such as faculties – through genetics. Moreover, one cannot deny the influence of the genetic factor on a child's personality. Therefore, we can choose a third moderate opinion which is that genetics, environment and upbringing - each – has a specific role in shaping a child's personality.

Lesson Seven

The Age Stages of a Child

Lesson Objectives

By the end of this lesson, the student should:

1. Determine the stages at which childhood begins and ends from a linguistic and contextual point of view.
2. Get acquainted with the age stages according to the narrative approach.
3. Get acquainted with the criteria of discernment in Islam.

Preamble

Childhood is the first stage in the life of the human being; and it requires care and attention – the most – from the guardians of the upbringing process (the father, the mother). Therefore, it is necessary to clarify the linguistic, contextual and situational meaning of childhood in order to facilitate the understanding of the upbringing process. Furthermore, it is necessary to learn about the age stages of the child due to its primary role in the success of the upbringing process and in achieving its desired objectives. This is because each stage has its specific approach which matches the intellectual, psychological and physical development of the human being.

There are many divisions adopted by psychologists and educators, in addition to different opinions in this regard. Nonetheless, the Islamic approach which is derived from the two weighty things, the Noble Qur'ān and the pure progeny ﷺ, remains the strongest approach within all the stages of the upbringing process. So, what do we mean by childhood? And what are the age stages of a child?

A Child from the Linguistic Point of View

A child, linguistically, is the youngster of everything or of the children of people particularly.

Al-Farāhidi (100-175 AH) said: "A child: the youngster of people's children..."[171]

[171] Al-Farāhidi, Al-Khalil ibn Ahmad, verified by Mahdī al-Makhzoumi and Ibrāhīm al-Samurrā'i, Iran, Institute of Dar al-Hijra, 1409 AH, 2nd edition, Vol. 7, p. 428

And Al-Feiruz Abādi (817 AH) said: "A child (pronounced *al-Tifl*) is the youngster of everything or the newborn."[172]

The Term 'Child' in the Noble Qur'ān

The term 'child' was mentioned four times in the Noble Qur'ān, three of which were in the singular form and one in the plural form; and they all indicated the child's age group which extends from birth until the age of puberty. This age group is:

1. God ﷻ said: ﴿*We indeed created you from dust, then from a drop of [seminal] fluid, then from a clinging mass, then from a fleshy tissue, partly formed and partly unformed, so that We may manifest [Our power] to you. We establish in the wombs whatever We wish for a specified term, then We bring you forth as infants*﴾[173]

2. ﴿*It is He who created you from dust, then from a drop of [seminal] fluid, then from a clinging mass, then He brings you forth as infants...*﴾[174]

3. ﴿*And not display their charms except to their husbands, or their fathers ... or children uninitiated to women's parts...*﴾[175]

---

172 Al-Feiruz Abadi, Muḥammad ibn Yaʿqūb, al-Qamous al-Muhit fi al-Lugha, Beirut, Dar al-Jeel, L.T, L.T', Vol. 4, p. 7

173 Sūrah al-Hajj, verse 5

174 Sūrah Ghāfir, verse 67

175 Sūrah al-Nūr, verse 31

4. ﴾*When your children reach puberty, let them ask permission [at all times] just as those who asked permission before them*﴿[176]

In addition to that, the Noble Qur'ān used some terms to refer to a young boy, some of which are:

a. Youth (*ghulam*): it seems from the Noble Qur'ān that the word boy is given to the young boy who is in his intermediate age stage right before the age of puberty. This is manifested in His saying ﷻ:

﴾*And there came a caravan, and they sent their water-drawer, who let down his bucket. 'Good news!' he said. 'This is a young boy!' So they hid him as [a piece of] merchandise, and God knew best what they were doing*﴿[177]

b. Boy (*sabi*): This was given to two childhood stages in the Noble Qur'ān:

﴾*Thereat she pointed to him. They said, 'How can we speak to one who is yet a baby in the cradle?'*﴿[178]

﴾*'O John!' [We said,] 'Hold on with power to the Book!' And We gave him judgment while still a child*﴿[179]

---

[176] Sūrah al-Nūr, verse 59

[177] Sūrah Yūsuf, verse 19

[178] Sūrah Maryam, verse 29

[179] Sūrah Maryam, verse 12

c. Child (walad): it was also mentioned in several verses such as "al-walad", "al-wildan" and "al-waleed", one of which is His saying ﷻ: *﴿...Did we not rear you as a child among us, and did you not stay with us for years of your life?﴾*[180]

d. Young: *﴿Lower the wing of humility to them, out of mercy, and say, 'My Lord! Have mercy on them, just as they reared me when I was [a] small [child]!'﴾*[181]

The Beginning of Childhood according to Linguistic and Religious Terminologies

It appears, from the sayings of linguistic scholars, that the beginning of childhood is the exit of the newborn from his mother's womb. For, a fetus isn't called a 'child' – except in condonation– just as a life-germ or an ovum isn't called a 'child'. Ibn Sīda (458 AH) said: "As long as the child is still in his mother's womb then he is a fetus..."[182]

And al-Zubeidi (1205 AH) said: "... a boy is called a child when he falls out of his mother's womb..."[183]

And if we track the Sunnah of the Prophet ﷺ and Ahl al-Bayt عليهم السلام, we will not find in their narrations anything that helps us determine the beginning of childhood. And perhaps the narrations didn't point this matter out due to the fact that it is

---

180 Sūrah Ash-Shu'arā, verse 18

181 Sūrah al-Isrā, verse 24

182 Ibn Sīda, al-Mukhassas, Vol. 1, p. 30

183 Al-Zubeidi, Taj al-'Arous, Vol. 15, p. 434

customarily clear. Therefore, we cannot refer to narrations in this regard due to the absence of any specific mentioning therein. Thereby, the reference that can be relied upon is the customary understanding.

The Beginning of Childhood from the Legal Point of View

Many opinions have been mentioned by jurists in regard to identifying the beginning of childhood, which led to a difference of opinion thereof. This difference can be restricted to three opinions which we will mention briefly:

The first opinion: "A child is the boy at the moment of falling out of his mother's womb until he reaches the age of puberty."[184]

The second opinion: It is mentioned in the Universal Declaration of the Rights of the Child[185] that "a child... needs protection and special care, including the appropriate legal protection before and after birth"[186]. One can assume that the term 'birth' implied the inclusivity of the fetus within the word 'child'.

---

184 Ibn 'Abidin, Muḥammad Amin, Radd al-Muhtar 'ala Durr al-Muhtar (footnotes of Ibn Abidin), supervised by the office of research and studies, Beirut, Dar al-Fikr, 1415 AH – 1995 AD, new edition, Vol. 2, p. 396, and Vol. 3, p. 672

185 Published upon a decision taken by the general assembly number, 1386 AH (D -14), dated 20, November, 1959 AD

186 Published upon a decision taken by the general assembly number, 1386 AH (D -14), dated 20, November, 1959 AD

The third opinion: it declared that "childhood includes the prenatal stage."[187]

The End of Childhood according to Religious Terminology

The end of childhood, according to religious terminology, is defined by its corresponding meaning which is puberty. For, puberty breaks the child out of childhood and enters him into a new stage which is the stage of duty (*al-taklif*). Some scholars and interpreters concluded from His ﷻ saying: ﴿*When your children reach puberty, let them ask permission [at all times] just as those who asked permission before them*﴾[188] that puberty is the end of childhood, based on the evidence of opposition between childhood and reaching puberty.

There are many criteria set by Islam for determining the stage of puberty[189], which are:

---

[187] Abdullah, Samar Khalil Mahmoud, A Comparative Study on The Rights of a Child in Islam and International Conventions, Master's thesis, National University of al-Najah, Faculty of Higher Education, Nablus, Palestine, 2003 AD, electronic copy, p. 30

[188] Sūrah al-Nūr, verse 59

[189] Review from the Imāmiyya scholars: al-Shahīd al-Thānī, Masālik al-Afhām ila Tankeeh Sharā'e' al-Islām, Vol. 4, p. 141, and form the books of the Sunnis: al-Shoukani, Muḥammad ibn 'Alī, Nayl al-Awtār min Aḥadīth Sayyid al-Akhbār, Beirut, Dal al-Jaleel, 1973 AD, L.T, Vol. 5, p. 370 and the pages that follow, and al-Jazeeri, Abdul Rahman, al-Fiqh 'ala al-Mathaheb al-Arba'a, printed with the book of al-Fiqh 'ala al-Mathaheb al-Arba'a wa Madhhab Ahl al-Bayt, Sayyid Muḥammad al-Gharawi and Shaykh Yaser Māzeh, Beirut, Dar al-Thaqalayn, 1419 AH – 1998 AD, 1st edition, Vol. 2, p. 411 and the following pages

The first sign: Germination, which means the germination of coarse hair on the pubis. This sign is common between males and females. Scholars have considered it one of the signs that can be relied upon as an indicator to religious puberty even in the absence of other indicators.

The second sign: The ejection of semen whether in waking or in dreams, and whether it resulted from intercourse or not. And it's also common between males and females.

The third sign (exclusive to females): Reaching the age of 9 (lunar years), i.e. approximately 8.8 Gregorian years.

For, females are distinguished from males by leaving childhood before them.

The fourth sign (exclusive to males): Reaching the age of 15 (lunar year), i.e. approximately 14.6 Gregorian years.

Based on the above, after – both – males and females leave the circle of childhood once they have reached the religious age of duty, they can no longer be treated – from a jurisprudential point of view – as children, but rather as dutiful adults who are obliged to follow the religious rulings and other rulings pertinent to the age of puberty.

As for the end of childhood in legal terminology, it's by completing 18 years of age.

The Division of Childhood Stages in Islamic Texts

Each of the upbringing stages through which a child passes has its specific upbringing rulings that are appropriate to the age stage of the child. One can observe the childhood stages in religious texts from two angles:

First: The Deductive Division:

This occurs through deducing the Islamic texts and reaching a conclusion in regards to the modality of dividing the age stages of a child. Afterwards, one can reach the following result:

a. The pre-marital stage which specializes in the proper selection of the spouse

b. The stage of sexual intercourse (before the establishment of the life-germ)

c. The germinal stage: the establishment of the life-germ and formation of the fetus, manifested in His ﷻ saying: *﴾So let man consider from what he was created. He was created from an effusing fluid. Which issues from between the loins and the breast-bones﴿*[190]

d. The embryonic stage which is the stage in of pregnancy

e. The postnatal stage which extends from the first until the seventh day of birth

f. The breastfeeding stage (two complete years)

g. The stage of custody from the first day until 2/7 years

h. The stage of discernment from 7 years until puberty

---

190 Sūrah al-Ṭāreq, verses 5-7

i. The stage of foolish puberty: a child's entry into the stage of puberty happens in two ways:

j. Immature foolish puberty where he cannot, at this stage, manage his affairs, money... etc., therefore it is considered – according to some jurisprudential rulings on upbringing – an extension to childhood.

k. Mature puberty: it's the stage in which the adult is capable of managing his affair, body and money...

And each of these stages has its own appropriate upbringing rights and characteristics.

Second: The Division Known as the 'Three Sevens':

This division can be concluded from religious texts in which it is referred to as the 'three sevens'.

It is narrated that the Prophet ﷺ said: "A child is a master for seven years, a servant for seven years, and a minister for seven years. If you are satisfied with his morals[191] until he reaches the age of 21 – otherwise you hit him on his sides[192] – then you are excused by God."[193]

---

[191] In the copy of Makārim al-Akhlāq, the term used is 'Akhlāqahu' meaning morals.

[192] In the copy of Makārim al-Akhlāq, the phrase used is 'hit him on his sides'.

[193] al-Ḥurr al-ʿĀmilī, Shaykh Muḥammad ibn al-Ḥasan, Tafsil Wasa'el al-Shia ila Tahsil Masā'il al-Shia, Vol. 21, p. 476, ḥadīth 27627, and al-Ṭabrisī, Shaykh al-Faḍl ibn al-Ḥasan, Makārim al-Akhlāq al-Akhlāq, p. 222

And it is narrated that Imām Ja'far al-Ṣādiq ﷺ said: "Let your child play for seven years, discipline him for seven years and keep him by your side for seven years. Then, he should succeed; otherwise, there's no good in him."[194]

The first seven: "the stage of play and grace (not negligence)":

This stage starts from 0 until 7 years. And it seems, from narrations, that this stage has its own specialty, whereby the child therein is weak, ignorant, lacking his actual perfection and unaware of his surroundings. Thus, he begins his exploration of all his surroundings according to the capacities and potentials that are appropriate to his age stage.

For, at this stage, he needs a margin of freedom to carry out his exploration under the supervision of the nurturer without adding a lot of restrictions which – if present – will limit his exploratory capacity that is given to him by God ﷻ through play and mobile activity.

Accordingly, narrations referred to this stage using terms such as: "the master child", "let your child", "give leeway to your child"... etc.

The second seven: "the stage of teaching and discipline":

This stage is considered a groundwork and a foundation in the upbringing process. For, we find narrations that emphasize the matters of teaching and discipline in a detailed manner, where the nurturer has an effective role in this stage in which the child's personality is being shaped in a way that prepares him to

---

[194] al-Kulaynī, Shaykh Muḥammad ibn Ya'qūb, Al-Kāfī, Vol. 6, p. 47

become mature, developed and effective in society in the following stages. Therefore, narrations referred to this stage using terms such as: "servant", "learns", "disciplined"...etc., after referring to him during his first seven years as "master". This indicates the qualitative transformation in the upbringing process during the second seven years.

Narrations pointed out the particularity of this stage due to its accuracy, such that several narrations were mentioned in regards to sexual education and religious upbringing... etc. It is narrated that the Prophet ﷺ said: "Separate your children in bed once they complete seven years of age."[195]

And it is narrated that Imām al-Ṣādiq (ع) said: "... Order your boys to pray when they reach seven years of age."[196] It is obvious that these narrations and others draw the pathway of the child's upbringing process at this stage.

The third seven: narrations referred to it using several expressions such as "keep him by your side", and in a narration "and a minister for seven years". We gather, from these two citations and others, that the requirement at this stage is to befriend the child and – gradually – train him on bearing responsibility and choosing life.

The Criteria of the Stage of Discernment

A child, in the stage of the second seven of the "three sevens", becomes in most cases a discerning child. And if we look up – in

---

[195] al-Ṭabrisī, Shaykh al-Faḍl ibn al-Ḥasan, Makārim al-Akhlāq, p. 223

[196] al-Kulaynī, Shaykh Muḥammad ibn Ya'qūb, Al-Kāfī, Vol. 3, p. 409

religious texts –the term "discerning child" or "discernment", we will not find it in any of these texts. Therefore, one must go back to identifying the criteria given to this stage by scholars through deducing their texts, which will result in the following opinions:

The first criterion (criterion of time): from 6 or 7 years until puberty.

Some scholars considered that the stage of a child's discernment extends from the age of 6 or 7 until puberty. And it is likely that the foundations of their evidence are the narrations mentioned by Ahl al-Bayt ﷺ from which one can conclude that the age of seven for a child involves a lot of worshiping and behavioral guidance which require discernment of the child so he can carry them out.[197]

The second criterion: distinguishing the beautiful from the ugly. There are declarations by some scholars in this regard such as:

"A discerning child is he who is capable of identifying the ugly and the beautiful."[198]

It is not required from a discerning child to be able to distinguish the beautiful from the ugly, and the harmful from

---

197 al-Khoeī, Ayatullāh Sayyid Abū l-Qāsim al-Mūsawī, and Tabrīzī, Ayatullāh Mīrzā Jawād, Sirat al-Najat fi Ajwibat al-'Istifta'at, collected by Mūsā Mufīd al-Dīn 'Assi, Beirut, Dar al-Mahajja al-Bayda', Dār al-Rasoul al-Akram, 1418 AH – 1997 AD, 1st edition, Vol. 6, p. 65

198 Arākī, Ayatullāh Muḥammad 'Alī, al-Masa'el al-Wadiḥa, Qom, the Islamic Media Office, 1414 AH, 1st edition, Vol. 2, p. 91

the beneficial in a detailed manner. General distinction is rather sufficient.

The third criterion: "The reference in regards to a discerning child is custom..."[199]

The fourth criterion: the variation of discernment according to the variation of the object of duty. For, in the case of the permissibility of looking at his or someone else's private parts, a discerning child – here – would be the person who is affected by looking at – his or someone's – private parts. And in the case of the validity of the acts of worship, it is the person who can distinguish the duties, comprehend that it comes from God ﷻ and carry the intention of divine proximity...[200]

The fifth criterion: the variation of the discerning child according to the variation of time, location and individuals.

Sayyid 'Alī al-Khāmina'ī was asked: Some rulings mentioned that the discerning boy is the boy who can distinguish the beautiful from the ugly, what is – then – meant by beautiful and ugly? And what is the age of discernment?

He replied: "The intended (meaning) from (the words) beautiful and ugly is what is customarily known to be so, while taking into consideration the circumstances of the boy's life, habits, etiquettes and local traditions. As for the age of

[199] Al-'Amilī, Sayyid Muḥammad Jawād, Muftah al-Karama fi Sharh Qawa'ed al-Alāma, verified by Muḥammad Bāqir al-Khalisī, Qom, Institute of Islamic Publishing, 1430 AH, 2nd edition, Vol. 6, p. 432

[200] Sīstānī, Ayatullāh Sayyid 'Alī al-Ḥusaynī, al-'Istifta'āt, L.M, L.N, L.T, L.T', p. 125-126

discernment, it varies according to the variation of people's potential, perception and intelligence."[201]

Conclusion

Though the scholars' sayings in regards to the child's age of discernment appears to be vary through different expressions, nonetheless it is all capsuled into one criterion which is:

That the child reaches an age stage where he develops the capacity to distinguish – in a general manner – the beautiful from the ugly, and the harmful from the beneficial in life. And there is no doubt that the areas of discernment vary according to the variation of their objects – whether they are sexual, political, financial, acts of worship ...etc.

Therefore, the age of discernment will vary from one child to another; and the reference for determining this age will be the customary and social perception of the environment in which the child moves and interacts with the rest of the members of his community.

Main Concepts

A child, linguistically, is the newborn until he reaches puberty. And childhood is a stage which extends from birth until puberty.

---

201 al-Khāmina'ī, Sayyid 'Alī al-Ḥusaynī, 'Ajwibat al-'Istifta'at, Vol. 2, p. 300, issue 822

The child terminologically: he is a world of complex unknowns like the vast oceans in which the more the researchers dive, the more the treasures and new scientific truths they discover.

The term 'child' was mentioned in the Noble Qur'ān in different expressions such as youth, boy, child and young...

According to the Imāmiyyah's terminology: both males and females break out of childhood after reaching the religious age of duty.

The narrative division of the age stages is known as the "three sevens", derived from the saying of Imām 'Alī ☙: "A boy is brought up for seven years, disciplined for seven years and employed for seven years..."[202]

The child's age of discernment is determined by his completion of 6 or 7 years of age, regardless of the cognitive state of a seven year old; for, this is a matter of worship according to the religious text.

---

[202] al-Ṣadūq, Shaykh Muḥammad ibn 'Alī, Man La Yaḥdaruhu al-Faqīh, Vol. 3, p. 493, ḥadīth 4746

Lesson Eight

Educational Justice

Lesson Objectives

By the end of this lesson, the student should:

1. Get acquainted with the meaning of educational justice.
2. Realize the importance of implementing educational justice in the upbringing of the family.
3. Believe in the positive distinction given by Islam to girls.

Preamble

The Utterly Just is considered one of God's names ﷻ. And due to its importance of Justice, it was made the second branch of the five branches of Islam. A believer must adorn himself with God's ﷻ qualities and His most beautiful names including The Utterly Just. The Qur'ān associated justice with piety; for, God ﷻ says: ﴾*Be fair; that is nearer to God-consciousness, and be wary of God. God is indeed well aware of what you do*﴿[203]

The absence of justice between children is considered one of the most prominent issues experienced by some Muslim families, such that we find that there is discrimination between children within the same household; and sometimes, boys are distinguished from girls. The upbringing approach in Islam emphasized on the issue of educational justice and considered it a high educational value. It is narrated that the Prophet ﷺ said: "...Fear God and act justly with your children..."[204]

Educational Justice between the Two Genders

The Islamic upbringing approach emphasized on the principle of equality between the male and female child. It is narrated that the Prophet ﷺ said: "He who has a daughter and has not buried her, insulted her or favored his son over her, God enters him into Heaven."[205]

---

203 Sūrah al-Mā'ida, verse 8

204 Al-Muttaqi al-Hindi, Kanz al-'Ummāl, Vol. 16, p. 445

205 Al-'Aḥsa'i, 'Awāli al-La'āli', Vol. 1, p. 181

The same case applies to the son as well. It is narrated that Sa'd ibn Sa'd al-'Ash'āri said: I asked Abā al-Ḥasan al-Riḍā ..., so I said: May I be sacrificed for you, are a man's daughters dearer to him than his sons? Al-Riḍā said: "Girls and boys are equal in this regard. They are as dear to him as God has set them to be."[206]

It is worthy to note that the emotional nature of a girl requires empathy and mercy more than a boy. This is indicated, as well, in the Islamic upbringing approach, where it is narrated that Abi al-Ḥasan al-Riḍā said: the Messenger of God said: "God (the Blessed and Exalted) is more empathetic with females than He is with males. There isn't any man who brings joy to a woman who is his *maḥram*[207] except that God brings him joy on the day of resurrection." [208]

The Meaning of Educational Justice

Man is innately enamored with the love of his children. This is considered a natural thing within every human being. Accordingly, love is of ranks and degrees which vary in intensity and weakness.

Based on this premise: when we speak of educational justice, are we speaking of justice in love and affection or of justice in behavior and actions?

---

206 al-Kulaynī, Shaykh Muḥammad ibn Ya'qūb, Al-Kāfī, Vol. 6, p. 51, i.e. his love for them is as much as God made place for it in his heart.

207 A *maḥram* is an unmarriageable kin with whom marriage or sexual intercourse would be considered forbidden in Islam.

208 Ibid., Vol. 6, p. 6

The answer to this question depends on presenting a structured introduction which clarifies the difference between two things:

1. The actions of the heart

2. The actions of the body (organs)

In regards to the actions of the heart: Not all the actions of the heart fall under man's power, choice and free will. An example of this would be justice amongst women in the case of polygamy, where God ☙ pointed out to this in His ☙ saying: *❨You will not be able to be fair between wives❩* [209] Hisham ibn al-Hakam asked Imām al-Ṣādiq ☙ about the meaning of this verse, to which he ☙ responded: "It means in affection". [210]

Accordingly, discrimination in heart-felt emotions may get out of man's control and will, where he may love one child more than the other, either for a known reason – such as the distinction of the child – or an unknown reason where, for example, he might have received - in his heart - the love of one child more intensely than the other. The actions of the heart aren't always optional to man; accordingly, justice is not demanded from him in a matter which doesn't always fall under his choice.

As for the actions of the body (organs) which means the actual treatment: he is ordered to carry them out justly because they fall under man's choice. So, the demand here is that the educator's behavior in raising his children is just, in the sense

---

[209] Sūrah al-Nisaa, verse 129

[210] Ibid., Vol. 5, p. 363

that he doesn't distinguish between them in a practical way. So, he doesn't show it in his behavior and actions; since showing behavioral favoritism in this case creates envy amongst siblings and leaves – therein – enmity and hatred. Moreover, the Second Martyr (al-Shahīd al-Thāni) justifies the disapproval of favoring some children over others by saying: "... because favoritism leaves enmity and tension amongst children, which has been observed in reality –past and present -, and due to the fact that it indicates the yearning of the father towards the favored (child) which triggers envy which results in cutting the ties of kinship."[211]

This was suggested in the story of Prophet Yūsuf ﷺ, where the assumption of the sons of Prophet Yaʿqūb ﷺ that the latter favors Yūsuf over them led them to conspire and plot against him. God ﷻ says as He narrates this story: ﴾*In Joseph and his brothers there are certainly signs for the seekers. When they said, 'Surely Joseph and his brother are dearer to our father than [the rest of] us, though we are a hardy group. Our father is indeed in manifest error.' 'Kill Joseph or cast him away into some [distant] land, so that your father's love may be exclusively yours, and that you may become a righteous lot after that'*﴿[212] It is worthy to note that Prophet Yaʿqūb ﷺ didn't behave in a manner that was contrary to the demands of justice and fairness while raising his children; rather, it was only out of sympathy for them because they were young and weak. However, due to the ignorance of his other children, the weakness of their character and their envy, they did what they did with their brother Yūsuf ﷺ. For, Prophet Yaʿqūb didn't deal with Yūsuf and his brother

---

[211] al-Shahīd al-Thānī, Masālik al-Afhām, Vol. 6, p. 28

[212] Sūrah Yūsuf, verses 7-9

Benyamin – who were children – except with the logic of childhood.

In this context, we notice that Imām al-Ṣādiq ﷺ said: My father said: "By God, I would sweet talk one of my children, sit him on my lap, give him a lot of love and praise, while another one of my children is more entitled to it. However, I do so to protect him from this child and others, so they do not do to him what Yūsuf's brothers did to Yūsuf. For, God did not send down Surat Yūsuf except as an example so that we do not envy one another as Yūsuf's brothers envied Yūsuf and violated him."[213]

It is worthy to note that even if a child carries out several undesired actions, the father or mother's emotional state must not reach the extent of hating or loathing him; they must rather only hate his actions as per the narrations mentioned in this regard. One of it is the narration by Imām al-Ṣādiq ﷺ where he said: "God loves a servant and hates his action, and He hates a servant and loves his action."[214]

Justice versus Equality in the Upbringing Process

It is said that justice is "giving every entitled person his right." And due to the fact that children differ in their gender and age, then justice demands that they are treated differently. So, how can one balance between distinction and the principle of equality?

---

[213] Al-'Iyāshi, Tafsir al-'Iyāshi, Vol. 2, p. 166

[214] al-Ṭūsī, Shaykh Muḥammad ibn al-Ḥasan, al-'Amāli, p. 411

To answer this question, it is necessary to differentiate between two types of equality:

The first type: the equality which is demanded by justice and is associated with it.

The second type: the equality which differs from justice

Every child has his own needs which are suitable to the age stages of his life. For example, a one year old needs his parents to hold him, put him in bed, hand-feed him and wash his hands... etc. Whereas, a seven year old goes to bed by himself and sleeps in it, is able to eat and wash his hands by himself...etc. And these are shades of natural distinction based on its reasons.

Therefore, educational justice doesn't mean that the educator should treat them both equally, such that he carries the seven year old, put him in bed, feed him his food and then wash his hands; for, this goes against the demands of upbringing which aims at leading the child towards his perfection which is appropriate to his age stage. He can, however, take a middle road in this area where he can place the second child as the intermediary between the first child and himself, thus giving the former a sense of responsibility towards his brother and making feel that he needs his care. Then, he is given the duty of taking care of him in regards to the matters that are appropriate to his age stage such as talking to him or playing with him...etc.

Based on that, the difference between justice and equality becomes clear.

For, justice means giving every entitled child his right, in the light of the optional excellences which he seeks to acquire such as knowledge, good manners, good skills, abiding by general etiquettes, working hard and putting effort to develop himself and improve his personality.[215] It should be clarified for his siblings that this distinction is not for their sibling – as a person – but rather for his action, and that they can – through performing this action – acquire the same distinction on the basis of: "and for the likes of this, let the competitors compete."

As for equality, it is not synonymous with justice. For, equality amongst children who belong to different age stages on one hand, and carry out different actions on another, is considered oppressive towards them; and this conflicts with educational justice.

It seems, from some narrations, that the principle of distinction doesn't contradict with the principle of justice, such as:

It is narrated that Sa'd ibn Sa'd al-Ash'ari said: "I asked Aba al-Ḥasan al-Riḍā ﷺ can a man love some of his children more than others, and prioritize some over others.

He ﷺ said: "yes, Abu Abdillah ﷺ did that when he gifted Muḥammad, and Abu al-Ḥasan ﷺ did that when he gifted Ahmad something; so, I managed and acquired it for him.[216]"[217]

---

[215] This also shows the difference between discriminating amongst children on an initial basis, and in terms of punishment for misbehavior. For the former conflicts with justice; however, distinguishing amongst children as a form of reward for doing good lies at the core of justice.

[216] It means that I managed what my father gifted my brother and I compiled it for him because he was a child.

[217] al-Kulaynī, Shaykh Muḥammad ibn Ya'qūb, Al-Kāfī, Vol. 6, p. 51

The Pre-Islamic Discriminatory Perception against the Female Child

The Noble Qur'ān condemned the discriminatory perception against females by the people of Jahiliyyah.[218] God ﷻ said: ﴾*When one of them is brought the news of a female [newborn], his face becomes darkened and he chokes with suppressed agony. He hides from the people out of distress at the news he has been brought: shall he retain it in humiliation, or bury it in the ground! Look! Evil is the judgment that they make*﴿[219] For, they used to welcome the newborn girl with a darkened face out of grief, to the extent that makes them hide from people in humiliation, which led some of them in the end to bury their daughter alive. ﴾*When the girl buried-alive will be asked. For what sin was she killed*﴿[220] This perception remained rooted in the lives of Muslims and believers where they would look at the girl with indignation, hatred and resentment. For, "when the Prophet ﷺ received the good tidings of a newborn girl, he looked at his companions' faces and saw hatred therein..."[221]

Unfortunately, some people still carry within themselves the customs and traditions of the Age of Jahiliyyah in regards to newborn girls. And if we look closer at the Islamic values, we will realize that Islam has raised the status of females and encouraged that through the following steps:

---

218 The Pre-Islamic age referred to as the Age of Ignorance

219 Sūrah al-Nahl verses 58-59

220 Sūrah al-Takwir, verses 8-9

221 al-Ṣadūq, Shaykh Muḥammad ibn ʿAlī, Man Lā Yaḥḍuruh al-Faqīh

First: emphasizing the prohibition of burying girls alive

Second: accentuating the fact that loving children is an innate thing and that parents shouldn't burry this primordial nature underground, especially loving girls whose hatred is prohibited in Islam; and laying emphasis on the fact that they (girls) are blessed and the best of children at home.

Third: viewing girls - according to the scale of Hereafter – as good deeds to be rewarded for by God ﷻ, in contrast to boys who are a blessing for which God will judge and hold accountability...etc.

Fourth: God ﷻ is more sympathetic with girls than with boys. And a girl can be more beneficial to her parents than a boy. God ﷻ said: ﴾*Your parents and your children —you do not know which of them is likelier to be beneficial for you*﴿[222].[223]

We find these meanings in several narrations that encourage taking care of girls, some of which are:

1. Forbidding the Burial of Girls while They are Alive:

It is narrated that the Messenger of God ﷺ said: "God ﷻ forbade dishonoring mothers and burying girls alive."[224]

---

[222] Sūrah al-Nisā', verse 11

[223] al-Kulaynī, Shaykh Muḥammad ibn Ya'qūb, Al-Kāfī, Vol. 6, p. 5

[224] al-Ṣadūq, Shaykh Muḥammad ibn 'Alī, Ma'ani al-Akhbār, commented on by al-Akbar al-Ghafāri, introduced by Ḥusayn al-'A'lami, Beirut, al-'A'lami Printing Institute, 1410 AH – 1990 AD, 1st edition, p. 280

2. The Prohibition of Hating Girls:

It is narrated that the Messenger of God ﷺ said: "Do not hate girls; for, they are the affable precious ones."[225]

3. The Prohibition of Wishing Girls Dead:

It is narrated that Jaroud said: I said to Abi Abdillah ؑ: I have girls, so he ؑ said: "Perhaps you wish for their death. In case you wished for their death and they died, you wouldn't be rewarded and you would meet God ﷻ when you meet Him as a sinful man."[226]

4. Following the Steps of the Messenger of God ﷺ:

It is narrated that Abi Abdillah ؑ said: "The Messenger of God ﷺ was a father of girls."[227]

5. Adopt the Morals of God in Regards to Sympathizing with Girls:

It is narrated that Abi al-Ḥasan al-Riḍā ؑ said: the Messenger of God ﷺ said: "God (the Blessed and Exalted) is more sympathetic with girls than He is with boys."[228]

---

225 al-Ṭabarāni, Sulaymān Ibn Ahmad, al-Mu'jam al-Kabir, verified by Hamdi Abdul Majid al-Salafi, L.M, Dar 'Ihya' al-Turath al-'Arabi, 1404 AH – 1984 AD, 2nd edition, Vol. 17, p. 310

226 al-Kulaynī, Shaykh Muḥammad ibn Ya'qūb, Al-Kāfī, Vol. 6, p. 5

227 Ibid.

228 al-Kulaynī, Shaykh Muḥammad ibn Ya'qūb, Al-Kāfī, Vol. 6, p. 6

6. The Blessedness and Mercy of the House that has (within it) a Girl:

It is narrated that the Messenger of God ﷺ said: "There isn't any house that has (within it) girls except that everyday twelve blessings and mercies descend upon it. And angels cease not to visit this house and write for their father, every day and night, the reward of a year of worship."[229]

7. The Best of Children are the Girls:

It is narrated that the Prophet ﷺ said: "He who has one girl, she is better for him than a thousand pilgrimages, a thousand conquests, a thousand sacrifices and thousand hospitable banquets."[230]

8. Girls are Blessed and Affable:

It is narrated that the Prophet ﷺ said: "May God have mercy on the father of girls; for, girls are blessed and lovely. Boys bring good tidings; and they (girls) are the everlasting good deeds."[231]

---

229 Burūjirdī, Ayatullāh Sayyid Ḥusayn, Jāmiʿ Aḥādīth al-Shīʿa, Vol. 21, p. 303

230 Ibid., Vol. 21, p. 302

231 Ibid.

9. Considering Girls as Good Deeds for which One is Rewarded:

It is narrated that Imām al-Ṣādiq said: "Girls are good deeds, and boys are a blessing. Indeed, good deeds are rewarded and blessings are accounted for."[232]

10. Girls are Shields from Hellfire and a Reason for Heaven's Entry:

It is narrated that the Prophet said: "He who has three girls and is patient with their tight livelihood, affliction and comfort, they become his shields on the day of Resurrection."[233]

11. Considering a Young Girl as a Sweet Basil Flower:

The Prophet received good tidings of having a newborn girl, so he looked at his companions' faces and saw hatred therein. Then he said: "What's the matter with you! (She's) a flower that I smell whose sustenance comes from God."[234]

12. Treating Girls with Kindness Enters One into Heaven:[235]

It is narrated that the Prophet said: "He who has two sisters or daughters whom he treats with kindness, he and I will be

---

[232] al-Kulaynī, Shaykh Muḥammad ibn Yaʻqūb, al-Kāfī, Vol. 6, p. 8

[233] al-Ṣadūq, Shaykh Muḥammad ibn ʻAlī, Al-Khiṣāl, p. 174

[234] al-Ṣadūq, Shaykh Muḥammad ibn ʻAlī, Man La Yaḥdaruhu al-Faqih, Vol. 3, p. 481

[235] Al-ʻAḥsāʼi, ʻAwāli al-Laʼali', Vol. 1, p. 253

together in Heaven like these two – and he pointed out to his index and middle fingers."

13. Provision for Girls Enters One into Heaven:

It is narrated that the Messenger of God ﷺ said: "He who provides for three daughters is given three gardens in Heaven, such that each garden is vaster than the world and all that dwells in it."[236]

14. God ﷻ Supports the Person who has Daughters:

It is narrated that the Prophet ﷺ said: "He who has a daughter, God supports him, makes him victorious, blesses him and forgives him."[237]

15. Contentment with the Choice of God ﷻ:

God ﷻ said: ﴾*To God belongs the kingdom of the heavens and the earth. He creates whatever He wishes; He gives females to whomever He wishes, and gives males to whomever He wishes*﴿[238]

---

[236] Burūjirdī, Ayatullāh Sayyid Ḥusayn, Jāmiʿ aḥādīth al-Shīʿa, Vol. 21, p. 303

[237] al-Mirzā al-Nūrī, Mustadrak al-Wasāʾil, Vol. 15, p. 115

[238] Sūrah al-Shura, verse 49

16. The First-Born Female is a Blessing for her Mother:

It is narrated that the Messenger of God ﷺ said: "It is a woman's blessing to have a bondmaid as an eldest child, which means to have a girl as her first-born child."[239]

17. The Supplication of Prophet Ibrāhīm in which He Asks for a Daughter:

It is narrated that Abi Abdillah ؑ said: "My father Ibrāhīm ؑ asked his Lord to grant him a daughter so that she would cry and lament over him after his death."[240]

Based on the above: One of the requirements of educational justice is that one doesn't discriminate between a male and a female child; one must rather provide each of them with the type of upbringing that is appropriate to their nature and realize the characteristics and features of each of the two genders.

Main Concepts

Justice is considered one of God's names ﷻ. And due to its importance it was made the second branch of the five branches of Islam. A believer must adorn himself with God's ﷻ qualities and His most beautiful names including the Just. The Qur'ān associated justice with piety; for, God ﷻ says: ﴿*Be fair; that is nearer to God-consciousness, and be wary of God. God is indeed well aware of what you do*﴾[241]

---

[239] Al-Rawundi, al-Nawāḍir, p. 151

[240] al-Kulaynī, Shaykh Muḥammad ibn Ya'qūb, Al-Kāfī, Vol. 6, p. 6

[241] Sūrah al-Mā'ida, verse 8

The Islamic upbringing approach emphasized on the principle of equality between the male and female child. It is narrated that the Prophet ﷺ said: "He who has a daughter and has not buried her, insulted her or favored his son over her, God enters him into Heaven."

Discrimination in heart-felt emotions may get out of man's control and will, where he may love one child more than the other, either for a known reason – such as the distinction of the child – or an unknown reason where, for example, he might have received - in his heart - the love of one child more intensely than the other. The actions of the heart aren't always optional to man; accordingly, justice is not demanded from him in a matter which doesn't always fall under his choice.

As for the actions of the body (organs) which means the actual treatment: he is ordered to carry them out justly because they fall under man's choice. So, the demand here is that the educator's behavior in raising his children is just, in the sense that he doesn't distinguish between them in a practical way. So, he doesn't show it in his behavior and actions; since showing behavioral favoritism in this case creates envy amongst siblings and leaves – therein – enmity and hatred.

Justice means giving every entitled child his right, in the light of the optional excellences which he seeks to acquire such as knowledge, good manners, good skills, abiding by general etiquettes, working hard and putting effort to develop himself and improve his personality.

As for equality, it is not synonymous with justice. For, equality amongst children who belong to different age stages on one hand, and carry out different actions on another, is considered oppressive towards them; and this conflicts with educational justice.

Lesson Nine

The Value of Custody in Islam

Lesson Objectives

By the end of this lesson, the student should:

1. Be able to define custody linguistically and terminologically.
2. Know the reasons for which the mother is given the right to custody.
3. Realize the importance of harmony between the parents during the custodian period.

Preamble

A child's need for care and attention due to his weakness gives the upbringing process a special joy which can only be tasted by someone who has drunk from its waters. Imām Ja'far al-Ṣādiq ﷺ pointed out to this meaning in his saying: "... Had – the newborn – been born with complete intellect and independence, then the joy of raising children would have gone, the parents wouldn't have had any interest in working on the child which would subsequently entitle them to being honored and cared for by their children when needed, for which the latter would therefore be rewarded. Then, the children wouldn't have familiarized themselves with their parents nor the parents with their children. For, children would have dispensed with their parents' upbringing and care and thus split away from them when they were born; and no man would have known his father and mother..."[242]

For, a child – in the first years of his life – needs special care and attention such as providing what he needs for nutrition, clothing, shelter, medication... And this type of attention and upbringing has been referred to, terminologically, as custody.

So, what is the right to custody? And who was given this right?

Custody in its Linguistic Meaning

Custody, linguistically, is derived from 'al-ḥiḍn' (the place that is under the arms) which means 'to preserve something and

---

[242] Al-Ja'fi, al-Mufaddal ibn Omar, Al-Tawḥīd, commented on by Kazem al-Muẓaffar, Beirut, al-Wafa' Institute, 1404 AH – 1984 AD, 2nd edition, p. 15-16

maintain it.'[243] And when a woman holds her child, it means that she brought him close to her and carried him in her arms.

Custody in Religious Terminology

Custody is given, in religious terminology, numerous definitions which are all rooted in one.

In regards to its definition, Allāmah al-Hilli said: "Custody: the upbringing of a child and his preservation, putting kohl in his eyes, oiling his head and hair, cleaning him, washing his clothes, and the likes of that. It is derived from al-ḥiḍn, which is the area that lies under the armpit, thus resembling the way a bird takes care of the eggs and chicks."[244]

For, custody is a form of raising a child, except that it involves – exclusively – the first age stage which is related to the physical needs of the child.

---

[243] Ibn Zakariyyah, Dictionary of Maqayees al-Lugha, Vol. 2, p. 73

[244] al-Ḥillī, al-'Allāma al-Ḥasan ibn Yūsuf, Tahrīr al-Ahkām al-Shar'iyyah 'ala Madhhab al-'Imāmiyyah, verified by Ibrāhīm al-Baḥaderi, supervised by Ja'far al-Subḥani, Qom, Imām al-Ṣādiq Institute, 1420 AH, 1st edition, Vol. 3, p. 93

The Reasons behind Granting the Mother – not the Father – the Right to Custody

God ﷻ sent down the Islamic religion such that it matches the human primordial nature.[245] And due to the fact that the innate nature of the mother encompasses special emotional qualities – that are more present in her than in a man -, she was delegated the custodial mission for being more sympathetic, gentle, patient and enduring in this regard. On the other hand, the mission of educational guardianship and bearing the external responsibilities of the child - such as alimony and others - are delegated to the father.

The Financial Alimony is the Father's Responsibility

When Islam granted the mother the right of custody in its physical aspect, it didn't burden her with the responsibility of spending on the child. It rather casted the responsibility of financial alimony on the father's shoulders. Therefore, all the requirements of the child such as food, clothes, medicine...must be provided by the father; and the mother is not obliged, religiously or legally, to spend anything in this regard except what she spends by her own choice with delight.[246]

---

245 Ṭabāṭabā'ī, al-'Allāma Sayyid Muḥammad Ḥusayn, Al-Mīzān fī Tafsīr al-Qur'ān, Tehran, Dar al-Kutub al-Islāmiyya, 1372 AH, L.T', Vol. 1, p. 389, and Vol. 2, p. 274, and Vol. 7, p. 247, and Vol. 9, p. 241, and Vol. 16, p. 178 and what follows.

246 al-Shahīd al-Thānī, Masālik al-Afhām, Vol. 8, p. 421

Between Custody and the Right of Guardianship

The question raised in this regard would be:

If the father – not the mother – has the right to guardianship over the child, how can the mother – and not the father – be granted the right to custody?

This can be answered in two ways:

First: It is true that guardianship over a child is generally granted to the father; however, every general rule has its specifics. For, there is an exception in this case which lies in granting the right of custody to the mother due to its suitability with her formative nature as mentioned earlier.[247]

Second: Some scholars considered that custody doesn't fall under the issue of guardianship and that it is rather concerned with the mother's right in managing the physical nurturing that is specific to the child in this regard. As for the actions that are related to the educational guardianship, it remains of the father's specialties. Therefore, there isn't any contradiction between the two.[248]

The Importance of Harmony between the Spouses during the Custodian Mandate

Harmony during the custodian mandate has a positive effect on the child from an upbringing perspective. Parents must

---

[247] al-Ḥillī, al-Sarā'er, Vol. 2, p. 653

[248] Ibid.

constantly pursue harmony in upbringing (their child), be it at times of agreement or spouse separation through divorce. This is because disagreement in this area has negative effects on the child which puts him in a state of anxiety and leads him to an unbalanced personality.

Therefore, parents must agree on the custodial issue in the light of the moral and value-based system, rather than legal provisions that are rather dry and lacking the spirit of values.

Agreement always takes precedence over conflict even in the case of separation. For, the child's interest and collaboration on raising and nurturing him take precedence over taking matters to court and putting the child in front of the most difficult decision – his father or mother.

For, the upbringing process involves numerous responsibilities that are shared between the spouses even in the case of divorce. Therefore, they must provide a positive environment for the child and overlook their personal affairs for the benefit of the child, so he can develop in a healthy way far from the atmosphere of tension and anxiety.

Moreover, the spouses mustn't forbid each other to visit the child or meet up with him while he is in the custody of the other (spouse). For, when the child is in the custody of the father or mother, none of them has the right to prohibit the other from visiting him or talking to him or checking up on him when he gets sick...due to the impact it has on cutting kinship ties and the harm it inflicts on either of them...[249]

---

[249] al-Jawāhirī, Shaykh, Jawāhir al-Kalām, Vol. 31, p. 292

Therefore, granting the right of custody to the mother, in the aforementioned way, doesn't eliminate the father's role in the upbringing process. She must, rather, practice this right at home in partnership with the father. And scholars emphasized on the importance of agreement between the parents in regards to custody and on basing every behavior thereof on the consensus of both. "When the spouses are together, there should be no talk about the child being between them; they must rather – each – do what is required of them in his upbringing."[250]

The Custodial Duration

Scholars agreed that the mother is more entitled to the child's custody for the entire duration of breastfeeding, which is for two complete years, whether the child is a boy or a girl. Sayyid al-Khumaynī ﷼ says: "The mother is more entitled to the child and his upbringing and all that benefits his preservation for the total duration of breastfeeding, which is two years; if she is a reasoning free Muslim woman, whether the child is a boy or a girl..."[251]

There's a question that is raised here: Does the mother have guardianship over the child after the breastfeeding period is completed? And for how long does this guardianship extend?

---

250 Al-Suyouri, Miqdad ibn Abdullah, al-Tanqeeḥ al-Ra'e' li-Mukhtasar al-Shara'e', verified by Abdul Lateef Ḥusaynī, Qom, Library of Ayatullah al-Mar'ashi, Al-Khiam Printing Press, 1404 AH, 1st edition, Vol. 3, p. 271

251 al-Khumaynī, Sayyid Rūhullāh al-Mūsawī, Taḥrīr al-Wasīlah, Vol. 2, p. 312

In answering this question, scholars suggested numerous opinions[252], which we will briefly present in the following paragraph:[253]

The first opinion: is that the mother has no right after two years.

The second opinion: is that the mother is more entitled to the boy and girl up until seven years.[254]

The third opinion: is that the mother is more entitled to the boy or girl up until the mother gets married.[255]

The fourth opinion: is that the mother is more entitled to the boy up until two years, and to the girl up until seven years.

---

252 For these opinions, review: Shaykh al-Ṭūsī, al-Mabsout, Vol. 6, p. 39, and al-Ḥillī, Ahmad ibn Muḥammad, al-Muhazzab al-Bare' fi Sharḥ al-Mukhtasar al-Nafe', verified by Mujtaba al-Iraqi, Qom, Institute of Islamic Publishing related to the group of teachers in the honorable city of Qom, 1411 AH, L.T', Vol. 3, p. 427

253 There are many jurisprudential details in regards to this matter which can be reviewed in specialized books.

254 al-Ṣadūq, Shaykh Muḥammad ibn 'Alī, Man Lā Yaḥḍuruh al-Faqīh, Vol. 3, p. 436

255 Ibid.

The fifth opinion: is that the mother is more entitled to the boy up until seven years, and to the girl as long as the mother is unmarried.[256]

The Conditions that Must be Met in Order to Assume Custody[257]

The presence of some qualities and characteristics within the parents has an effective and quite important role in the upbringing process, regardless of the absolute jurisprudential ruling. That's why scholars have emphasized on the necessity of meeting several conditions, the most important of which are:

1. Islam: Custody represents one of the forms of guardianship. Therefore, the woman must be a Muslim since guardianship over a child is not permissible for a non-Muslim woman if his father is a Muslim. Moreover, both parents must ensure a religious and suitable environment

---

256 al-Ṭūsī, Shaykh Muḥammad ibn al-Ḥasan, al-Khilaf, verified by a group of editors, Qom, Institute of Islamic Publishing related to a group of teachers in the honorable city of Qom, 1407 AH, L.T', Vol. 5, p. 131

257 For custody conditions, review: al-Shahīd al-Thānī, Masālik al-Afhām, Vol. 8, p. 422 and what follows, and Al-Tabataba'i, Sayyid 'Alī, Riyad al-Masa'il, Qom, Institute of Islamic Publishing related to the group of teachers in Qom, 1422 AH, 1st edition, Vol. 10, p. 523 and what follows, and Shaykh al-Jawāhiri, Jawaher al-Kalam, Vol. 31, p. 287 and what follows.

for the child. And this cannot be achieved in the custody of a woman who is distant from religion...[258]

2. Intellect: in the sense that a mother must be sane. For, custody is not allowed for an insane woman.

3. Physical health: the mother must have good health and wellbeing; and she shouldn't be infected with any contagious disease that can prevent her from taking care of her child and nurturing him. Some scholars rejected this condition; for, they considered that the mother – in this case – delegate this matter to someone else;in which case, the mother's custody over the child is not lost.[259]

4. Trustworthiness: This is an essential and important trait. For, a person who doesn't possess this trait is capable of betraying that which was entrusted to him. But if the mother possesses this trait, then she will not neglect the child during this period and she will take care of him and his affairs.

---

[258] It is narrated that the Messenger of God ﷺ said: "There isn't any child except that is born upon the primordial nature; then his parents turn him into a Jew or a Christian." Al-Bukhāri, Sahih al-Bukhāri, Vol. 7, p. 211. Ibn Hanbal, Musnad Ahmad, Vol. 2, p. 315. al-Ṣadūq, Shaykh Muḥammad ibn ʿAlī, Man Lā Yaḥḍuruh al-Faqīh, Vol. 2, p. 49, ḥadīth 1668

[259] In this condition, the opinion of Shaykh al-Jawāhirī appears, whereby he considers that custody is not a guardianship but rather a right which belongs to the mother. Accordingly, if she doesn't have the ability to practice this right, no one else takes her role. But rather, the guardianship and choice belongs to the father who can decide to delegate whoever he finds suitable to take custody of his child.

5. Justice and refraining from debauchery: This is because the child will get affected by the upbringing approach and the traits of the nurturer. Al-Shahīd al-Thāni pointed this out by saying: "No custody is permissible for the licentious woman. For, a licentious person is not entitled to guardianship, and she cannot be trusted with preserving him (the child), and the child has no fortune under her custody because he will be brought up in her path. For, a child's soul is like an empty land which receives whatever is placed in it.[260]"[261]

Main Concepts

A child's need for care and attention due to his weakness gives the upbringing process a special joy which can only be tasted by someone who has drunk from its waters.

Custody, linguistically, is derived from '*al-ḥiḍn*' (the place that is under the arms) which means 'to preserve something and maintain it. Whereas, in religious terminology, it is specifically related to the physical needs of the child during his first age stages.

When Islam granted the mother the right of custody in its physical aspect, it didn't burden her with the responsibility of spending on the child. It rather casted the responsibility of financial alimony on the father's shoulders.

---

260 This points out to what was mentioned by Imām 'Alī ﵇: "Indeed, the heart of a child is like an empty land which receives whatever is placed in it." Nahj al-Balāghah, from his will to his son al-Ḥasan, he wrote it to him in Hadirīn as he was leaving Siffīn, number 269, p. 526

261 al-Shahīd al-Thānī, Masālik al-Afhām, Vol. 8, p. 422

Harmony during the custodian mandate has a positive effect on the child from an upbringing perspective. Parents must constantly pursue harmony in upbringing (their child), be it at times of agreement or spouse separation through divorce.

Whether the law grants the mother the right of custody individually or in partnership with the father, the partnership takes precedence due to its positive impact on the child.

The custodial duration that is agreed upon by the scholars is two complete years whether the child is a boy or a girl.

The presence of some qualities and characteristics within the parents has an effective and quite important role in the upbringing process. And these traits are very important regardless of the absolute jurisprudential ruling: such as Islam, intellect, physical health, trustworthiness and justice.

Lesson Ten

The Father's Guardianship over the Child's Upbringing

Lesson Objectives

By the end of this lesson, the student should:

1. Get acquainted with the meaning and concept of guardianship.
2. Get acquainted with the reasons for granting the father guardianship over the upbringing (of the child).
3. Distinguish between guardianship over the upbringing and the upbringing itself.

Preamble

The true religion of Islam granted the father guardianship over the child's upbringing, which places him before a great deal of responsibility. For, he must strive to carry out this guardianship through the proper upbringing of the child and through working on managing his affairs in a way that is suitable with the child's interests on one hand–and contributes to shaping his personality in a balanced form, so that he can take his hand and guide him towards a virtuous upbringing and development–on the other.

Then, what is the concept of guardianship? And does someone else – besides the father – have the right of guardianship over the child or is it exclusively the father's right? This is what we will shed light on in this lesson.

Guardianship in its Linguistic and Terminological Meanings

Guardianship, linguistically, indicates closeness and proximity[262]. Every person who manages people's affairs is considered to be their guardian.[263] And guardianship means the most entitled to manage (someone's) affairs.

Linguistically, it is a form of power, operation, government, care and management.

---

262 Ibn Manẓūr, Lisān al-ʿArab, Vol. 15, p. 407

263 Al-Farāhīdī, al-ʿAyn, Vol. 2, p. 240

In jurisprudential terminology, it is a form of dominance and power for a person which gives him the right to manage another person's affairs and arrange it. And as Sayyid al-Khumaynī ؒ says: "Guardianship is the authority to manage affairs, or an addition between the guardian and the person under his protection which gives the former authority over the latter's affairs."[264]

Therefore, guardianship is a religious position granted by God ﷻ; and whoever assumes guardianship, by the will of God, must observe the limitations of guardianship that are drawn out by God ﷻ, and thus bear the responsibility according to the religious rules and moral system.

Guardianship over Family Management

Man is a social being by nature. Therefore, it's not possible for people to coexist with each other without the presence of a guardian and caretaker who handles the responsibility of decision making and managing the affairs of the group in a positive manner. It is narrated that the Prophet ﷺ said: "If three people were traveling, they should appoint a leader from amongst them."[265]

The family (father/mother/children) is the nucleus of society, and therefore, cannot be left without a guardian. The question

---

[264] al-Khumaynī, Sayyid Rūhullāh al-Mūsawī, al-Rasā'el, with the notes of Mujtabā al-Tehrāni, L.M, the Ismaili Institute for Printing, Publishing and Distribution, 1385 AH, L.T', 1st edition, p. 272

[265] Al-Sajistāni, Abi Dawoud, verified by Sa'id Muḥammad al-Lahhām, Beirut, Dar al-Fikr, 1410 AH – 1990 AD, 1st edition, Vol. 1, p. 587

that is raised here is: who is the person who was granted, by the Islamic religion, the right of guardianship within the family?

God, the Exalted, divided the responsibilities within the family. He carried out the physical upbringing of the child which includes nutrition, clothing, cleaning, nursing and keeping him comfortable... one of the mother's roles and responsibilities within the family. Accordingly, He granted her custody over the child's upbringing in regards to these matters, due to the traits given to her by God ﷻ such as love, patience, and tolerance in regards to the child from this particular aspect during the first age stages. And He granted the father the right to manage and take decisions regarding the child's different affairs, in addition to managing his diverse conditions. And in reality, this right is not an honorary; it is rather a duty, trust and responsibility which puts on the father's shoulders a heavy burden.[266]

Evidence for Granting Guardianship over the (Child's) Upbringing to the Father rather than the Mother

Jurists agree that according to the Islamic religion, the general right of guardianship over the child - within the family - centers around the father. And they claim that the mother doesn't have any legal guardianship over the child, by resorting to the following proofs:

266 Review: al-Ghurawi, 'Alī, the encyclopedia of Imām al-Khoeī, Ayatullāh Sayyid Abū l-Qāsim al-Mūsawī, al-Tanqih fi Sharh al-Makāsib, al-Bay', the report of Imām al-Khoeī's research, Qom, the Institute of 'Ihya' Athar al-Imām al-Khoeī, 1425 AH – 2005 AD, 1st edition, Vol. 37, p. 136

1. The jurists unanimously agreed that: "There is no guardianship for the mother or her parents over the young child."[267]

2. The absence of any proof within narrations of the mother's guardianship; it was rather specialized for the father or paternal grandfather.

Jurists inferred that the right of guardianship was granted to the father from several proofs, some of which were:

First: A rational biography which is based on the fact that the father is the one who has the right to manage his children's affairs.

Second: The deductive reading of diverse narrative texts in several jurisprudential chapters.[268] Al-Khonsari said: "In regards to the guardianship of the father and paternal grandfather, there is no problem and no disagreement about their guardianship in general. This is indicated in separate chapters."[269]

Third: Direct inference through narrative texts from which some jurists concluded the general guardianship of the father

---

[267] al-Jawāhirī, Shaykh, Jawāhir al-Kalām, Vol. 29, p. 234

[268] Review: al-Ghurawi, al-Tanqih fi Sharh al-Makaseb, al-Bay', Vol. 37, p. 136

[269] Al-Khonsarī, Ahmad, Jame' al-Madarik fi Sharh al-Mukhtasar al-Nafe', verified and commented on by 'Alī Akbar Ghafari, Tehran, al-Sadūq Library, 1405 AH, 2nd edition, p. 95

over his children[270], some of which was narrated by Muḥammad ibn Muslim on behalf of Abi Ja'far al-Bāqir ﷺ – in regards to a man who gave alms to his mature children - , he said: " If they don't receive it before death then it is an inheritance, And if he gave alms to his undiscerning child then it is permissible because his father is the person who manages his affairs..."[271]

Who Besides the Father may Assume Guardianship over the Child

Guardianship is a form of authority that is related to planning, taking decisions and assuming the appropriate stance in regards to the child's affairs in any field in life. As for the upbringing, it is related to the practical and executive aspect which specializes in the steps that are required to lead the child to the perfection for which is prepared. And here comes the question, is this guardianship exclusive to the father only?

The popular opinion of jurists claim that this guardianship exceeds the father to include the paternal grandfather – while excluding the maternal grandfather. Therefore, if they both agree on decisions that are specifically related to the upbringing of the child, then it will be indisputably valid from an upbringing aspect.

---

[270] Rohānī, Sayyid Muḥammad Ṣādiq, Fiqh al-Ṣādiq, Qom, Institute of Dar al-Kitab, 1412 AH, 3rd edition, Vol. 20, p. 313, and al-Ḥakīm, Muḥammad Saʿīd al-Tabātabāʾī, Misbah al-Minhaj, chapter of al-Tijara, L.M, Institute of al-Hikmah lil Thaqafa al-Islamiyya, 1428 AH – 2002 AD, 2nd edition, Vol. 2, p. 377

[271] al-Kulaynī, Shaykh Muḥammad ibn Yaʿqūb, Al-Kāfī, Vol. 7, p. 32

However, there was a discussion regarding the case where the father and grandfather have different points of view, such that the father finds the child's interest in a certain matter, whereas the grandfather sees that there isn't any interest thereof. In this case, whose opinion takes precedence over the other, the guardianship of the father or the paternal grandfather?

They said that the grandfather's right of guardianship in regards to management takes precedence over the father's[272]; and they based their opinion on several narrations such as:

It is narrated on behalf of 'Obeida ibn Zurarah: I said to Abi Abdillah ﷺ: "A father wants to marry off his bondmaid to a man, and her grandfather wants to marry her to another man. He ﷺ said: The grandfather is more entitled in doing so, as long as it is not harmful and the father hadn't married her off before him. Her marriage by her father and grandfather is permissible."[273]

Yes, "... the father and grandfather are each, autonomous, in their guardianship. For, it is not mandatory for them to collaborate or take permission from one another. Whoever takes initiative first, while observing what needs to be observed, doesn't leave space for the other. And the grandfather takes

---

272 al-Khumaynī, Sayyid Rūhullāh al-Mūsawī, Kitab al-Bay', Tehran, verified and published by the institute of the organization and publishing of Sayyid al-Khumaynī's work, 1421 AJ, 1st edition, Vol. 2, p. 593

273 al-Kulaynī, Shaykh Muḥammad ibn Ya'qūb, Al-Kāfī, Vol. 5, p. 395

precedence in cases of disagreement."[274] (That is, when any disagreement arises, the grandfather takes precedence.)

Is the Father's Guardianship Absolute or Conditional?

A disagreement arose in regards to whether the guardianship of the father over the (child's) upbringing is absolute without any condition or restriction, or conditional on justice or interest for instance? Jurists were divided into two groups, and each had his own specific proofs:

The first opinion: Claiming absolute guardianship: It means the guardianship that isn't restricted by any additional limitation or conditional on anything such as justice or interest.

They inferred their opinion from the absence of any restriction within the religious texts which hadn't restricted this matter by justice or otherwise, especially if we take into consideration the fact that the father is born with an innate love for their children and sympathy towards them.[275]

And according to the reasonable tradition, the licentious father also takes guardianship over his child's affairs without any denial from the side of the legislator. Moreover, giving guardianship to someone other than the father is more harmful to the child than the harms of a licentious father, especially that licentiousness doesn't negate empathy and mercy on children and the proper

---

274 Al-Ansarī, Muḥammad 'Alī, al-Mawsou'a al-Fiqhiyya al-Muyassara, L.M, Mujamma' al-Fikr al-Islami, 1415 AH, 1st edition, p. 148

275 Al-Karakī, the editor 'Alī ibn al-Ḥusayn, Jami' al-Maqasid fi Sharh al-Qawa'id, Qom, verified and published by the institute of Al al-Bayt li –'Ihya' al-Turath, 1411 AH, 2st edition, Vol. 11, p. 276

guardianship over them. This is additional to the consequences of giving the guardianship to someone other than the father, such as battles, conflicts and social problems amongst the members of the same community.

Yes, there is no doubt that the condition of justice which was adopted by those who shared the second opinion establishes a moral value in the father's ascension towards a more virtuous behavior in regards to the upbringing of the child. And the religious judge maintains the right to terminate the father's guardianship if he sees that he is behaving against the interest of the child in a way that causes him harm, as Sayyid al-Khumaynī ﷺ pointed out: "It seems that justice isn't a condition to the guardianship of the father and grandfather. Therefore, the judge doesn't assume guardianship when they are licentious. However, when he discovers – even through circumstantial evidence – that they are causing the person under their guardianship harm, he terminates their guardianship and prohibits them from management."[276]

The second opinion: Conditional guardianship: It means that the guardianship is conditional on specific requirements such as justice, and it isn't absolute.

Some jurists adopted the requirement of justice in regards to the father's guardianship over the (child's) upbringing (in terms of the father not being oppressive or licentious). For, they considered that when Islam granted the father guardianship over the child, it wasn't solely due to his fatherhood. It rather demanded that justice be added to fatherhood, in order to validate the guardianship. Therefore, "It – the guardianship –

---

[276] al-Khumaynī, Sayyid Rūhullāh al-Mūsawī, Taḥrīr al-Wasīlah, Vol. 2, p. 14

becomes problematic in the case of a licentious father... and the father regains his guardianship through repentance."[277]

Those who adopted this opinion inferred it from the Noble Qur'ān in His saying ﷻ: *﴾And do not incline toward the wrongdoers, lest the Fire should touch you﴿*[278] For, they considered that giving guardianship to an oppressive father is a form of leaning towards him.[279]

The Condition of Interest and Non-Corruption

One of the things that were subject to disagreement in regards to the father's guardianship was the condition of interest or non-corruption.

Two opinions were mentioned by jurists in this regard:

The First Opinion: Taking the Child's Interest into Consideration in the Matter of Guardianship

Taking the child's interest into consideration means that the guardian must study the choice that holds the interest of the child and act upon this choice, such that his guardianship gets terminated if he doesn't take this approach. And some jurists see that the wisdom behind legislating guardianship over the child, in the first place, is observing his interest in all matters.

---

[277] al-Ḥillī, al-'Allāma al-Ḥasan ibn Yūsuf, Qawa'ed al-Ahkam fi Ma'rifat al-Halal w al-Harām, Qom, the institute of Islamic publishing, 1413 AH, 1st edition, Vol. 2, p. 564

[278] Sūrah Hūd, verse 113

[279] Al-Khumaynī, Sayyid Rūhullāh al-Mūsawī, Kitab al-Bay', Vol. 2, p. 599

Therefore, the father's guardianship is conditional on observing the child's interest; otherwise, his right of guardianship will be taken away from him.

The Second Opinion: Considering Non-Corruption in the Matter of Guardianship

This means that the guardian must not carry out any action that harms the child. The popular opinion of the jurists is that wisdom requires the absence of any corruptive act towards the child and that the child's guardianship is not conditional on his interest. Moreover, it is not necessary for an act that is void of any benefit for the child to result in corruptive acts towards him. For, the act can be void of both – interest and corruption.

Main Concepts

The true religion of Islam granted the father guardianship over the child's upbringing, which puts him in front of a great deal of responsibility. For, he must strive to carry out this guardianship duly through the proper upbringing of the child.

Guardianship, linguistically, indicates closeness and proximity. And every person who manages people's affairs is considered to be their guardian.

Guardianship is a religious position granted by God ﷻ; and whoever assumes guardianship, by the will of God, must observe the limitations of guardianship that are drawn out by God, and thus bear the responsibility according to the religious rules and moral system.

God ﷻ granted the father the right of guardianship over the child's upbringing; and this right, in reality, is not an honorary. It is rather a duty, trust and responsibility which puts on the father's shoulders a heavy burden.

The popular opinion of jurists claim that this guardianship exceeds the father to include the paternal grandfather – while excluding the maternal grandfather.

A disagreement arose in regards to whether the father's guardianship is absolute or conditional. Both groups provided proof for their opinions.

The fundamental meaning of the guardianship over the (child's) upbringing is transference of the child from deficiency to perfection – and so on.

Lesson Eleven

Nurturing Intellect and Developing Cognitive Skills

Lesson Objectives

By the end of this lesson, the student should:

1. Realize the meaning of nurturing the intellect upon thinking.

2. Get acquainted with the upbringing approaches for developing a child's intellect.

3. Clarify the role of moral upbringing in cognitive development.

The Definition of the Intellect

It is narrated that Imām ʿAlī ﵇ said: "The best of gifts is the intellect."[280] For, intellect is the best gift granted by God ﷻ to man. And the intellect is the faculty of reasoning which distinguishes man from other living creatures. Imām ʿAlī ﵇ said: "Man is (distinguished) by his intellect."[281]

The intellect is God's ﷻ most favored creations. For God ﷻ addressed it by saying: "By my Honor and Majesty, I haven't created a creation that is more favorable to Me than you."[282]

That's why the intellect must be brought up and guided towards Divine objectives.

Raising the Intellect and Reason and its Objectives

Educating the intellect and reason is a process through which the child is led to the stage where he is capable of employing his intellect to perceive the reality of things, distinguish between conditions of perfection, deficiency, beauty and ugliness and invest it in a positive way which allows him to attend to his role through a series of cognitive activities such as: saving and preserving information, recalling and retrieving it, comparing things, controlling the self and leading it towards the purpose of its creation.

---

[280] Al-Wasitī, ʿOyoun al-Hikam w al-Mawāʾez, p. 237

[281] Ibid., p. 61

[282] al-Kulaynī, Shaykh Muḥammad ibn Yaʿqūb, Al-Kāfī, Vol. 1, p. 10

Therefore, the education of the intellect and reason aims at actualizing several faculties for the child; the most important of which are:

a. Accurate sensory observation (through the senses) and contemplation of his surroundings such as natural phenomena and creatures, in addition to the situations he encounters and experiences he acquires.

b. Activating man's cognitive capacity and encouraging it to receive, contain and understand through recalling and retrieving information, in addition to comparing things and identifying the link between them... etc.

c. The art of processing, analyzing and arranging information in a way that allows him to generate new and organized ideas, resolve problems and confront difficulties with different skills.

Sayyid al-Khāmina'ī emphasized on the necessity of teaching a child reasoning and philosophy, where he says: "Many people in our society don't even think of philosophy as an important subject for a child. For, some people imagine that philosophy is a sort of joke, and others take notice of it in their older age; however, this isn't the case. Philosophy is the shaping of thought, teaching of comprehension and accustoming the mind to thinking and understanding which must be present from the beginning of childhood. The framework and form are important, in children's philosophy, and so is the content and substance; however, the basis is the approach, which lies in accustoming the child from the beginning of his childhood to thinking and reasoning."[283]

The Impact of Raising the Intellect towards Achieving the Objectives of Upbringing

The noblest aim of the process of educating the child's intellect lies in achieving the final purpose of his existence, which is pointed out in the Noble Qur'ān *﴾I did not create the jinn and the humans except that they may worship Me﴿*[284], that is to know and worship God ﷻ. Thus, a link must be made between the child's cognitive skills and the discovery of God ﷻ and His traits in nature and the universe. Sayyid al-Khāmina'ī says: "Nurturing the faculties of cognition and reason in society is the key to resolving problems, self-restraint and setting the grounds for man to worship God."[285]

For, man cannot reach the perfection of his soul and knowledge of the truth of things except by the intellect through which he can distinguish between righteousness and falsehood. It is narrated that the Prophet ﷺ said: "The intellect is a light in the

---

283 al-Khāmina'ī, Sayyid 'Alī al-Ḥusaynī, the guardian's speech 2021, prepared by Noun Center for Authoring and Translation, Beirut, The Islamic and Cultural Association of al-Maāref, 2013 AD, 1st edition, p. 456, Sayyid al-Khāmina'ī speech (May God prolong his life) in a meeting with university teachers in North Khorasan on 11/10/2012 AD

284 Sūrah al-Dhāriyat, verse 56

285 The official website of Sayyid al-Khāmina'ī

heart that distinguishes between righteousness and falsehood."[286] This is from the theoretical point of view.

As for the practical aspect, through his intellect, man is capable of controlling himself, adhering it to the exterior of the Islamic Sharia, adorning himself with moral virtues and abandoning vices, in order to reach the knowledge of God ﷻ and connect to Him.

It is narrated that Imām Ja'far al-Ṣādiq ﵇ said: "... through the intellect, the servants knew their Creator and the fact that they were created, that He is the manager of their affairs and they are the managed, that He is perpetual and they are mortal; and they inferred –through their intellects – what they saw of his creation, from his sky and land, sun and moon, and day and night, and that it (the intellect) and they have a Creator and Manager who still exists and forever remains. Through it (the intellect), they know beauty from ugliness, that darkness lies in ignorance and light in knowledge. This is what the intellect has shown them..."[287]

The Noble Qur'ān encouraged, in tens of verses, thinking, contemplation, looking deeply, reasoning and maintaining insight...etc., in addition to the narrations that were mentioned on behalf of Ahl al-Bayt ﵈ which emphasized on the correlative relationship between the intellect and religion. It is

---

[286] Al-Daylami, al-Ḥasan ibn Muḥammad, Irshad al-Quloub, Qom, Intisharat al-Sharif al-Radi, 1415 AH, 2nd edition, Vol. 1, p. 198

[287] al-Kulaynī, Shaykh Muḥammad ibn Ya'qūb, Al-Kāfī, Vol. 1, p. 29

narrated that Imām al-Ṣādiq ☙ said: "He who reasons has a religion, and he who has a religion enters Heaven."[288]

The Role of Questions in the Cognitive Upbringing of the Child

Throughout the intellectual and cognitive upbringing of the child, the nurturer must use the approach of raising a bunch of questions by tracking the child's cognitive habits in relation to things, and then he must look for their answers. For example:

Does my child raise questions and have a lot of inquiries?

Does he ask about the things which he doesn't understand and get convinced by the answer he receives?

Does he memorize information quickly or need to repeat it several times?

Does he have a keen sensory observation and contemplate the situations he encounters, or does he show no interest?

Does he have the capacity of comparing between things?

Does he support his opinions with testimonies and evidence?

Does he take decisions by himself or rely constantly or mostly on others?

Does he surrender to the problems he faces or come up with solutions and diverse alternatives?

---

[288] Ibid., p. 11

Does he transfer ideas to behavior?

Does he learn from his mistakes and never repeat them?

The Approaches towards Developing the Right Way of Thinking

There are many approaches that must be adopted by the educator/nurturer in order to develop the right way of thinking for the child, the most important of which are:

Encouraging the Child to Ask Questions

A child is born with a mind that is empty of knowledge – which plays a fundamental role in the process of thinking. At the same time, enclosed within him is the love of knowledge which must be activated by encouraging him to ask questions. For, a question is a key to the treasures of sciences, as mentioned by the Messenger of God ﷺ: "Knowledge is a treasure, and its key is inquiry."[289]

Therefore, training on inquiry during childhood leads the child to becoming one of the people who provide answers when he's older. It is narrated that Imām 'Alī said: "He who asks when he's young answers when he's older."[290]

Therefore, the nurturer must encourage the child to ask questions and raise inquiries about everything that surrounds

[289] Al-Radi, Muḥammad ibn Ḥusayn, al-Majazāt al-Nabawiyya, verified by Ṭāha Muḥammad al-Zayni, Qom, published by Basirati Library, L.T, L.T', p. 209

[290] Al-Wasitī, 'Oyoun al-Hikam w al-Mawa'iz

him in life, without shyness, so he doesn't close on himself the door of knowledge. It is narrated that Imām al-Bāqir ﷺ said: "Ask and do not disdain or be shy; for, this knowledge cannot be learned by someone who is arrogant or shy."[291]

On the other hand, he (the nurturer) must interact positively with the child's questions and make him feel that his question is important and admirable. And he mustn't treat his questions with sarcasm and ridicule; for, the purpose – especially in early childhood – isn't to discover the child's skills in raising questions but rather to develop his sense of initiating a question regardless of its nature.

At a later stage, he seeks to develop the child's (skill in) raising good questions; for, "in good questioning lies half of knowledge"[292], as narrated on behalf of the Messenger of God ﷺ. In pursuit of realizing this purpose, one can resort to the approach of rephrasing the child's question in a better way in front of him rather than putting him down.

As the child's age stage advances, one must move progressively with him by teaching him the etiquettes of questioning and the fact that his primary purpose from asking should be the acquisition of knowledge, rather than to embarrass and prove wrong the teacher or parents or friend. It is narrated that Imām al-Ṣādiq ﷺ said: "Ask the scholars about what you are ignorant

[291] al-Ṣadūq, Shaykh Muḥammad ibn 'Alī, 'Ilal al-Sharā'i', Vol. 2, p. 606

[292] Al-Karajki, Muḥammad ibn 'Alī, Kanz al-Fawā'ed, verified by Abdullah Ne'ma, Beirut, Dar al-Adwa', 1985 AD, 1st edition, p. 287

of; and never ask them out of stubbornness and experimentation..."[293]

Moreover, the nurturer mustn't leave the child's question pending and unanswered; and he must be extremely keen not to provide the child with incorrect answers that would distort his understanding. Therefore, if he doesn't have the answer ready in his mind, he must aim at taking the child on a journey of joint-search for the answer, or he must consult the experts, specialists and people of knowledge regarding questioning in front of the child, so he can hear the answer from them and understand – indirectly – that asking others is a natural thing.

Strengthening the Child's Sensory Observation

One of the important approaches in the process of cognitive development is strengthening the child's sensory observation; for, man – generally – and a child – particularly – is a sensory more than a mental being.[294] Accordingly, he (the nurturer) must accustom the child to pay attention to all the details without losing sight of any of it, for which he can resort to several methods such as placing a painting in front of the child or sitting with him in nature – or even in a room in the house – and asking him to describe what he sees, portray what exists in the room and write it down on paper in order to assess the accuracy of his observation and narration of details.

---

[293] al-Ṭabrisī, Shaykh 'Alī, Mishkāt al-Anwār fi Ghurar al-Akhbār, verified Mahdī Hoshmand, L.M, Dar al-Ḥadīth, 1418 AH, 1st edition, p. 564

[294] Al-Sadr, Sayyid Muḥammad Bāqir, Mūjaz fi 'Usūl al-Din, verified and studied by Abdul Jabbar al-Rifa'i, L.M, Shari'at Printing, 1422 AH – 2001 AD, p. 224-225. Review: p. 224-240; for, it's a nice study on the topic.

Moreover, the Noble Qur'ān urged man towards sensory thinking, contemplation and observation; for, sometimes it urges him to look at the camel, as mentioned in His ﷻ saying: *Do they not observe the camel, [to see] how she has been created* [295], and at the wind, as per His ﷻ saying: *And We send the fertilizing winds and send down water from the sky providing it for you to drink and you are not maintainers of its resources* [296], and the planets and plants... pointing out to the fact that this type of contemplation on prospective verses connects man to the knowledge of God ﷻ.

Activating Brainstorming Skills

Accustoming the child to brainstorming and sharing ideas with a group or children opens up his horizons of knowledge and guides him towards the right opinion, in addition to the fact that it encourages him to express his opinion, discuss it with others, try to persuade them by using proofs and respect others' opinions despite their diversity.

It is narrated that Imām 'Alī ؑ said: "Confront some opinions with others; and righteousness will be conceived thereof."[297]

Moreover, training the child on brainstorming will weaken his love of control, obsession with his thoughts and imposing them

---

[295] Sūrah al-Ghashiya, verse 17

[296] Sūrah al-Hijr, verse 22

[297] Al-Wasitī, 'Muḥammad al-Hikam w al-Mawa'ez, p. 91

on others. It is narrated that Imām ʿAlī ﷺ said: "He who obsesses with his opinion perishes."[298]

Developing the Sense of Dealing with Information

There are several approaches in this regard, the most important of which are:

Accustoming the child to admitting his ignorance. It is narrated that Imām ʿAlī ﷺ said: "The purpose of the intellect is to admit ignorance."[299]

Accustoming the child to understanding the information rather than merely memorizing them. It is narrated that Imām ʿAlī ﷺ said: "Indeed, there is no good in knowledge without understanding."[300]

Accustoming him to verify the authenticity of the information he receives and guiding him towards the most important resources in which he can look for information. It is narrated on behalf of Zayd al-Shahham, on behalf of Abi Ja'far ﷺ, in regards to His ﷻ saying: ﴾*So let man consider his food*﴿[301], he (Zayd) said: I said (to the Imām): What is his food? He ﷺ said: "The knowledge that he receives, who he receives it from."[302]

---

298 Nahj al-Balāgha, part 4, a chosen chapter from the sayings of Imām ʿAlī ﷺ, saying 161

299 Al-Wasitī, ʿOyoun al-Hikam w al-Mawa'ez, p. 241

300 al-Kulaynī, Shaykh Muḥammad ibn Yaʿqūb, Al-Kāfī, Vol. 1, p. 36

301 Sūrah ʿAbas, verse 24

302 al-Kulaynī, Shaykh Muḥammad ibn Yaʿqūb, Al-Kāfī, Vol. 1, p. 50

Accustoming the child to consider the opinions in themselves, when assessing their precision and error, regardless of whom they came from.

It is narrated that Imām ʿAlī ※ said: "Take the wise saying from the person who brings it to you, and consider what is being said without considering who is saying it."[303]

Training him on discovering the contradictions in information, opinions and situations, so he doesn't get easily deceived by tricks and fallacies. It is narrated that Imām ʿAlī ※ said: "The corruption of the intellect leads to getting deceived by tricks."[304]

Encouraging the child to engage in personal experiences in discovering things and building experiences." It is narrated that Imām ʿAlī ※ said: "Intellect is an instinct nurtured by experiences."[305]

Teaching him how to arrange his priorities in terms of important and more important on one hand, and bad and worse on the other hand. It is narrated that Imām ʿAlī ※ said: "The reasonable man is not he who knows good from evil; rather, he is the one who knows the better of two evils."[306]

---

[303] Al-Wāsitī, ʿUyūn al-Hikam w al-Mawāʿez, p. 241

[304] Ibid., p. 357

[305] Ibn Abi Hadid, Abdul Hamid ibn Hiba God al-Madāʾeni, Sharh Nahj al-Balāgha, commented on by Ḥusayn al-Aʾlami, Beirut, al-Aʾlami Institute, 1415 AH – 1995 AD, 1st edition, Vol. 20, p. 341

[306] Al-Shāfiʾi, Muḥammad ibn Talha, Matālib al-Suʾoul fi Manāqib Al al-Rasoul, verified by Mājed Ahmad al-Atiyyah, L.M, L.N, L.T, L.T', p. 250

The Role of Ethics and Manners in the Development of Intellect and Cognition

One of the important and outstanding Islamic principles in nurturing – man and – a child's intellect and cognition is training the child on adorning himself with virtues and abandoning vices due to its close connection to the process of developing positive thinking and eliminating negative thinking. It is narrated that Imām 'Alī ؏ said: "He doesn't benefit from wisdom who has an intellect contaminated with anger and lust."[307]

Therefore, 'Allāma Tabataba'i says: "If man's innate religion corrupts and he doesn't nourish himself from religious piety, his internal powers that are touched by lust, anger, love, hatred and others will not be balanced. And under the imbalance of these powers, the faculty of theoretical perception doesn't do its job in a satisfactory way."[308]

The Role of Nutrition in Cognitive Development

One of the essential factors that contribute to the child's cognitive development is the nature of his nutrition. For, many foods and drinks play an important role in activating his mental faculties; and one can consult specialists in medicine and nutrition in this regard. Some ḥadīths and narrations

---

[307] Al-Tamimi al-Amidi, Abdul Wahed ibn Muḥammad, category of Ghurar al-Hikam wa Durar al-Kalim, verified and corrected by Mustapha Darāyti, Iran, Qom, office of Islamic press, 1407 AH, 1st edition, p. 65

[308] Ṭabāṭabā'ī, al-'Allāma Sayyid Muḥammad Ḥusayn, Al-Mīzān fī Tafsīr al-Qur'ān, Vol. 5, p. 311

mentioned some types of foods and drinks such as pumpkin, quince, celery, frankincense, honey, pomegranate, vinegar, chickpeas, rue[309], ...etc., we will mention some of it briefly:

It is narrated that Imām Abi al-Ḥasan Mūsā al-Kāẓim 🌸 said: "One of the things that were recommended by the Messenger of God 🌸 to ʿAlī 🌸 is that he said to him: O' ʿAlī, you should have pumpkin; eat it. For, it increases in the brain and intellect."[310]

It is narrated that the Messenger of God 🌸 said: "You should have celery; for, if there is anything that increases one's intellect it would be it."[311]

It is narrated that the Messenger of God 🌸 said: "You should have frankincense; for, it ... increases one's intellect, raises the mind's intelligence, clarifies the vision and eliminates forgetfulness."[312]

It is narrated that the Messenger of God 🌸 said: "You should have chickpeas; for, it is that which raises the intelligence

---

[309] Rue: It's a type of plant.

[310] al-Kulaynī, Shaykh Muḥammad ibn Yaʿqūb, Al-Kāfī, Vol. 6, p. 371

[311] Mustaghfirī, Abu al-Abbas, Tobb al-Nabi, L.M, Intisharat Radi, 1362 AH, 1st edition, p. 31

[312] al-Majlisī, al-ʿAllāma Muḥammad Bāqir, Biḥār al-Anwār, al-Jamiʾa li Durar Akhbār al-Aʾimma al-Aṭhār, verified by Ibrāhīm al-Mayanji and Muḥammad Bāqir al-Bahboudi, Beirut, al-Wafaʾ Institute, 1403 AH-1983 AD, 2nd edition, Vol. 59, p. 300

(*mukyisa*)[313]. If there was anything that would increase one's intellect it would be it."[314]

It is narrated that Imām al-Ridā ﵇ said: "You should have quince; for, it increases one's intellect."[315]

Main Concepts

It is narrated that Imām 'Alī ﵇ said: "The best of gifts is the intellect." For, intellect is the best gift granted by God ﷻ to man. And the intellect is the faculty of reasoning which distinguishes man from other living creatures. Imām 'Alī ﵇ said: "Man is (distinguished) by his intellect."

Educating the intellect and reason is a process through which the child is led to the stage where he is capable of employing his intellect to perceive the reality of things, distinguish between conditions of perfection, deficiency, beauty and ugliness and invest it in a positive way which allows him to attend to his role through a series of cognitive activities.

For, man cannot reach the perfection of his soul and knowledge of the truth of things except by the intellect through which he can distinguish between righteousness and falsehood. It is narrated that the Prophet ﷺ said: "The intellect is a light in the heart that distinguishes between righteousness and falsehood." This is from the theoretical point of view.

---

313 *Mukyisa*: it is derived from intelligence and cleverness.

314 Al-Barqi, Ahmad ibn Muḥammad ibn Khāled, al-Mahāsin, Beirut, al-A'lami Printing Institute, 1429 AH – 2008 AD, 1st edition, Vol. 2, p. 517

315 al-Ṭabrisī, Shaykh al-Faḍl ibn al-Ḥasan, Makārim al-Akhlāq, p. 172

As for the practical aspect, through his intellect, man is capable of controlling himself, adhering it to the exterior of the Islamic Sharia, adorning himself with moral virtues and abandoning vices, in order to reach the knowledge of God ﷻ and connect to Him.

One of the important approaches in the process of cognitive development is strengthening the child's sensory observation; for, man – generally – and a child – particularly – is a sensory more than a mental being. Accordingly, he (the nurturer) must accustom the child to pay attention to all the details without losing sight of any of it.

One of the important and outstanding Islamic principles in nurturing – man and – a child's intellect and cognition is training the child on adorning himself with virtues and abandoning vices due to its close connection to the process of developing positive thinking and eliminating negative thinking. It is narrated that Imām 'Alī ؑ said: "He doesn't benefit from wisdom who has an intellect contaminated with anger and lust."

Lesson Twelve

Theological Upbringing

Lesson Objectives

By the end of this lesson, the student should:

1. Realize the importance of the Islamic theological upbringing of the child.
2. Get acquainted with the best approach to transfer the theological concepts to the child.
3. Get acquainted with the methods of theological upbringing.

Preamble

One of the most important rights of the child upon his parents is raising him upon true religion and cultivating firm belief in his mind and heart so he can become insightful in the matters of his religion and worldly affairs. Narrations pointed out to this issue; as it is narrated that Imām al-ʿAskarī ☙ said: "God ☙ covers some parents with a garment that is worthier than this world and all that it encompasses, for which all creations look up to them and honor them; and they look at themselves in surprise, so they said: "Our Lord, how did we attain this when our deeds didn't earn them? ... So it is said: it is by teaching your child the Qurʾān and making him insightful of the Islamic religion..."[316]

Therefore, parents must give religious upbringing special attention. This upbringing includes these aspects: theological upbringing, moral upbringing and jurisprudential upbringing. And on top of the pyramid lies the theological upbringing.

The Impact of Theological Upbringing on a Child

The theological upbringing of the child entails two aspects:

First, positive: It is concerned with preparing the child and strengthening his capacity to accept the righteous beliefs and disciplines that are related to God ☙ and his traits, prophethood, Imāmate and the hereafter.

Second, negative: That is, to keep the child away from the environment which encompasses false or perverted beliefs.

---

[316] al-Majlisī, al-ʿAllāma Muḥammad Bāqir, Biḥār al-ʾAnwār, Vol. 7, p. 306

Theological upbringing plays a lively role in shaping a child's identity; and it aims at answering many inquiries raised by him, especially those related to the unseen world, such as his questions on the Creator ﷻ or death... Therefore, the answers provided by the Islamic religion in this regard are sufficient to grant the child a feeling of security and tranquility which removes anxiety and fear of the unknown future from the child's heart. This is what we sense in the life of Prophets ﷺ; for, Yūsuf ﷺ was nine years old when his brothers left him at the bottom of a well. And when the by-passers picked him up and he ﷺ left the well, someone said to them: Treat this stranger well; then Yūsuf told them: "He who is with God doesn't encounter any estrangement."[317]

The Approaches Towards Theological Upbringing

Some people consider that the religious and theological upbringing of the child surpasses his mental capacities and exceeds his level of comprehension, and that it leads to negative repercussions on building his character, or it robs him of the freedom of choosing the theological belief which he wants after research and scrutiny.

It is the right of the educational researcher to raise the likes of these questions on the theological upbringing of the child: does the child comprehend theological matters so that we can raise him upon them? And at what age stage do we start with the process of the theological upbringing of the child? And what is

---

[317] Al-Zamakhshari, Rabee' al-Abrar wa Nusous al-Akhbār, verified by Abdul Amir Mhanna, Beirut, al-A'lami Printing Institute, 1412 AH – 1992 AD, 1st edition, Vol. 3, p. 5

the nature of these theological issues to which we will start introducing him? ... Etc.

The paths towards God ﷻ are as many as the breaths of his creations. And one can deal with the issue of God's ﷻ existence using several approaches; the two most important of which are:

First: the theoretical approach which is adopted by philosophers through the provision of proofs of intellectual reasoning to know God ﷻ, where they gather evidence which requires cognitive effort in order to prove the existence of God ﷻ. This approach is distant from the understanding of common people, let alone the minds of children.

Second: the approach of the primordial human nature which aspires to speak to the internal primordial nature of the human being, due to the fact that it is created upon faith in God ﷻ. This approach was adopted by most people throughout their spiritual lives in regards to their relationship with God ﷻ. Moreover, it was adopted by Ahl al-Bayt عليهم السلام during the course of theological upbringing. A man said to Imām Ja'far al-Ṣādiq عليه السلام: "O' son of the Messenger of God, guide me to God, what is He; for, debaters spoke a lot (on the matter) and confused me.

So he said to him: O' servant of God, have you ever been on a boat? He said: Yes.

He said: Did it break while you were on it, leaving you with no boat to save you or swimming skills to rescue you? He said: Yes.

He said, "Did your heart then get attached to the hope that something is capable of saving you from your dilemma?" He said: Yes. Al-Ṣādiq عليه السلام said: "That thing is God who has the power to save where no savior exists, and to rescue where no rescuer exists."[318]

If we carry out an induction of the Qur'ānic texts and the approach of Ahl al-Bayt, we will see that they emphasize on the effectiveness of both approaches being used jointly. This means that there is no conflict between the two approaches and that man needs them both.

Therefore, since the upbringing process is gradual and considerate of the child's level of understanding and perception, the most appropriate modality of raising the child theologically would be to start with the innate/natural approach, and later on move gradually with him in order to reach that knowledge through theological proofs.

And due to the fact that children are born with innate monotheistic belief in God, the nurturer – thus – should merely develop those tendencies that exist within them. It is narrated that Abi Abdillah said: "Mūsā ibn Imran said: O' Lord, which deeds are most favored by you? He said: loving children; for, I have created them upon monotheism, and if I ended their lives, I would enter them into Heaven with my mercy."[319]

God prepared the heart of the child in a way that he is innately guided towards the knowledge of God and believing in Him. Nonetheless, the primordial nature is not a sufficient

---

318 al-Ṣadūq, Shaykh Muḥammad ibn 'Alī, Al-Tawḥīd, verified by 'Alī Akbar al-Ghafāri, Beirut, al-A'lami Printing Institute, 1427 AH – 2006 AD, 1st edition, p. 231

319 Al-Barqi, al-Mahāsin, Vol. 1, p. 293

and independent factor - by itself. Therefore, the child still needs – in pursuit of reaching the knowledge of God – external support, which is the guidance of the nurturer who works on the nourishment of that primordial nature, as an internal source of energy which dwells within the child, in light of what is required by his nature and self. Accordingly, the nurturer must adopt the approach of the monotheistic primordial nature by exciting this knowledge about God ﷻ that is hidden deep within the child.

The Necessity of Keeping the Child Away from Theologically-Perverted Environments

Islam emphasized on the importance of securing the appropriate environment for raising the child form a theological perspective on one hand; and it highlighted the necessity of keeping him distant from theologically-perverted environments on another hand. It is narrated that Imām ʿAlī ؑ said: "Teach your boys (from our knowledge) that through which God benefits them, so that the Murjites don't conquer them."[320]

Al-Fayd al-Kashani said in his commentary on this narration: "It means teach them in the beginning of their youth, nay in their primary days of perception when they reach the age of discernment which allows them to identify from a narration that which guides them towards the knowledge of the Imāms ؑ and Shiism, before the opponents tempt them and lead them into their misguidance, after which it becomes difficult to dismiss them thereof."[321] This means that parents must keep

320 Ibn Sha'ba al-Harāni, Tuhaf al-'Uqūl, p. 104

321 al-Fayḍ al-Kāshānī, Mullā Muḥammad, al-Wāfī

their children away from theologically-perverted environments, and choose well the environment that is appropriate for a wholesome theological development – be it an environment of residence, school, scouts, sports... etc.

The Methods of Theological Upbringing

It has become clear that a child is created with an innate proclivity towards a monotheistic upbringing, and that the nurturer can stimulate this primordial nature which dwells within the child and activate the potentials therein. This raises several inquiries such as: How can the nurturer stimulate the monotheistic nature that lies within the child? And at what age stage does this process begin?

Answering this question, one can suggest several methods that can benefit the nurturer in the theological upbringing of the child. And it is as follows:

1. The Method of Verbal Indoctrination

This method entails accustoming the child to the repetition of some sentences and phrases on a verbal level, even if he doesn't understand their meaning, such as repeating the saying: there is no God but God or Muḥammad is the Messenger of God...; for, this repetition – in itself – has its special role and impact in activating the sense of belief in God ﷻ.

The nurturer must use this method in early childhood (3 years). It's the method that was adopted in the narration of Ahl al-Bayt ؏. For, it is narrated on behalf of Abdullah ibn Fudala, on behalf of Abi Abdillah and Abi Ja'far ؏ that he said: I heard him say: "When a child completes three years of age, he is told: say: 'there is no God but God' seven times..."[322]

And it is narrated that he (the Prophet) ﷺ said: "Make your boys' first words be there is no God but God".[323]

2. The Method of Learning the Law of Causation

Raising the intellect by thinking about things, finding links between them and getting to know their reasons plays a role in developing the feeling of God's ﷻ presence.

The child pays attention to sounds and links them to their sources; and if this proves anything at all it'll be the fact that the law of causation is present innately within him. And the nurturer must develop this feeling within the child and, gradually, transfer it into a conscious feeling.

In the beginning, the nurturer must develop – within the child – the sense of knowledge and discovery, and make him realize that behind every phenomenon there's a reason that inspires its existence; for, the sound of barking is caused by a dog... etc. Then, he can move with him gradually through the process of connecting things together then to the process of linking the specifications of things and their causes, in the sense that if he sees a beautiful painting he realizes that the painter is skillful, in contrary to the case where it's not beautiful then he realizes that

---

[322] al-Ṣadūq, Shaykh Muḥammad ibn 'Alī, Man Lā Yaḥḍuruh al-Faqīh, Vol. 1, p. 281, ḥadīth 863

[323] Al-Mubārak al-Fawri, Muḥammad ibn Abdul Rahmān ibn Abdul Raḥim, Tuḥfat al-Ahwadhi, explained by the collector of al-Tarmadhi, Beirut, Dar al-Kutub al-'Ilmiyyah, 1410 AH – 1990 AD, 1st edition, Vol. 4, p. 46

the painter is unskilled. Therefore, he must seek to develop this sense within the child at every age stage; and gradually this state will grow with him until he realizes that every phenomenon in life has a God and a Creator and that He is the Cause of all Causes. This is what we feel in the approach of Ahl al-Bayt 🕊; for, when Imām 'Alī 🕊 was asked to prove the existence of a creator, he responded: "The ungulate denotes (the existence of) the ungulate, the dung denotes the donkeys and the footprints denote the walk; then how can a superstructure with such gentleness and a lower center with such intensity not denote the Subtle, the All-knowing?"[324]

3. The Method of Developing the Tendency Towards Sensory Experience

Man is, generally, a sensory – more than a mental – being, let alone the child whose sensory component is strongly prominent and present. Sensation is more capable of raising a human being than intellectual and abstract theory; and it occupies more aspects of his being, personality, emotions, feelings and reactions than intellect does.[325]

The nurturer's role is to work on developing the child's sensual tendency and take his hand so he can discover the creatures that surround him and link them to each other, and then to gradually help him to contemplate the wonders of the creatures and the meticulousness of their creation. The Noble Qur'ān, the Prophet 🕊 and Ahl al-Bayt 🕊 adopted this approach

---

[324] al-Majlisī, al-'Allāma Muḥammad Bāqir, Biḥār al-Anwār, Vol. 3, p. 55

[325] al-Ṣadr, Ayatullāh Shahīd Sayyid Muḥammad Bāqir, al-Mūjāz fī 'Uṣūl al-Dīn, p. 224-225; and review: p. 224-240, for it's an interesting study.

which suggests that sensory observation and visualization, proceeded with contemplation, examination and observation of the wonders of God's ﷻ creation – such as contemplating the difference between night and day and stars and giving life to plants – bear the fruit of knowing God ﷻ and His traits and connecting with Him. Amīr al-Mu'minīn ﷺ expresses this point in one of his speeches, where he says: "The perfection of its creation (the things and creatures) is sufficient to consider it a sign."[326]

And God ﷻ invites us to contemplate the signs in the horizons and ourselves, where He says: ﴿*Soon We shall show them Our signs in the horizons and in their own souls until it becomes clear to them that He is the Real. Is it not sufficient that your Lord is witness to all things?*﴾[327]

The way through which the child gets to know himself is one of the most important ways of theological upbringing. And the nurturer must never lose sight of this. Ahl al-Bayt adopted this approach in teaching and theological upbringing – so did the students who graduated from their schools. For, it is narrated that Hisham ibn al-Hakam said: If someone asks: Through which tool did you know your Lord? Say: I knew God ﷻ through myself, because it is the nearest thing to me... God ﷻ says: ﴿*And in your souls [as well]. Will you not then perceive?*﴾[328]

Therefore, developing the child's experiential sense by introducing him to the systems and subtleties of things...

---

326 al-Ṣadūq, Shaykh Muḥammad ibn 'Alī, al-Tawḥīd, p. 71

327 Sūrah Fussilat, verse 53

328 Sūrah al-Dhāriyyat, verse 21

reinforces – within himself – faith in God ﷻ. And contrary to the assumption of some people, reinforcing this aspect will not lead to the nourishment of the tendency towards atheism and denying the existence of God ﷻ.

4. The Method of Practicing Worship

One of the methods of raising a child on establishing a relationship with God ﷻ and developing a sense of religious faith within him is to make him – when he reaches the age of discernment (7 years) and afterwards – perform the acts of worship such as prayer, fasting, almsgiving and others... And "the child might not understand the expressions that he mumbles during prayer; however, he understands the meaning of directing one's self towards God and whispering to him..."[329] For, prayer, fasting and other forms of worship make the child live in a state of submission to the greatness of God ﷻ.

5. The Method of Raising (the Child) on the Love of the Prophet ﷺ and Ahl al-Bayt ﷺ

It is narrated that the Prophet ﷺ said: "Discipline your children upon three traits: the love of your Prophet ﷺ, the love of his progeny and reading the Qur'ān..."[330]

One of the most beneficial methods of this type of theological upbringing of the child is to read him the stories and biographies ﷺ that are suitable for children, such as making the Prophet ﷺ lovable to the child's heart by highlighting his

---

329 Falsafi, Muḥammad Taqi, al-Tifl bayn al-Wirātha wal-Tarbiya, Vol. 2, p. 150

330 al-Suyūṭī, ʿAbd al-Raḥmān ibn Abī Bakr, al-Jāmiʾ al-Saghīr, Vol. 1, p. 51

empathetic, sympathetic, loving and merciful interaction with his sons al-Ḥasan and al-Ḥusayn ﻋﻠﻴﻬﻤﺎ ﺍﻟﺴﻼﻡ...etc.

6. The Method of Raising (the Child) on the Belief in the Hereafter

It is frequent for a child, during the second stage of his childhood i.e. starting the age of six and above, to ask about death especially if he lost any of his relatives. For, he would ask 'where is he? Will he come back? How do we see him?' It is important that we present – to the child – the concept of death in a way that is related to the continuity of life, and that the dead person lives a second life and sees and hears us if we pray for him...etc.

One can resort to the sensory approach in the attempt of making the child understand the idea of death. The Noble Qur'ān tackles this issue in His saying: *﴾It is God who sends the winds and they raise a cloud; then We drive it toward a dead land and with it revive the earth after its death. Likewise will be the resurrection [of the dead]﴿*[331] amongst other verses.

It is also important to present the day of Return by picturing it as a day of harvesting the results after which one either fails or succeeds. However, one must be attentive not to turn the matter into the approach of threatening the child with punishment in the Hereafter, such as saying the expression: "if you do this, God will choke you", "God will burn you in Hellfire"...etc. and other expressions. This is considered as an

---

[331] Sūrah Fāter, verse 9

impermissible lie – even when used with a child[332]-; for, if God doesn't address the child with the speech of eternal punishment, then why would the nurturer?

Main Concepts

One of the most important rights of the child upon his parents is raising him upon true religion and cultivating firm belief in his mind and heart so he can become insightful in the matters of his religion and worldly affairs.

The theological upbringing of the child entails two aspects:

First, positive: It is concerned with preparing the child and strengthening his capacity to accept the righteous beliefs and disciplines that are related to God ﷻ and his traits, prophethood, Imāmate and the hereafter.

Second, negative: That is, to keep the child away from the environment which encompasses false or perverted beliefs.

A child is created with an innate proclivity towards a monotheistic upbringing, and that the nurturer can stimulate this primordial nature which dwells within the child and activate the potentials therein.

There are many methods for theological upbringing which are concluded from the narrations of Ahl al-Bayt عليهم السلام, the most important of which are: the method of verbal indoctrination, the method of nurturing the intellect in a way that allows it to

332 al-Khoeī, Ayatullāh Sayyid Abū l-Qāsim, and Tabrīzī, Ayatullāh Mīrzā Jawād, Sīrat al-Najāt fi Ajwibat al-'Istifta'āt, Vol. 3, p. 298, question 920

make connections amongst things, developing the sensual and experiential tendency, practicing acts of worship, raising (the child) on the love of the Prophet and Ahl al-Bayt ﷺ and raising (the child) on the belief in the Hereafter.

It is also important to present the day of Return by picturing it as a day of harvesting the results after which one either fails or succeeds. However, one must be attentive not to turn the matter into the approach of threatening the child with punishment in the Hereafter.

Lesson Thirteen

Raising by Example

Lesson Objectives

By the end of this lesson, the student should:

1. Realize that man is a sensual being more than he is mental.
2. Realize that raising by example through a behavioral idol is one of the most important method of upbringing.
3. Be able to differentiate between self-discipline and objective external discipline.

Preamble

Man cannot experience the interaction with values as abstract meanings unless they are represented and embodied in reality. For, if man observes - through his senses - values such as righteousness, honesty, bravery and generosity... embodied and characterized in reality in a certain person, this will make him interact with them in a more positive way than learning them – theoretically – as abstract meanings and concepts. Therefore, man gets attached to characters who embody values and can be regarded as role models he can follow in his path and conduct. Moreover, Islam has invited us to emulate the personality of the noble Prophet ﷺ and Imāms ﷷ, since they are examples who embodied those values and others within their personalities – in the real sense of the term 'embodiment', ﴾*In the Apostle of God there is certainly for you a good exemplar*﴿[333]

Sayyid Muḥammad Bāqir al-Ṣadr says in this regard: "... Sensation is more capable of raising a human being than abstract intellectual theory; and it occupies a larger space in the aspects of his being, personality, feelings, emotions and reactions than the intellect 'the abstract theoretical concept'. Based on this premise, man needed to have a nurturing sensation."[334] For, he considers that this nurturing sensation is the great Messenger and the infallible Imāms ﷷ.

---

[333] Sūrah al-Aḥzāb, verse 21

[334] al-Ṣadr, Ayatullāh Shahīd Sayyid Muḥammad Bāqir, al-Mūjāz fi 'Usūl al-Dīn, verified and studied by Abdul Jabbār al-Rifā'i, p. 224-225; and review: p. 224-240; for, therein lies an interesting study on this topic.

Sensory Model Upbringing

The presence of a sensory and behavioral model has its effective impact in the upbringing process. That's why the prophetic upbringing of ʿAlī ؏ is considered as a sensory and behavioral model upbringing. Imām ʿAlī ؏ describes this by saying: "And you have known my position from the Messenger of God ﷺ by close kinship and special status. He put me in his lap when I was a child, held me close to his chest and placed me in his bed. I could touch his body and smell his perfume.[335] He used to chew on a thing [food] and then feed it to me. He never found a lie in my speech or deceit in my actions. God paired him ﷺ – ever since he was a weaned child – with the greatest angel amongst His angels who paved for him – day and night – the path of nobilities and virtuous morals. I used to follow him as a calf would follow his mother. He would increase my knowledge, every day, by his morals, and command me to follow his steps…"[336]

The Sensory Approach in the Noble Qurʾān

The Noble Qurʾān used the sensory upbringing approach in presenting the concepts and values - intended to be transferred to people - through 'education by storytelling'. God ﷻ said: *Whatever We relate to you of the accounts of the apostles are those by which We strengthen your heart*[337]

---

[335] Perfume: his good smell.

[336] Nahj al-Balāghah, Vol. 2, p. 175

[337] Sūrah Hud, verse 120

The Imāms of Ahl al-Bayt ﷺ emphasized on having the invitation towards religion and dissemination of God's ﷻ message adopted and embodied through action and behavior before the verbal invitation; as it is more impactful on people's hearts.

It is narrated that Imām Ja'far al-Ṣādiq ﷺ said: "Invite people towards your religion without the use of your tongues, so they can see - in you - piety, diligence, prayer and goodness; for, that would be a missionary."[338]

Role Models and their Impact on a Child's Upbringing

Al-Rāghib al-Asfahānī defined having a role model as: "the state in which a person follows another, in doing good or ugly."[339] Upbringing by example and by providing the sensual role model is considered one of the best methods in raising a child due to the following reasons:

First: the sensual tendency that is present particularly in the child.

Second: the child's possession of a high capacity for imitating and mimicking.

Third: the impact of the embodiment of meanings and concepts in a sensual example on the spectator and recipient.

---

[338] al-Kulaynī, Shaykh Muḥammad ibn Ya'qūb, Al-Kāfī, Vol. 2, p. 77

[339] Al-Rāghib al-Asfahānī, Mufradāt Alfāz al-Qur'ān, p. 76

Therefrom arises the importance of having the father and mother as good examples for the child who mimics them in speech, action, morality and conduct. This, accordingly, puts them under the responsibility of monitoring themselves, acting in a moral and positive way in front of the child and concealing (from him) the immoral and negative conduct.

This is due to the fact that a child cannot comprehend – by himself – the reason for which his parents prohibit from doing something which they – themselves – carry out, for example when the father or mother forbids the child from lying or swearing and cursing his brother...etc., when they –themselves – carry out this swearing, cursing and screaming in the house.

For, in addition to his ability to mimic and imitate, a child has a deep attachment and strong connection to his parents, which increases his likelihood of copying their behavior.

Sayyid al-Khumaynī ☙ says in this regard: "Children are always or mostly with their parents; therefore their upbringing must be practical, in the sense that – assuming the parents do not have virtuous morals and good deeds – they must manifest virtue within themselves in front of the child, in which case the children will be practically well-brought up and refined. And perhaps this – in itself – will be the start of the parents' reform; for, that which has been crossed is a real bridge, and carrying out a certain trait is the path to acquiring it... Virtuous parents who raise well (their children) are of the fateful blessings and un-optional joys that can be destined for a child. On the other hand, their corruption and deficient upbringing is of the grievances and fateful agreements to which a person is bound with no choice of his own."[340]

Self-discipline and External Objective Discipline

Raising by a behavioral example supports the child's self-discipline and external discipline.

Self-Discipline: It means the action and behavior of the child, which originates from his wholesome primordial nature, where he performs good behavior as a result of his conviction which stems from within, and refuses to act badly with internal conviction due to the moral values he sees embodied within his parents' behavior. For, raising (a child) by providing a practical example embodied in the nurturer (the parents) embeds in the child high morale which guides him properly without imposing on him things in a mandatory way or making him feel robbed of his freedom. He, rather, carries out proper behavior and stays away from bad behavior with his own will and personal conviction without external pressures. The Noble Qur'ān calls this process of self-discipline 'al-tazkiyah'.

Objective-External Discipline: It expresses an external force that defines and controls behavior within the moral bounds. This external force is manifested in:

---

340 al-Khumaynī, Sayyid Rūhullāh al-Mūsawī, Junoud al-'Aql w al-Jahl, translated to Arabic by Ahmad al-Fahri, Beirut, al-A'lami Printing Institute, 1422 AH – 2001 AD, L.T, p. 142

First: direct orders and prohibitions

Second: penal law for misconducts[341]

The external disciplinary factor cannot carry out its required task without the factor of self-discipline.

Islamic upbringing differs from other forms of upbringing because it aspires to have behavior stem from an internal value-based force. For, it aims at having the child's behavior activated by the internal moral force so that he can manifest it through external practical behavior. For example, Islam doesn't want the child to stand respectfully for someone out of fear or greed while he curses him on the inside; it rather wants him to stand up respectfully due to the value of respect which lives within him as a personal energizer that mobilizes external behavior.

Raising by Example Starts with Self-Discipline

It is narrated that Imām ʿAlī ﵇ said: "He who appoints himself as a leader of the people must start with teaching himself before others; and he must discipline others through his own conduct before disciplining them by his tongue. He who teaches and disciplines himself is more entitled to respect that he who teaches and disciplines others."[342] Accordingly, parents must discipline themselves before embarking on the process of raising a child; otherwise, one cannot give from what he lacks.

---

341 This was extracted based on what benefits our study from the book: al-Ṣadr, Ayatullāh Shahīd Sayyid Muḥammad Bāqir, Iqtiṣāadunā, p. 282-284

342 Nahj al-Balāghah, the chapter of chosen sayings by Imām ʿAlī ﵇, p. 640-641, ḥadīth 73

This type of discipline isn't specific to the father and mother; it rather involves every teacher and nurturer. For, if the nurturer doesn't act according to his knowledge, he will not inspire others.

al-'Allamah Sayyid Muḥammad Ḥusayn al-Tabātabā'ī says in this regard: "It is mandatory for the nurturing teacher to act upon his knowledge; for, knowledge has no impact unless accompanied by action...

That's why we see that people's hearts do not soften and they do not allow themselves to be guided by teachings and advice if they find the preacher or advisor abandoning these actions and deserting patience and steadiness in his path. They may have said: if what he's saying is the truth, he would've acted upon it... For, one of the conditions of a virtuous upbringing is that the nurturing teacher – himself – adheres to what he describes for the learner and acts according to what he wants the latter to act..."[343]

Therefore, if the nurturer doesn't believe in what he says and doesn't act according to his knowledge, no good can come out of him.

---

343 God ﷻ said: ﴿*That, then, is God, your true Lord. So what is there after the truth except error? Then where are you being led away?*﴾ Sūrah Yūnus, verse 32, and He said: ﴿*Will you bid others to piety and forget yourselves, while you recite the Book? Do you not apply reason?*﴾ Sūrah al-Baqara, verse 44. And He narrated Shou'eib's saying to his people: ﴿*He said, 'O my people! Have you considered, should I stand on a manifest proof from my Lord, who has provided me a good provision from Himself? I do not wish to oppose you by what I forbid you. I only desire to put things in order, as far as I can, and my success lies only with God: in Him I have put my trust, and to Him I turn penitently*﴾ Sūrah Hūd, verse 88.

Sayyid al-Khāmina'ī: The Teacher's Role Towards the Child

In a speech for Sayyid 'Alī al-Khāmina'ī in which he clarifies the teacher's role towards the child, he says: "If we consider education in its expansive meaning, it includes these three field:

First: teaching knowledge, i.e. teaching the contents of books and sciences that must be learned by our children – our country's future men and women.

Second: And it is more important than the first; it is the teaching of thinking. Our children must learn how to think – the right and logical thought – and they must be guided towards proper thinking... For, benefiting from knowledge can only be made possible by thinking.

Third: It includes behavior and ethics, i.e. teaching behavior and ethics... Teaching ethics and behavior doesn't resemble the teaching of knowledge where a person only reads and studies books. A lesson in ethics cannot be transferred by books; for, behavior is more impactful than a book and a speech. This means that when you are in class and amongst your students, you are teaching them by your behavior. Surely, speaking and clarifying by words is mandatory as well, in addition to giving advice; however, the impact of behavior is deeper and more thorough. Man's behavior manifests the truthfulness of his speech."[344]

Main Concepts

Man cannot experience the interaction with values as abstract meanings unless they are represented and embodied in reality. Moreover, Islam has invited us to emulate the personality of the noble Prophet ﷺ and Imāms ؑ, since they are examples who embodied those values and others within their personalities – in the real sense of the term 'embodiment', ﴿*In the Apostle of God there is certainly for you a good exemplar*﴾[345]

The presence of a sensory and behavioral model has its effective impact in the upbringing process. That's why the prophetic upbringing of 'Alī ؑ is considered as a sensory and behavioral model upbringing.

The Noble Qur'ān used the sensory upbringing approach in presenting the concepts and values - intended to be transferred to people - through 'education by storytelling'. God ﷻ said: ﴿*Whatever We relate to you of the accounts of the apostles are those by which We strengthen your heart*﴾[346]

---

[344] al-Khāmina'ī, Sayyid 'Alī al-Ḥusaynī, the guardian's speech 2014, prepared by the Noun Center for Publishing and Translation, Beirut, al-Maaref Islamic and Cultural Association, 2015 AD, 1st edition, p. 225-226, from a speech by Sayyid 'Alī al-Khāmina'ī in a meeting with teachers and educators on the occasion of teacher's day, on 7/5/2014 AD

[345] Sūrah al-Aḥzāb, verse 21

[346] Sūrah Hūd, verse 120

It is important that the father and mother act as good examples for the child who mimics them in speech, action, morality and conduct. This, accordingly, puts them under the responsibility of monitoring themselves, acting in a moral and positive way in front of the child and concealing (from him) the immoral and negative conduct.

Self-Discipline: It means the action and behavior of the child, which originates from his wholesome primordial nature, where he performs good behavior as a result of his conviction which stems from within, and refuses to act badly with internal conviction due to the moral values he sees embodied within his parents' behavior.

Objective-External Discipline: It expresses an external force that defines and controls behavior within the moral bounds. This external force is manifested in:

First through direct orders and prohibitions, and second by a penal law for misconducts.[347]

---

[347] This was extracted based on what benefits our study from the book: al-Ṣadr, Ayatullāh Shahīd Sayyid Muḥammad Bāqir, Iqtiṣādunā, p. 282-284

Lesson Fourteen

Raising by Love

Lesson Objectives

By the end of this lesson, the student should:

1. Realize the importance of raising by love for a child.
2. Realize that love lies within man's primordial nature.
3. Get acquainted with the methods of a love-based upbringing.

Preamble

Love is a thing that is realized by every person through presence-based (or experiential) knowledge. For, it is an emotional trait which he experiences through his heart; we do not need logic to define it. Human love can be verbally defined as the heart-based inclination and emotional attraction towards something that gives the lover pleasure and joy.

The positive investment of this innate feeling by using it in shaping the child's identity is considered one of the most important foundations of raising a child. It is what we refer to as 'raising by love'.

In other words, what we mean by 'raising by love' is: using methods which include love, mercy, sympathy, affability, tenderness, gentleness and kindness...in building the child's balanced personality from an emotional perspective and shaping the features of his character in its different aspects.

The Objectives of Raising by Love

The process of raising by love aims at achieving several objectives, such as:

a. The proper emotional development of the child and the satisfaction of his sentimental needs, straying far from mental health disorders and complexities.[348]

---

[348] Banbila, Ḥasan ibn Abdullah, Usūl al-Tarbiya lil Tufūla fi al-Islām, al-Riyād, al-Rush Nashirūn library, 2009 AD, L.T', p. 221

b. Strengthening the relationship and connection between the child and the nurturer in a way that strengthens the latter's impact on the child's personality, such that the child accepts what he receives from him, listens to his words and obeys his orders.

c. Contributing to the healthy development of the other aspects of a child's identity including the mental, physical and moral development...

The Child's Need for Affection

The child is – by creation – a gentle, sensitive and emotional being. Therefore, he needs someone who can quench his emotional thirst on one hand, in addition to his need to feel that he is loved, cared for, attended to, nurtured, appreciated and respected... "For, a child needs to feel others' love for him and their contentment with him, especially his parents and teachers. He needs to be accepted and wanted by his parents and others."[349]

Loving a child is a two-faced coin: one face is positive, in the sense that it grants him positive energy, provides him with a feeling of happiness and allows him to experience joy, pleasure and delight. These are all necessary needs for a healthy emotional development.[350] Another face is depriving, in the sense that it eliminates (from him) the negative energy and

---

349 Mursi, Muḥammad Sa'īd, Fan Tarbiyat al-Awlād fi al-Islām, Cairo, Dar al-Tawzi' w al-Nashr, 2012 AD, L.T', p. 27

350 Mursi, Muḥammad Sa'īd, Aḥdath al-Asalīb al-Tarbawiyya al-Fa'ala lil Abā' wal-Ummahāt, Cairo, Dar al-Tawzī' w al-Nashr, 2012 AD, L.T', p. 27

contributes to reducing anxiety, anger, aggression and sleeplessness in his personality.

Parents must aim at satisfying the child's emotional and sentimental needs by resorting to all possible methods, so that their child can develop emotionally, mentally and physically in a healthy way.

Loving Children is of Man's Primordial Nature

Loving children is considered one of the things that are embedded in the human psyche and must be attended to and preserved. Religious texts have encouraged the love of children and considered it as the best of deeds. It is narrated that Imām Ja'far al-Ṣādiq ۩ said: "Mūsā ibn Imran said: O' Lord, what are the most favored deeds to You? He ۩ said: "Loving children..."351

The nurturer is required to strive for preserving the feeling of love towards the nurtured (children) within him, especially fathers and mothers. Narrations have pointed out the blessings of this love that befall the nurturer as well; for, it is narrated that Imām al-Ṣādiq ۩ said: "God has mercy on a servant due to the intensity of his love for his child."352

Love between Excess and Deficiency

Love is essential and fundamental in the upbringing process. Nonetheless, when speaking of loving children, it is required to

---

351 Al-Barqi, al-Mahāsin, Vol. 1, p. 200, the chapter of loved actions, ḥadīth 15

352 Ibid., p. 50

have equilibrium and balance in order to maintain a positive love. And any diversion from equilibrium – towards either extremes – will turn love into a negative factor. The danger that lies in this sort of negative love – in regards to upbringing – is that it leads to the adoption of wrong methods therein, such as the method of excessive pampering and spoiling by being lenient with the child and encouraging him to satisfy his desires... This method has negative effects on the child's personality; for, thus, he will be brought up as a selfish individual who doesn't care about anyone, and who is eager to fulfill his desires and acquire everything he wants."[353]

This is in regards to excess; the same thing applies to deficiency. For, any deficiency in providing love for children will lead to the adoption of several negative approaches, such as: the controlling approach, i.e. to control the child's actions, speech and desires in a way that aligns with the parents' desires regardless of the child's needs and demands..."[354]

The best way of raising (a child) by love is for the nurturer to adopt the joint approach of firmness and softness. Many narrations have mentioned that one of the traits and signs of a believer is that he is firm and soft[355], whereby he is lenient when

---

[353] Ajami, Samer, Uqūbat al-Tifl fi al-Tarbiya al-Islamiyya, center of educational studies and research, Beirut, Dar al-Balāghah, 1435 AH – 2014 AD, L.T', p. 199-200

[354] Ibid.,,, page 200

[355] It is narrated that Imām 'Alī said: "it is one of their (the pious) signs to see him strong in his religion, and firm in his softness." Nahj al-Balāghah, Vol. 2, p. 163. And it's narrated that Imām al-Ṣādiq said: "The believer is strong in his religion and firm in his softness." Al-Kulaynī, Shaykh Muḥammad ibn Yaʿqūb, Al-Kāfī, Vol. 2, p. 231

the situation demands it and firm when the child's interest requires it. Neither his love prevents him from being firm, nor does his firmness make him harsh-hearted.

It is important to pay attention to the difference between firmness and harshness[356]. For, firmness, love and mercy can come together; whereas harshness is tightness of the heart, which is incompatible with love and mercy. God ﷻ says: *﴾so woe to those whose hearts have been hardened﴿*[357]

It is narrated that the Messenger of God ﷺ said: "Those who are furthest from God are (those who have) a hardened heart."[358]

Ways of Expressing Love

The feeling of love isn't a sufficient factor in the process of raising with love. Rather, the most important thing is showing this internal feeling and transferring it to others. This is done through several ways, most of which were inspired from religious texts.

The way of the loving gaze: when the nurturer looks at the nurtured (child) with love, it brings happiness and joy to the latter's heart and makes him feel cared for, attended to and loved. The Prophet ﷺ considered the loving gaze from a father

---

[356] For harshness, its reasons and results, review Ajami, Samer Tawfiq, al-'Ibra fi al-Bukā 'ala Sayyid al-Shuhadā, Beirut, Dar al-Walā', 2012 AD, 1st edition, p. 35 and what follows.

[357] Sūrah al-Zumar, verse 22

[358] al-Ṭūsī, Shaykh Muḥammad ibn al-Ḥasan, Al-'Amālī, p. 3

to his child a form of worship. It is narrated that the Prophet ﷺ said: "A father's loving look towards his child is worship."[359]

The way of words of love: The nurturer must express his love for the child by telling him phrases that show love, due to the good effect it has on the child. An example of talking with love would be when the nurturer makes a request to the child in a kind manner such as saying: "if you please, if you grace me with, can you..." For this has a great role in raising the child, in addition to building his emotional connection with the nurturer.

The way of the loving and merciful kiss: A kiss on a child's cheek or forehead or hand is one of the highest forms of expressing love and mercy. The Prophetic upbringing approach emphasized this approach through speech and action. For, the Messenger of God ﷺ used to constantly kiss his sons, al-Ḥasan and al-Ḥusayn عليهما السلام.

The way of hugging a child: Hugging and smelling a child is one of the original ways of showing love and mercy. And the child's need for them matches his need for air, food and water. One of the Prophet's ﷺ traits was to seat al-Ḥasan and al-Ḥusayn عليهما السلام on his thighs and bring them close to him, as a way of expressing his love and emotional connection to them.

The way of smiling: It is considered one of the ways through which love is expressed. The Prophetic approach emphasized on the general recommendation of smiling in the face of one's brothers. It is narrated that Imām al-Ṣādiq عليه السلام said: "A believer's

[359] al-Mirzā al-Nūrī Mustadrak al-Wasā'il, Vol. 15, p. 170, ḥadīth 17894

smile in the face of his brother is a good deed."[360] How then would the case be in regards to smiling in the face of children?!

The way of wiping the child's head: Once the Prophet ﷺ woke up, he used to wipe the heads of his children and grandchildren.[361]

The way of being gentle with the child: It is one of the important approaches in raising a child. Gentleness means being lenient and soft. Using gentleness in upbringing leads to achieving the desired goals and aspired objectives. This has been emphasized by narrations; for, it is narrated that the Messenger of God ﷺ said: "God loves gentleness and supports (one) in achieving it."[362]

The way of forgiving the child: It is narrated that the Messenger of God ﷺ said: "May God have mercy on he who assists his child in honoring him, and this is through forgiving his wrongdoing and praying for him – in his private supplication to God."[363]

The way of concealing the child's mistakes: Among the methods of raising (a child) with love, is the method of concealing his mistakes, lapses and slip-ups especially that concealment (of error) is of the Godly traits. It is narrated that

---

[360] al-Ṭabrisī, Shaykh al-Faḍl ibn al-Ḥasan, Mishkāt al-Anwār fi Ghurar al-Akhbār, p. 316

[361] al-Ḥillī, Aḥmad ibn Fahd, ʿUddat al-dāʿī wa najāḥ al-sāʿī, Iraq, al-Rasoul al-A'thām Institute, 2010 AD, 1st edition, p. 87

[362] al-Kulaynī, Shaykh Muḥammad ibn Yaʿqūb, Al-Kāfī, ḥadīth 12

[363] al-Ḥillī, Aḥmad ibn Fahd, ʿUddat al-dāʿī wa najāḥ al-sāʿī, page 86

Imām al-Ṣādiq ﷺ said: "God is a concealer who loves concealment."[364] Therefore, if a child makes a certain mistake, he shouldn't be defamed because this hurts his feelings, harms him and leads to his repulsion from the nurturer after which he will no longer admit to him his mistakes and will rather conceal everything from him. Accordingly, the nurturer will be deprived of the opportunity of adjusting the child's behavior.

The way of overlooking: Overlooking some of the child's mistakes and refraining from taking account of every little thing are considered one of the most important methods of raising with love. It is narrated that Imām Zayn al-'Ābidīn ﷺ said: "Son, let it be known to you that the good of this world, in its entirety, is in two words: Fixing the matter of livelihoods is two-thirds in prudence and one-third in overlooking; for, man only overlooks what he has recognized and comprehended." [365]

The way of honoring the child: One of the ways of raising with love is honoring the child and making him feel appreciated and respected, and that he has a high status and position in the nurturer's heart. It is narrated that the Prophet ﷺ said: "Honor your children and discipline them well, and you will be forgiven."[366]

The way of gifting: Gifting is also one of the approaches of raising with love, especially on some occasions that require it,

---

364al-Kulaynī, Shaykh Muḥammad ibn Ya'qūb, Al-Kāfī, Vol. 5, p. 555

365 Al-Khazaz al-Qommi, 'Alī ibn Muḥammad, Kifayat al-Athār fi al-Naṣṣ 'ala al-A'imma al-'Ithnay 'Ashar, verified by Abdul Latif al-Ḥusayni, Qom, Intishārāt Bidar, al-Khiam printing press, 1401 AH, L.T', p. 240

366 al-Ṭabrisī, Shaykh al-Faḍl ibn al-Ḥasan, Makārim al-Akhlāq, p. 222

such as his success or accomplishment of a certain thing. For, it is narrated that Abi Abdillah ﵇ said: "The Messenger of God ﷺ said: "Exchange gifts and you will exchange love. Exchange gifts, for, it eliminated grudges."[367]

The way of satisfying the child: It is desirable that the father or mother takes the initiative to satisfy the child, make him happy and bring joy to his heart, especially before sleeping. For, it is dangerous to let the child sleep while he experiences negative energy from sadness and grief. It is narrated that the Messenger of God ﷺ said: "... He who attempts to satisfy a young boy of his offspring until he is satisfied, God will attempt to satisfy him on the day of resurrection until he is satisfied."[368]

The way of keeping a promise: Usually a person promises his children something such as buying him something and then goes back on his promise. The nurturer must be attentive to the danger of going back on a promise and not fulfilling it, in terms of tainting an honest and trustworthy image in the child's mind, and of the theological effects of this wrongful act – committed by the nurturer – on the meaning of sustenance. It is narrated that the Messenger of God ﷺ said: "Love the boys (children) and have mercy on them; and if you promise them anything, keep your promise. For, they believe that you provide their sustenance."[369]

---

367 Ibid., p. 222

368 Ibn Askar, 'Alī ibn al-Ḥasan, Tarīkh Madinat Dimashq, studied and verified by 'Alī Chiri, Beirut, Dar al-Fikr, 1415 AH, L.T', Vol. 52, p. 363

369 al-Kulaynī, Shaykh Muḥammad ibn Ya'qūb, Al-Kāfī, Vol. 6, p. 49

The way of being playful and childish with the child: The nurturer must play with his children and interact positively with them in their activities which include different games. There are many narrations that encourage the father to play with the child and act childishly with him. It is narrated that the Messenger of God ﷺ said: "Let he who has a child act childishly with him."[370]

The way of praying for the child not against him: One of the approaches of raising with love is to pray for the child and bring him up constantly in parents' supplications (for their child), and to refrain from praying against him when being angry with him for whatever behavior he performs. He must rather pray for his guidance and reform. It is narrated that the Messenger of God ﷺ said: "May God have mercy on whoever assists his child in honoring him, and this is by forgiving his wrongdoing and praying for him to God."[371]

The way of justice and equality between children: The nurturer mustn't discriminate amongst children and must rather treat them justly, even in kisses or gifts, as mentioned in narrations. It is narrated that the Prophet ﷺ saw a man among the companions who had two children kissing only one of them without the other. So he ﷺ said: "Will you treat them equally."[372]

---

[370] al-Ṣadūq, Shaykh Muḥammad ibn ʿAlī, Man Lā Yaḥḍuruh al-Faqīh, Vol. 3, p. 483, ḥadīth 4707

[371] al-Ḥillī, Aḥmad ibn Fahd, ʿUddat al-Dāʿī wa Najāḥ al-Sāʿī, p. 86

[372] al-Majlisī, al-ʿAllāma Muḥammad Bāqir, Biḥār al-Anwār, Vol. 101, p. 99

The way of well-receiving (welcoming) the child when the parents or the child comes home: The same applies when bidding farewell to the child before leaving the house... The Prophet ﷺ used to adopt this approach with the children of his household. It is narrated that Abdullah ibn Ja'far said: "When the Messenger of God ﷺ came from travel, he would meet with the boys of his household, he said: He came from travel and approached me before I reached him and held me in his arms, then one of Fatima's sons came so he placed him next to him, he said: Then, the three of us entered the city on a camel."[373]

The way of honoring the child and assisting him in honoring (the parents): It is narrated that the Messenger of God ﷺ said: "May God have mercy on he who assists his child in honoring him."[374]

The way of laying duties on the child according to his capacity: It is one of the important methods of raising with love. For, the child must not be burdened with responsibilities that exceed his endurance. It is narrated on behalf of Yunus ibn Rabat, on behalf on Imām al-Ṣādiq ؑ, that the Messenger of God ﷺ said: "May God have mercy on he who assists his child in honoring him. He said: I said: How does he assist him in honoring him? He said: He accepts the little which he offers, overlooks his

373 Al-Naysabouri, Sahih Muslim, Vol. 7, p. 132

374 al-Mirzā al-Nūrī, Mustadrak al-Wasā'il, Vol. 15, p. 168, ḥadīth 17885

shortcomings, refrains from exhausting him and doesn't degrade him."[375]

The way of familiarizing oneself with the child: He ﷺ said: "May God have mercy on he who assists his child in honoring him by treating him kindly, familiarizing himself to him, teaching him and disciplining him."[376]

The way of sympathy: It is narrated that Imām ʿAlī ؑ said: "You must be more sympathetic with your child than he is with you."[377]

Main Concepts

Love is a thing that is realized by every person through presence-based (or experiential) knowledge. For, it is an emotional trait which he experiences through his heart; we do not need logic to define it. Human love can be verbally defined as the heart-based inclination and emotional attraction towards something that gives the lover pleasure and joy.

---

[375] al-Ṭūsī, Shaykh Muḥammad ibn al-Ḥasan, Tahdhīb al-Ahkām fī Sharh al-Muqni'ah, verified by Ḥasan al-Mūsawi al-Khurasan, Tehran, Dar al-Kutub al-Islamiyya, 1365 AH, 4th edition, Vol. 8, p. 113, ḥadīth 390. Explaining the terms of the ḥadīth: "doesn't exhaust" him means not to oppress him or treat him unfairly or lay on him more than he can bear. And degradation here means stupidity and ignorance, i.e. refrains from attributing stupidity to him.

[376] Burūjirdī, Ayatullāh Sayyid Ḥusayn, Jāmiʿ Aḥādīth al-Shīʿa, Vol. 21, p. 411

[377] Sharḥ Nahj al-Balāghah, part 20, the sayings attributed to Imām ʿAlī ؑ, ḥadīth 152

The process of raising by love aims at achieving several objectives, such as:

The proper emotional development of the child and the satisfaction of his sentimental needs, straying far from mental health disorders and complexities, strengthening the relationship and connection between the child and the nurturer and contributing to the healthy development of the other aspects of a child's identity.

The child is – by creation – a gentle, sensitive and emotional being. He needs to feel others' love for him and their contentment with him. He needs to be accepted and wanted by his parents and others.

Loving children is considered one of the things that are embedded in the human psyche and must be attended to and preserved. Religious texts have encouraged the love of children and considered it as the best of deeds.

Love is essential and fundamental in the upbringing process. Nonetheless, when speaking of loving children, it is required to have equilibrium and balance thereof.

There are many methods of raising with love which can be concluded from religious texts.

Lesson Fifteen

The Economic Upbringing of a Child

Lesson Objectives

By the end of this lesson, the student should:

1. Get acquainted with economic upbringing and its objectives.
2. Realize the father's economic responsibility.
3. Learn the child's economic rights from narrations.

Preamble

The economic factor in a person's life has its dynamic role in the advancement of human societies. The following saying by the Messenger of God ﷺ serves as a sufficient indicator to the importance of the economic factor in man's life: "O' God, bless our bread and do not separate between us; for, if it weren't for bread, we wouldn't have fasted or prayed or performed the obligations demanded by our Lord."[378]

Islam focuses on the father's obligation of shouldering his economic responsibilities towards the child. For, this is one of his rights upon his guardian. Moreover, it has a great effect on shaping the child's identity and developing it.

So, what is economic upbringing? And what are its objectives and approaches?

Economic Upbringing

It occurs when the child's guardian exerts the greatest efforts and energy for the sake of securing the child's livelihood needs in different areas, and fulfills his role in providing the child with a set of knowledges and directions, and accustoming him to behaviors and training him on skills that will make his economic activities and transactions in line with the religious value-based system and divine legislations on one hand, and enables him to invest possessions and gain money in the future, and to use it in a balanced way which leads him to a decent living and proximity to the Generous Lord.

---

[378] Al-Barqi, al-Mahāsin, Vol. 2, p. 586

The study of upbringing involves two main chapters:

First: the responsibilities and procedures that must be carried out by the guardian and nurturer towards the child in regards to the economic aspect.

Second: the economic values, manners, legislations and skills upon which the child must be raised.

The Objectives of Economic Upbringing and the Need for It

The economic upbringing of a child aims at achieving a set of educational objectives, the most important of which are:

a. The flourishing of earth and linking economic development to the worship of God ﷻ

God ﷻ says: ﴿*Worship God. You have no other god besides Him. He brought you forth from the earth and made it your habitation*﴾[379]

b. The launching of economic activities in accordance with the system of religious values and the rulings of the Islamic Sharia

c. The wise employment of monetary and economic resources – as opposed to the imprudent management thereof

[379] Sūrah Hūd, verse 61

God 🕮 says: *Do not give the feeble-minded your property which God has assigned you to manage: provide for them out of it, and clothe them, and speak to them honorable words* [380]

The Economic Responsibilities of the Guardian Towards the Child

There are several responsibilities shouldered by the child's guardian in the economic field. We will mention the most important ones:

First: Providing for the Child (Alimony)

It is narrated on behalf of Hureiz that Abi Abdillah 🕮 said: "I said to him: Who am I obliged to support financially? He 🕮 said: The parents, child and wife."[381]

The most important and superior economic right of a child – which is emphasized by the Islamic viewpoint – is the obligation of the guardian to provide financially for the child. This means that the guardian must shoulder the responsibility of providing everything the child needs in his life and requires in reality such as shelter, food, drinking, clothing, medication, education, entertainment and toys... The Islamic Sharia hasn't determined a specific fixed criterion in regards to the required amount of alimony for the child; it rather considered it a matter of custom which must take into consideration the requirements

---

[380] Sūrah al-Nisā', verse 5

[381] al-Ṭūsī, Shaykh Muḥammad ibn al-Ḥasan, Tahdhīb al-Aḥkām fī Sharh al-Muqni'ah, Vol. 6, p. 293

of the child's age stages, in addition to the circumstances and environment in which he lives.

Second: Being Generous in Providing for Children

Moreover, it is recommended to provide generously for the child – all in accordance with one's capacity – as mentioned in the narrations of Ahl al-Bayt ﵈. For example, it is narrated that Imām ʿAlī ibn al-Ḥusayn ﵇ said: "The most pleasing of you to God are the most generous with their children."[382]

Islam emphasizes on the importance of having the guardian exert his utmost efforts in pursuit of making money to support his children in accordance with what pleases God ﷻ. For, if a person exerts his highest efforts and still doesn't manage to do it, then he is excused in front of God ﷻ. "His sustenance is limited, and he is poor, thus he cannot provide generously; in this case, he is to provide in proportion to what God has given him of money, that is, according to his capacity."[383]

Whereas, if God ﷻ provides a person with abundant sustenance, and he acts in a stingy and ungenerous manner with his children, God ﷻ will punish him in this world by taking away his blessing.

It is narrated that Abi al-Ḥasan Mūsā ibn Ja'far ﵇ said: "A man's children are his captives; therefore he who God has blessed him with a blessing should be generous with his captives

---

382 al-Kulaynī, Shaykh Muḥammad ibn Yaʿqūb, Al-Kāfī, Vol. 4, p. 11

383 Ṭabāṭabā'ī, al-ʿAllāma Sayyid Muḥammad Ḥusayn, Al-Mīzān fī Tafsīr al-Qur'ān, Vol. 19, p. 318

[children]. And if he doesn't, then his blessing is on the verge of being taken away."[384]

Moreover, a father must make his children feel that he is financially capable; for, this will make them trust him and feel safe, secure and at peace in his presence. It also brings happiness to the father himself. It is narrated that Imām al-Ṣādiq ؏ said: "One of man's joys is to be the guardian over his children."[385] And he must not make his children resort to someone beside him; for, the worst father is he whose children resort to someone beside him.

It is narrated by Jaber ibn Abdillah that the Messenger of God ﷺ said: "Should I inform you of the best of your men? We said: Yes, O' Messenger of God. He said: The best of your men is he who is pious, pure and generous, who is pure in both sides, honors his parents and doesn't make his children resort to someone beside him."[386]

Jurists considered that providing generously for one's children is the greatest form of almsgiving[387], and that "it's better than

---

[384] al-Ṣadūq, Shaykh Muḥammad ibn 'Alī, Man Lā Yaḥduruh al-Faqīh, Vol. 3, p. 556

[385] Ibid., p. 168

[386] al-Kulaynī, Shaykh Muḥammad ibn Ya'qūb, Al-Kāfī, Vol. 2, p. 57

[387] al-Shahīd al-Awwal , al-Durour al-Shar'iyyah fi Fiqh al-Imāmiyya, the institute of Islamic publishing, Qom, the institute of Islamic publishing which is related to the group of teachers in the honorable city of Qom, 1417 AH, 2nd edition, Vol. 1, p. 255

giving alms to others beside them."[388] For, there is no value for any gift to others, even if it was almsgiving, if it was on the account of the children's needs. The Messenger of God ﷺ recommended this to Imām 'Alī ؑ: "O' 'Alī, no alms is to be given while a kin is in need."[389] This shows that Islam has given priority to the generous provision for one's children and giving them precedence over others.

It is important to pay attention to the fact that the praiseworthy act, according to the Islamic vision of upbringing, is the generous provision which coincides with balanced spending and doesn't trespass that towards overspending or wastefulness. It must rather be carried out in a balanced way, as indicated in the Noble Qur'ān in the context of mentioning the traits of the servants of the Compassionate: ﴿*Those who, when spending, are neither wasteful nor tightfisted, and moderation lies between these [extremes]*﴾[390]

Third: Good Management

Islam emphasizes on good management especially that it leads to preserving the blessing and increasing it. This occurs through the good management of financial resources by spending on needs in light of arranging the priorities. For, spending according to one's capacities isn't stinginess, but rather economical. Narrations have pointed to spending in light of

---

388 al-Ḥakīm, Ayatullāh Sayyid Muḥsin al-Tabātabā'ī, Minhāj al-Ṣāliḥīn, Beirut, Dar al-Ta'āruf for Printing, 1980 AD, L.T', Vol. 2, p. 272

389 al-Ṣadūq, Shaykh Muḥammad ibn 'Alī, Man Lā Yaḥḍuruh al-Faqīh, Vol. 4, p. 270

390 Sūrah al-Furqan, verse 67

determining the priorities according to circumstances of time, place and others. For example, Imām al-Ridā ؏ said: "A believer must reduce his children's food intake during winter and increase the fuel that keeps them warm."391

One of the distinguishing factors of the Islamic vision of upbringing is that it takes two things into consideration in regards to the economic aspect of raising a child:

1. The money from which one provides for the child must be good (halal) money

2. The nature of the job chosen by the father must be permissible (halal); and he must stay away from prohibited acts. Noble narrations have indicated the good impact of halal sustenance; for, it is narrated that Imām 'Alī ؏ said: "The light of the heart comes from eating halal."392

On the other hand, it pointed out to the fact that eating from forbidden money makes the result of the upbringing process as shaky as the person who builds on sand. It is mentioned that the Messenger of God ؾ said: "Worshiping, while eating from that which is prohibited, is like building on sand."393

---

391 al-Kulaynī, Shaykh Muḥammad ibn Yaʿqūb, Al-Kāfī, Vol. 4, p. 13

392 Al-ʿAmili, Muḥammad ibn al-Ḥasan al-Ḥusaynī, al-Mawaʾez a;-ʿAdadiyya, edited by al-Mirza ʿAlī al-Mashkini al-Ardabili, Qom, al-Hādī, 1406 AH, 1st edition, p. 58

393 al-Ḥillī, Aḥmad ibn Fahd, ʿUddat al-Dāʿī wa Najāḥ al-Sāʿī, p. 141

Managing the Child's Economic Affairs

One of the child's economic rights is that his guardian must carry out the management of the child's financial and economic affairs in the manner that best serves his (the child's) interest.

For, a child can acquire wealth in a certain way, such as inheriting money as a result of one of his relative's death– his mother for example – or receiving a monetary gift from someone...etc. It is the child's right upon his father to manage – well – the child's wealth in a way that serves the child's interest or doesn't lead to any damage or corruption thereof.

In this context, the guardian must observe God's rights in regards to the child's money, in the sense of taking from it Zakat for example and other financial rights that are related to the child's possessions.

The Relationship between Economic and Theological Upbringing

The nurturer must seek to connect economic upbringing to theological upbringing[394], such that he makes the child feel that everything he owns including food, drinks, clothes, toys and gifts... belong to God and are of his blessings so that the child's emotional connection to God and love for Him increases. At the same time, the guardian must be aware of making the child feel that poverty is from God, lest he blames

394 Review on this topic: al-Ṣadr, Ayatullāh Shahīd Sayyid Muḥammad Bāqir, Iqtiṣāduna (Our Economics), p. 296 and what follows, under the title: the connection between Islamic Economics and other factors of Islam.

God ﷻ for his pain and deprivation which will lead to his repulsion from Him ﷻ.

This idea can be explained to the child by telling him, for example: you own this toy and you are responsible for it; if another kid wants to play with it, don't you feel that he must ask for your permission? And if you allow him to play with it, don't you think that he must play with it in the manner that you love and are pleased with? God ﷻ is the Creator and Owner of this universe; therefore, if we – or you – want to use his sustenance and wealth, it must be with his permission and consent ﷻ.

Strengthening the Connection between Faithful Values and Economic Upbringing

On another hand, the nurturer must gradually raise the child's awareness to the fact that Islam encourages the flourishing of the earth and economic development, emphasizes the values of work, struggle and making effort, and condemns laziness and sluggishness. One can benefit – in pursuit of achieving these claims – from the following methods:

1. The method of upbringing through storytelling, by providing examples from the Qur'ān, narrations and biography (of the infallibles) of the Prophets' عليهم السلام and Imāms' عليهم السلام work in shepherding, irrigation, iron and different commercial transactions... etc.[395]

---

[395] al-Kulaynī, Shaykh Muḥammad ibn Ya'qūb, Al-Kāfī, Vol. 5, p. 74

2. The method of memorizing and indoctrination, by encouraging the child to memorize some ḥadīths and narrations through which the Prophet and Imāms show how they raise people on economic values and manners.[396]

3. The method of raising by example, where the religious father can benefit from his personal struggle and hard work to make an income - that is witnessed by his child – to raise him on being aware of making a connection between faith and economic development.

The Financial Upbringing of a Child

It means creating a specific way in which a child sees the nature of money, employs, invests and spends it.

We will present the nature of the Islamic view of money in several points:

1. All wealth belongs to God ﷻ.

2. Using money requires the permission and contentment of God ﷻ.

3. Making sure that money isn't regarded as an ends in itself, but rather a means to a good and decent living, and it must be employed in serving people's happiness so that it acts as sustenance for man in this world and the Hereafter.

4. Emphasizing the necessity of positive investment of money after acquiring it. It is narrated that Imām 'Alī ibn al-

---

[396] This is concluded from the ḥadīths mentioned in this lesson.

Ḥusayn said: "The investment of money signifies the fulfillment of chivalry."[397]

5. Preserving money, taking care of it and refraining from losing it; it is narrated that a man asked Imām al-Ṣādiq: "If a man has money and loses it; does it go away? He said: "Preserve your money; for, it is the pillar of your religion."[398]

6. Employing money in the right – rather than corrupt – places; it is narrated that Imām ʿAlī said: "He of you who has money must be aware of corruption..."[399]

7. Seeking to form sound economic concepts and rectify wrong economic concepts related to the criteria for richness and poverty. Financial status is not the distinguishing criterion amongst people; man must rather be respected for his knowledge, morals, piety and the richness of his soul...

It is narrated on behalf of Abi Dharr (May God be pleased with him) that he said: "The Messenger of God said: O' Aba Dharr, do you see richness in abundant wealth? I (Abu Dharr) said: Yes, O' Messenger of God. He said: Then you see that lack of wealth is poverty? I said: Yes, O' Messenger of God. He said: "Richness is but the richness of the heart, and poverty is the poverty of the heart."[400]

---

[397] al-Kulaynī, Shaykh Muḥammad ibn Yaʿqūb, Al-Kāfī, Vol. 1, p. 20

[398] al-Ṭūsī, Shaykh Muḥammad ibn al-Ḥasan, Al-'Amālī, p. 679

[399] al-Kulaynī, Shaykh Muḥammad ibn Yaʿqūb, Al-Kāfī, Vol. 4, p. 32

[400] Ibn Habban, Sahih ibn Habban, verified by Shu'eib al-Arna'out, L.M, al-Risāla Institute, 1414 AH – 1993 AD, 2nd edition, Vol. 2, p. 461

Economic Values and Behaviors Upon which to Raise the Child

There are many economic behaviors that must be raised during the process of the child's economic upbringing, such as:

First: To Spend within the Bounds of his Actual Needs in a Balanced and Moderate Manner.

It is narrated that Imām al-Ṣādiq ﷺ said: "All money (wealth) belongs to God. He entrusted it to his creations as deposits, ordered them to eat from it in moderation, drink from it in moderation, wear from it in moderation, get married with it in moderation, ride from it in moderation and give the rest of it to the faithful poor."[401]

Second: Accustoming him to the Fact that Economic Situations Fluctuate

Thus, tight situations mustn't lead to stinginess and cheapness but rather to cautiousness and good management. Likewise, increase (in sustenance) mustn't lead to wastefulness and overspending, but rather to financial prudence and saving.

It is narrated that the Messenger of God ﷺ said: "A believer has learnt a certain manner from God; if He increased his sustenance he became financially prudent, and if He reduced it he reduced his spending."[402]

---

[401] Burūjirdī, Ayatullāh Sayyid Ḥusayn, Jāmiʿ Aḥādīth al-Shīʿa, Vol. 17, p. 108

[402] Ibid., p. 106

And in these two contexts, many methods and procedures emerge such as:

1. Making the child live within the general standard of living held by his community members even if the father is rich, because "the little that suffices is better than the lot which distracts"[403], as narrated on behalf of the Messenger of God ﷺ.

2. Determining the purchase value of the child's daily needs at a specific and fixed price, and making him feel that not everything he asks for must be provided and secured.

3. Accustoming him to arrange the expenses and balance between them in light of the priorities, and gradually list the needs from most to least important.

4. Taking the child to the market and shops and giving him the chance to shop and carry out the purchasing process by himself, under their monitoring and supervision.

5. Refrain from getting embarrassed by the child's behavior in the market and his nagging and persistent demands through crying and screaming, which might lead the parents to buying whatever the child wants despite the fact that he doesn't need it.

6. Accustoming the child to save money for times of need and testing him by giving him a small amount of money and rewarding him if he spends it properly.

---

[403] al-Ṣadūq, Shaykh Muḥammad ibn ʿAlī, Man Lā Yaḥḍuruh al-Faqīh, Vol. 4, p. 376

Third: Acustoming the Child to Assess the Value of Things by Guiding him through the Modality in which Resources are Used According to the Need and Necessity.

Some procedures can be carried out in this area:

1. Introducing the child to the fact that overspending money doesn't only happen directly; it rather has other ways as well such as not taking care of school materials.

2. Accustoming the child not to take lightly the objects and money in the house, such as wiping his hands with the furniture after eating.

3. Training the child on preserving his stuff, toys and possessions, taking care of them, nurturing them and cleaning them.

Fourth: Accustoming the Child to Respect the Money, Property and Economic Rights of Others.

Respecting the financial rights of others is one of the important values in economic upbringing. The following steps can be taken in this pursuit:

1. Accustom him to the fact that the reality of stinginess is achieved by refraining from giving people their rights.

2. Avoid using other children's money (or property) without their permission.

3. Respect the property and possessions of public institutions such as schools, playgrounds, gardens, streets...etc.

4. Accustom the child, with affability and love, to respect the right of others in shared properties between himself and others, such as his siblings or generally the family members in the house.

5. Accustom him, for example, to return the money to the market owner if the latter gave him more than he is entitled to.

Fifth: Accustoming the Child to Carry Out Economic Activities that Have a Symbiotic Nature.

1. Instill in the child's heart softness and mercy towards the poor, needy, orphans and people with disabilities by imagining himself in their shoes.

2. Accustoming him to spend money on connecting kinship ties, good-deeds, hospitality and almsgiving, and on carrying out financial worshiping obligations such as paying alms and Khums (a fiscal purification which amounts to one fifth of the annual profits.)

Sixth: Accustoming the Child to Appreciate the Value of Halal (Permissible) Work

1. Condemn laziness and make it detestable to the child; and this can be presented to children through realistic stories on animals such as bees, ants and others. This can be concluded from a narration on behalf of Imām al-Ṣādiq ؏ where he said: "Can any of you be like the ant? For, an ant drags (its sustenance) to its hole."[404]

---

[404] al-Kulaynī, Shaykh Muḥammad ibn Yaʿqūb, Al-Kāfī, Vol. 5, p. 79

2. Keep the child away from toys that have the spirit of gambling.

3. Take him on frequent visits to work and introduce him to its environment, nature and circumstances.

4. Accustom the child to carry out some jobs that are appropriate to his age and that don't wear him out, and encourage him (at the right age) to work during summer break – without exhausting him – so he can feel the fatigue and struggle in pursuit of securing one's needs.

5. Make him feel the misconduct committed by the beggars in the streets, without complementing that feeling with arrogance.

Main Concepts

The economic factor in a person's life has its dynamic role in the advancement of human societies. The following saying by the Messenger of God ﷺ serves as a sufficient indicator to the importance of the economic factor in man's life: "O' God, bless our bread and do not separate between us; for, if it weren't for bread, we wouldn't have fasted or prayed or performed the obligations demanded by our Lord."

Studying upbringing involves two main chapters:

First: the responsibilities and procedures that must be carried out by the guardian and nurturer towards the child in regards to the economic aspect.

Second: the economic values, manners, legislations and skills upon which the child must be raised.

The most important and superior economic right of a child – which is emphasized by the Islamic viewpoint – is the obligation of the guardian to provide financially for the child. This means that the guardian must shoulder the responsibility of providing everything the child needs in his life and requires in reality such as shelter, food, drinking, clothing, medication, education, entertainment and toys.

Islam emphasizes on the importance of having the guardian exert his utmost efforts in pursuit of making money to support his children in accordance with what pleases God ﷻ. For, if a person exerts his highest efforts and still doesn't manage to do it, then he is excused in front of God ﷻ. "His sustenance is narrow and he is poor such that he cannot provide generously; in this case, he is to provide in proportion to what God has given him of money, that is, according to his capacity."

The nurturer must seek to connect economic upbringing to theological upbringing, such that he makes the child feel that everything he owns including food, drinks, clothes, toys and gifts... belong to God ﷻ and are of his blessings ﷻ so that the child's emotional connection to God ﷻ and love for Him increases.

The emphasis on the economic values and behaviors on which the child must be raised.

Lesson Sixteen

The Jihadi Upbringing

Lesson Objectives

By the end of this lesson, the student should:

1. Learn the objectives of a Jihadi upbringing.
2. Know the values of a Jihadi upbringing.
3. Understand the methods of a Jihadi upbringing.

Preamble

In our community, a child opens his eyes to scenes of murder and migration, hears that his father, brother or one of his relatives is battling with the Zionist enemy or Takfirist terrorism, and watches, in his cities and villages, the martyrs' bodies held up high by people's arms. In light of these scenes, we cannot raise the child on values, feelings and behaviors that are distant from the reality he experiences within his community.

A child who grows up in an environment of unsettled security which is militarily unstable, cannot be isolated by his parents from his society and its circumstances. For, wisdom demands that parents take all these factors into consideration during the upbringing of their child.

Thus, it becomes clear that a Jihadi upbringing is a fundamental issue in shaping the child's character, reinforcing the culture of resistance within him and implanting the specific Islamic values in this regard such as love of the homeland and hatred of the enemy, and in having him aim at becoming an effective factor in the movement of Jihad (struggle) and resistance in accordance with his personal tendencies and abilities – the very thing that contributes to helping the child adapt to this sort of challenges.

Presenting Jihad and Resistance to the Child at their Level of Understanding

The child's mental, psychological and sentimental characteristics have a tendency towards distraction, play and pursuing joy and pleasure. Therefore, in the primary stage of a child's life, the nurturer must present the idea of Jihad and the resistance culture in an image that fits his awareness and perception on one hand, and which doesn't terrify and scare him on another. For example, he can compare – for him – struggle or Jihad with the states of health and sickness which are encountered by the child's body. Then, he can show him – for instance – that a person's body might get infected with flu because of the cold weather or with diarrhea whenever he consumes contaminated foods or drinks...

And the child, in this regard, must take one of two paths in order to preserve the wellbeing of his body:

First: Prevention from all the factors that contribute to exposing his body to illness or weakness or powerlessness. He must, therefore, wear warm clothes in winter and refrain from leaving the house in the summer when the temperature is quite high.

Second: Treating the body from disease and enduring - with patience - the bitterness of medicine in pursuit of removing the illness and having the body recovered and back to normal.

The same applies to the homeland. For, like a person's body, it gets attacked by enemies such as Zionists and Takfirists and others. The homeland, thus, needs its people to defend it and cure it from the disease of Zionist and Takfirist violation in order to maintain its wellbeing. For, society is like one body, as narrated on behalf of the Messenger of God ﷺ and his grandson Imām al-Ṣādiq ؑ: "Believers - in honoring each other and being compassionate and sympathetic with one another – are like the body that complains causing its parts to suffer with sleeplessness and fever."[405]

Children must be gradually taught that a society's strength and honor can only be realized through sacrifices and enduring hardships, and that – on the other hand – abandoning Jihad bequeaths the nation humiliation.

It is narrated that Abi Abdillah ☙ said: the Messenger of God ☙ said: "... He who abandons Jihad, God dresses him with humiliation in himself, poverty in his livelihood and the annihilation of his religion. God (the Blessed & Exalted) honored my nation with its horseshoes and spear posts. "[406]

A Jihadi Upbringing through Play and Entertainment

Since the nature of the child is inclined towards play and fun, and since he needs amusement and entertainment, this can be invested positively through the following steps:

1. Encouraging the child to enroll in scouts associations such as the scouts so he can get accustomed to the scouts life which provides him with values, skills and several behaviors that make him experience the closest life styles to the Jihadi one.

---

[405] al-Kāfī, Ḥusayn ibn Sa'eed, al-Mu'min, Qom, the school of Imām Mahdī ☙ in the Hawza, 1404 AH, 1st edition, p. 40, and al-Bukhari, Sahih al-Bukhārī, Vol. 7, p. 78

[406] al-Ṣadūq, Shaykh Muḥammad ibn 'Alī, Al-Amālī, p. 673

2. Organizing Jihadi touristic trips for the child and taking him to Jihadi monumental places and introducing him to them, such as the touristic monumental place in Mlita.

3. Encouraging the child to watch TV and cinema shows, such as: the cartoon "the child and the occupation" aired on the children's TV channel "Tāha".

4. Encouraging the child to take part in dramatic works that have a Jihadi and resistant aspect.

In this regard, we emphasize on the importance of investing in art - such as cinema, cartoons, theater, music and anthems...etc - in reinforcing the culture of resistance within the child. For, the impact of these means is highly effective and leads to positive results in this regard.

5. Taking the child to activities, carnivals and celebrations related to the resistance, victory and liberation...

6. Taking the child on hunting trips where he gets accustomed to the culture of concealment and archery...

7. Motivating and training the child on physical sports which include martial arts and accustoming him to games of war.

We emphasize, in this context, on our children's need for electronic games that contribute to the reinforcement of the idea of resistance, instead of the games through which we are being subject to cultural invasion.

Parents' Fear of Conducting Jihadi activities with Children

Some parents may experience fear from the negative impact of the aforementioned Jihadi activities on the child's personality. Excess of this feeling might lead them to the level of depriving their child from participating in these activities, as they fall under the assumption that they will make the child aggressive without realizing that aggression doesn't result from these activities and games; it is rather the fruit of a set of familial, economic, social, political and security factors, such that the community in which the child lives – including the familial, social and educational one – is the one who bears responsibility for implanting the tendency towards violence within him.

Jihadi Values and Manners

The child must be trained on Jihadi values, faculties and manners, such as:

1. Developing the faculty of freedom within the child and accustoming him to defending himself, property and honor.

2. Accustoming him to the rejection of oppression in all its forms, supporting the oppressed and defending him.

3. Training him on challenging hardships and not being afraid of confrontation.

4. Encouraging him to get integrated within the lines of preparation and mobilization.

5. Encouraging him to refuse any form of imitating the enemies of God ﷻ in regards to clothing and food...etc.

Building a Connection between the Child and the Mujahideen (those who Struggle at the Battlefront) and Martyrs

One of the important methods in Jihadi upbringing is working on building an emotional and sentimental connection between the child on one hand, and the mujahedīn, captives, injured and martyrs on the other by adopting the following methods and procedures:

1. The child must constantly feel his parents' love for the mujahideen, captives, injured and martyrs...

2. Taking the child to visit the homes of the mujahideen, injured or captives, and participating in the martyrs' funerals and visiting their graves every now and then.

3. Accustoming the child to struggling (jihad) by money, for example through supporting the boxes of the support committee of the Islamic resistance, and by tongue, through praying for the victory of the mujahedīn, recovery of the injured and release of the captives, and accustoming him to praying for the defeat and humiliation of the enemy.

4. Having him memorize some verses and narrations that show the importance of Jihad and high status of the mujahedīn, and encouraging him to read the martyrs' stories and wills.

The Method of Jihad-based Storytelling

One of important methods in Jihadi upbringing is using the storytelling approach which narrates the biography of the mujahideen in a way that suits the child's age, language and imagination.

Moreover, the child must be taught – in parallel – that the Zionist enemy seeks to benefit from the literary storytelling method by implanting wrongful concepts within the mind of the Israeli child by presenting the Arab person as an occupying invader of their land which they had inherited from their ancestors, such that they must exterminate the Arab man who threatens the future of Israel.

Furthermore, the nurturer must benefit from the Jihadi biography of the Prophet ﷺ and Imāms of the Prophetic Household عليهم السلام, present it to the child in the framework of a story that matches his age stage, and encourage him to extract the morals and lessons from it, such as:

1. Stories and morals from the battles of the Messenger ﷺ (Uhud, Badr, al-Ahzab, Khaybar, the conquest of Mekkah...), and the battles of Imām Alī عليه السلام (al-Jamal, al-Nehrawan, Siffin).

2. Presenting the Qur'ānic stories in a way that suits the child's awareness and perception such as the story of Prophet

Dāwūd 🕮 (Talout and Jalout)... and others such as the Prophets Ibrāhīm and Mūsā 🕮.[407]

Connecting the Child to the Karbalā' of Imām al-Ḥusayn 🕮

One of the methods in Jihadi upbringing is to connect the child to the revolution of Imām al-Ḥusayn 🕮 through the following points:

1. Narrating the events of Karbalā' in a storytelling manner which aims at connecting the Ḥusaynī revolution to the Islamic resistance.

2. Encouraging the child to participate in the different activities of 'Āshūrā': Ḥusaynī mourning gatherings for children, lamentation gatherings, 'Āshūrā' marches...

3. Making the child understand the prominent Ḥusaynī slogans, such as: "Never to humiliation"[408] and "I shall not surrender as a humiliated person, nor shall I

---

[407] It is narrated that Imām Ja'far ibn Muḥammad said on behalf of his father 🕮: "The first of whom went into battle is Ibrāhīm 🕮, when the Romans captured Lut 🕮, thus Ibrāhīm repelled until he rescued him from their hands." al-Ṭūsī, Shaykh Muḥammad ibn al-Ḥasan, Tahdhīb al-Aḥkām fī Sharh al-Muqni'ah, Vol. 6, p. 170

[408] al-Ṭabrisī, Shaykh Aḥmad ibn 'Alī, al-Iḥtijāj, verified and commented on by Sayyid Muḥammad Bāqir al-Khurasan, al-Najaf al-Ashraf, Dar al-Nu'mān for printing and publishing, 1386 AH – 1966 AD, L.T', Vol. 2, p. 24

escape like a slave"[409], and that they have all lasted until our day and we must preserve it.

Introducing the Child to the Enemy by Knowing (the Affairs of) his Own Time

Introducing the child to his enemy, his objectives and history by knowing the happenings of his time will make him insightful. The Prophet ﷺ and the Imāms of the Prophetic household عليهم السلام emphasized on the necessity of being insightful of the happenings of one's time. It is narrated that the Messenger of God ﷺ said: "The man of intellect must be insightful of his time."[410]

Therefore, one of the important methods that can be used in Jihadi upbringing is the employment of history in pursuit of introducing the child of the history of his enemy, his objectives and his greedy plans in different areas, be it the Zionist enemy which started from the relationship between the Jews and the Prophets عليهم السلام and murdering the latter until they were known as 'the murderers of the Prophets' عليهم السلام, or the Takfirist enemy which started from the battle of Nehrawan with the Khawarej which was the launching point of their Takfirist agenda against Imām Alī عليه السلام, in addition to the disclosure of the crimes perpetrated by other enemies and other things committed against this oppressed nation under fake slogans.

---

[409] al-Mufīd, Shaykh Muḥammad ibn Muḥammad ibn al-Nuʿmān, Kitāb Al-Irshād, Beirut, al-A'lami Printing Institute, 1410 AH – 1989 AD, 3rd edition, Vol. 2, p. 98

[410] al-Ṣadūq, Shaykh Muḥammad ibn ʿAlī, Al-Khiṣāl, p. 525

Main Concepts

In our community, a child opens his eyes to scenes of murder and migration, hears that his father, brother or one of his relatives is battling with the Zionist enemy or Takfirist terrorism, and watches, in his cities and villages, the martyrs' bodies held up high by people's arms. In light of these scenes, we cannot raise the child on values, feelings and behaviors that are distant from the reality he experiences within his community.

The child's mental, psychological and sentimental characteristics have a tendency towards distraction, play and pursuing joy and pleasure. Therefore, in the primary stage of a child's life, the nurturer must present the idea of Jihad and the resistance culture in an image that fits his awareness and perception.

Children must be gradually taught that a society's strength and honor can only be realized through sacrifices and enduring hardships, and that – on the other hand – abandoning Jihad bequeaths the nation humiliation.

Some parents may experience fear from the negative impact of the aforementioned Jihadi activities on the child's personality. Excess of this feeling might lead them to the level of depriving their child from participating in these activities, as they fall under the assumption that they will make the child aggressive without realizing that aggression doesn't result from these activities and games; it is rather the fruit of a set of familial, economic, social, political and security factors...

One of important methods in Jihadi upbringing is using the storytelling approach which narrates the biography of the mujahedīn in a way that suits the child's age, language and imagination.

Moreover, the child must be taught – in parallel – that the Zionist enemy seeks to benefit from the literary storytelling method by implanting wrongful concepts within the mind of the Israeli child.

One of the important methods in Jihadi upbringing is working on building an emotional, sentimental and social connection between the child on one hand, and the mujahedīn, captives, injured and martyrs on the other hand.

One of the methods that can be used in Jihadi upbringing is the employment of history in pursuit of introducing the child of the history of his enemy, his objectives and his greedy plans in different areas.

Lesson Seventeen

The Sexual Upbringing of a Child

Lesson Objectives

By the end of this lesson, the student should:

1. Know the meaning of sexual upbringing and its objectives.
2. Learn the principles of Islamic sexual upbringing according to the religious texts.
3. Realize the difference between Islamic and Western sexual upbringing.

Preamble

The sexual upbringing of the child is considered one of the most difficult forms of upbringing, due to the misconception of sex and intense sensitivity towards the topic. Therefore, forming a correct idea of sex would be the first step in the path of being audacious in the field of sexual upbringing.

It is not specific to sex education; rather, it involves the guardian's execution of the procedures that guarantee the child's protection against sexual violence, enable him to defend himself and train him on handling well the different sexual situations in light of religious values.

For, the presence of fear and worry towards sexual education – in regards to some people – results primarily from the misunderstanding of the concept of sexual upbringing.

The Definition of Sexual Upbringing

Educators mentioned numerous definitions for sexual upbringing[411], the most important of which is that: sexual upbringing is a type of social nurturing which provides the individual with scientific information, righteous experience and healthy directions in regards to sexual matters, to an extent which is allowed and in accordance with his bodily, physiological, reactional and social development, and within the framework of religious teachings, social standards and the

411 Review: Cyril, Hātem, al-Tarbiya al-Jinsiyya fi al-Mujtama', translated by Nada Jaber Hatem, Beirut, Dar al-Kitāb al-Ḥadīth Institute, 1994 AD, L.T', and al-Khammāsh, Umaya, Psychologia al-Tarbiya al-Jinsiyya 'ind al-Atfāl, al-Quds, Association of Arabian Studies, 1962 AD, 1st edition.

prevalent ethical values within the community. This qualifies him for compatibility in sexual situations and for confronting his sexual problems in the present and future – in a realistic way which leads to psychological wellbeing.[412]

Sexual upbringing isn't limited to teachings about sex; it rather includes the guardian's undertaking of procedures that guarantee the child's protection against sexual violence[413], enable him to defend himself and train him on handling well the different sexual situations in light of religious values. And the child's guardian must accustom him to all the methods that enable him to defend himself.

And abandoning sexual upbringing is the same as the depriving sexual upbringing of the child, which leads the child into a wrongful sexual upbringing.

The Objectives of Sexual Upbringing

Sexual upbringing has several objectives which it aims at achieving, the most important of which are:

1. Protecting the child from all sorts of sexual abuse
2. The adaptability of the child to diverse sexual situations
3. Health care for proper sexual development

412 Review: al-Zo'bi, Ahmad Muḥammad, Psychologia al-Murāhaqa al-Nadhariyyāt – Jawānib al-Numuw – al-Mushkilāt wa Subul 'Ilājiha, Amman, Jordan, Dar Zahrān for publishing and distribution, 1431 AH – 2010 AD, 1st edition,

413 Child sexual abuse

4. The formation and activation of the faculty of sexual chastity

5. The adoption of religious sexual manners and behaviors

Sexual Upbringing of the Child in Religious Texts

The fundamental point in the beginning of the process of a child's sexual upbringing is convincing the nurturers themselves that the child has a special sexual feeling at an early stage in his life – though in a mild and unapparent way. And the private sexual life of a child requires – from the beginning – upbringing, guidance and direction. The avoidant approach and the ostrich policy doesn't work well with this issue.[414]

Religious texts have pointed out that the start of a child's sexual upbringing begins within the first months of his birth. It is narrated that Imām 'Alī said: "The Messenger of God prohibited the man from copulating with his wife while their son is in the cradle watching them."[415]

This narration – amongst others – points out to the parents' obligation to refrain from carrying out their private relationship

414 Review: Abla Marjān, al-Tarbiya al-Jinsiyya lil Atfāl Haq lahum Wajib 'Alayna, Abu Dhabi, UAE, Khalifa Educational Prize Printing, 2010-2011 AD, L.T'

415 al-Mirzā al-Nūrī, Mustadrak al-Wasā'il, Vol. 14, p. 228, ḥadīth 16568, and in al-Bahrani, Yūsuf, al-Hadā'eq al-Naḍira fi Ahkām al-'Itra al-Tāhira, Qom, the institute of Islamic publishing that's related to the group of teachers in the honorable city of Qom, L.T, L.T', Vol. 23, p. 136: It is narrated on behalf of Ja'far ibn Muḥammad, on behalf of his fathers that he said: the Messenger of God said: "A man is prohibited from copulating with his wife while the boy is in the cradle watching them."

in front of the child; it even emphasizes on the necessity of avoiding the case where a child can hear the expression of any sexual talk or hints - even if he is in the cradle. And this prohibition is one of the most prominent manifestations of sexual upbringing for children.

The Difference between Islamic and Western Sexual Upbringing

The ethical aspect of early sexual upbringing of the child constitutes one of the faces of difference and distinction from sexual upbringing in light of some philosophers and psychologists' perception in the West who want to forsake the upbringing of a child upon ethical values in regards to the sexual life, based on the excuse that it harms the wellbeing of his sexual development.

Betrand Russel says: "Early ethical upbringing becomes harmful especially in the field of sex... Do not teach the child any sexual manners before he reaches the age of maturity; and – carefully – refrain from passing to him the idea that there is something detestable or repelling about the natural functions of the body."[416]

They want to present religious sexual upbringing in a regressive image, the thing that corrupts the proper sexual concepts for the child. And on another hand, they encourage parents to attract their children towards perverted sexual activities and delighting in it.

---

416 Bertrand Russel, Ghazu al-Sa'āda (The Invasion of Happiness), p. 79-80

Larsen Olerstam says: "... Fathers and mothers must encourage their children's desire for learning about sexual affairs and delight in their sexual activity. Those who receive such an upbringing usually raise their children well and do not distort their sexual understandings; thus, the children develop in a natural way such that one needs not worry about them save from falling into the hands of a fanatic religious scholar."[417]

Therefore, between excess here and deficiency there, the theory of moderation must come to light; for, it sees that sexual upbringing, in light of religious concepts and values, is necessary and lively in shaping the child's health, value-based, physical and behavioral identity.

Sexual Chastity

One of the most important general principles of sexual upbringing is the nurturer's indoctrination of the child with concepts and values, and accustoming him to the behaviors that contribute to the formation of the faculty of chastity within him, in a way that allows him to live a state of mental, psychological, sentimental and behavioral moderation and balance towards the sexual situations which he encounters in his life.

That's why we notice that religious texts have focused on praising sexual chastity and acting in a chaste manner.

---

[417] Olerstam, Larsen, Homosexuals (al-Shadhoun al-Jinsiyyoun), p. 166

God ﷻ says: ﴾*Those who cannot afford marriage should be continent until God enriches them out of His grace*﴿[418] And it is narrated that the Messenger of God ﷺ said: "Be chaste, and abandon debauchery."[419]

Sexual chastity is the educational concept which is inclusive of all the sexual don'ts that are prohibited and defiant of ethical constraints and general manners: no to voyeurism, no to watching pornographic films, no to nudity, no to dirty talk, no to sexual harassment, no to masturbation, no to fornication, no to lesbianism, no to homosexuality...

The Methods of Sexual Upbringing

There are several methods that must be adopted by the nurturer to achieve the desired objectives of sexual upbringing according to the religious vision, the most important of which are:

Distancing the Child from the Parents' Private Relationship:

1. The parents must avoid having intercourse where they can be seen by the children, and must not take intimate positions which have sexual implications in front of them in the living room or anywhere else.

2. The child must not be allowed to get accustomed to sleeping with his parents – in their bed – after reaching the age of two.

---

418 Sūrah al-Nūr, verse 33

419 al-Kulaynī, Shaykh Muḥammad ibn Yaʿqūb, Al-Kāfī, Vol. 5, p. 554

3. Training children on asking for permission and knocking on the door before entering the private space of the father and mother, or any other family member.

On Bathing and Cleaning:

1. Accustoming the child to enter the bathroom by himself to do his thing and clean his organs, and to close the bathroom door after entering it and refrain from leaving it open.

2. Accustoming the discerning child to perform Friday's Ghusl (washing) in order to get used to Ghusl al-Janaba *(which is done after having a sexual relationship with one's spouse)* later on.

The Separation of Children in Bed:

Efforts must be made to separate males and females in bed from early childhood (two years), and males and males – and females and females – once they reach the age of discernment.

It is narrated that the Messenger of God ﷺ said: "Separate your children in bed once they reach the age of seven."

On Physical Touch:

1. The child must be introduced to the fact that there are sensitive areas in his body that are private to him and which no one has the right to approach. And in case someone approaches them, he has the right to express utmost annoyance and rejection.

2. The girl – especially the discerning one starting at the age of six – must be averted from every physical touch of any sort with a non-mahram, such as handshaking, kissing and sitting in his lap due to being a relative or her cousin or her father's friend... It is narrated that Abi Abdillah ﷺ said: "If the free bondmaid completes six years of age, you must not kiss her."[420] Avoid touching or playing with children's sexual organs, even as a joke or for the sake of making the child laugh. It is narrated that Imām ʻAlī ﷺ said: "A woman approaching her daughter who has reached the age of six is a division of fornication."[421]

Some scholars considered that approaching means touching the private parts.[422]

On Looking and Watching:

1. Accustoming the child to distinguish the organs which must not be looked at by any one such as his reproductive organs.

2. Avert the child from watching TV shows, series and movies which contain sexual scenes.

---

[420] al-Kulaynī, Shaykh Muḥammad ibn Yaʿqūb, Al-Kāfī, Vol. 5, p. 533

[421] al-Ṣadūq, Shaykh Muḥammad ibn ʻAlī, Man Lā Yaḥḍuruh al-Faqīh, Vol. 3, p. 436

[422] al-Majlisī, Muḥammad Taqi, Rawdat al-Muttaqin fi Sharḥ Man Lā Yaḥḍuruh al-Faqīh, commented on by Ḥusayn al-Mūsāwi al-Kirmāni, Qom, al-Maṭba'a al-ʻIlmiyya, 1398 AH, L.T', Vol. 8, p. 344

3. Accustom the child to lower his gaze away from other people's private parts.

4. Develop his sense of self-monitoring by training him on changing the TV channel whenever immoral scenes come up until he gets accustomed to doing that when he's alone.

On Covering Up and Clothing:

1. The parents must cover their private parts from the child especially when they reach the age of discernment.

2. The mother or sister must wear clothes that observe decency, especially once the spectating child reaches the age of discernment.

3. Accustom the child to wearing his underwear by himself and to refraining from nudity and taking off his clothes in front of anyone.

4. Accustom the child to closing the door on himself when he wants to take off his clothes or change them.

5. Warn the child not to allow anyone to take off his clothes...

6. Teach the child, through observation, to differentiate between the manifestations of mahrams and non-mahrams, like when he sees his mother taking off her hijab in front of her brother, father, maternal uncle, or paternal uncle, and wearing it in front of the neighbors or the maternal/paternal aunt's husband...

On Speech and Conversation:

1. Refrain from allowing the child to hear sexual hums and sounds whenever the spouses gather in private for marital intercourse.

2. They must avoid talking about what's going on in their sexual life in front of the children.

3. Observing manners when using phrases and words to talk about sexual affairs in front of the children.

4. Avoid the narration of jokes, witticisms and stories related to sexual matters in front of the children.

5. Avoid telling the child the names of his sex organs which are customarily frowned upon using in public.

The Particularity of Sexual Upbringing for the Female Child

Sexual upbringing for a girl has particularity which differs from that of a boy. For, girls realize the religious age of duty before boys, and need sexual awareness, such as:

1. Preparing the discerning girl and introducing her to menstruation and its provisions, and explaining it to her in a way that allows her to –readily – welcome the menstrual cycle without fear.

2. Accustoming the discerning girl to cover herself and wear the hijab, and to understand the religious boundaries such as: the prohibition of handshaking and touching a non-

mahram, refraining from showing her beauty/ornaments in front of him or from softening her voice when speaking to him.

3. Being aware of allowing the girl to play alone with her male paternal or maternal cousins.

4. Accustom the girl and teach her the manners of proper sitting, such that she doesn't sit in a position where her legs are open...

5. Make her understand the importance of remaining distant from girls who disseminate sex tapes or phone numbers to guys, and of only befriending those who have good ethics.

6. Warn her from talking to any boy or guy who tries to get acquainted with her.

Raising the Girl to be Modest

It is narrated that Abi Abdillah ؏ said: "Modesty is composed of ten parts, nine of which are in women and one is in men."[423] For modesty is something that God ﷻ has placed in the origin of creating girls. Nonetheless, this doesn't eliminate the fact that there are internal and external factors that play a role in weakening its presence. And it falls under the mother's responsibility primarily to familiarize her with the manners and behaviors that develop the faculty of modesty within her character; for, the continuity of modesty depends on chastity.

---

[423] al-Ṣadūq, Shaykh Muḥammad ibn ʿAlī, Al-Khiṣāl, p. 438

The sense of modesty must be embedded in a girl in a way that doesn't prevent her from raising issues boldly with her mother. For, the mother has an essential role in befriending her daughter and building trust with her so that she can be her secret keeper, such that the girl doesn't need to resort to someone besides the mother – especially her colleagues or relatives who are of her age or a bit more mature.

The Precautionary Measures of Sexual Upbringing

The sexual upbringing of a child require the parents' implementation of precautionary measures that protect the child from sexual exploitation by adults, and protects him from getting exposed to any sexual assault which has a negative impact on his character.

Amongst the most important measures are:

First: Building Trust between a Child and his Parents

Parents must build a relationship with their child that is founded on trust, allocate time to listen to him on a daily basis, express positive interaction with him and encourage him to speak – in utter frankness – about anything that happens with him especially whenever he gets exposed to any sexual abuse or harassment. Parents must take care not to interact with him negatively such as threatening or blaming him which leads to him refraining from opening up to them in the future.

They must rather make him feel the trust and comfort and that they are proud of him and guide him towards defending himself against any abuser.

Second: Monitoring which Aims at Building Relationships amongst Children within the Family

Parents must monitor the way in which children play with each other. For, a child may sometimes, out of curiosity, bring a few toys – innocently – and carry out some actions and suspicious relationships that have sexual implications without being aware of its purpose, such as kissing his sister on the mouth. These issues must be taken into consideration; for, neglecting them can lead the children to carrying out suspicious sexual relationships. On the other hand, one must monitor the behavior of others towards the child. For, it may be that the older or mature son exploits the child sexually without the parents noticing it due to their trust. And narration have warned of getting carried away with this trust, such as the narration on behalf of Imām al-Ṣādiq ﷺ where he says: "Do not trust your brother all the way; for, the swiftness of getting carried away cannot be recovered."[424]

Main Concepts

The sexual upbringing of the child is considered one of the most difficult forms of upbringing, due to the misconception of sex and intense sensitivity towards the topic. Therefore, forming a correct idea of sex would be the first step in the path of being audacious in the field of sexual upbringing.

Sexual upbringing includes the (child's) guardian's undertaking of procedures that guarantee the child's protection against sexual violence. And the child's guardian must accustom him to all the methods that enable him to defend himself.

---

[424] al-Kulaynī, Shaykh Muḥammad ibn Ya'qūb, Al-Kāfī, Vol. 2, p. 672

And abandoning sexual upbringing is the same as the depriving sexual upbringing of the child, which leads the child into a wrongful sexual upbringing.

God has placed, within the human being since childhood, many natural instincts that trigger him to move and strive to attain his lively needs, including the sexual feeling which starts to appear gradually in the first stage of a child's life. One of its forms is the child's early inclination towards the opposite sex and what comes along with that such as feelings of love and jealousy...etc.

Religious texts have pointed out that the start of a child's sexual upbringing begins within the first months of his birth. It is narrated that Imām 'Alī ؏ said: "The Messenger of God ﷺ prohibited the man from copulating with his wife while their son is in the cradle watching them."

The ethical aspect of early sexual upbringing of the child constitutes one of the faces of difference and distinction from sexual upbringing in light of some philosophers and psychologists' perception in the West who want to forsake the upbringing of a child upon ethical values in regards to the sexual life, based on the excuse that it harms the wellbeing of his sexual development.

Lesson Eighteen

Social Upbringing

Lesson Objectives

By the end of this lesson, the student should:

1. Be able to define social upbringing and its objectives.
2. Understand the principles of social upbringing.
3. Get acquainted with the role of the family in social upbringing.

Preamble

Man is a social being by nature; and he cannot do without living with others and building different relationships with them. For, it is narrated that Imām al-Ṣādiq ؏ said: "No one can do without people in his life; and people are in need of one another."[425]

The preservation of human gathering requires the existence of a system of laws and values that allows for the possibility of their cohabitation. And Islam is the righteous religion for leading man's social life in all its aspects.

The Definition of Society

There are many definitions for society that were mentioned in books of sociology. In turn, we define society as a group of individuals who live in one geographical space and are connected to each other through private relationships in light of agreed-upon laws, values, customs, and traditions. Through their collaboration, they form and divide - amongst each other - roles and jobs as one interactive and organized entity which allows them to realize their goals, fulfill their needs and secure their requirements to a large extent.

Societies vary in simplicity, complexity, vastness and narrowness, in addition to the fact that there is a virtual society represented by the world of internet and social media platforms and a real world represented by different forms such as the village, city, school...etc. And the child grows within the social

---

[425] al-Kulaynī, Shaykh Muḥammad ibn Yaʿqūb, Al-Kāfī, Vol. 2, p. 635

environment that plays a role in building his character and shaping his identity.

Social Upbringing and its Objectives

Social upbringing is the process in which a child is transferred from an individual life to a social one, according to the religious system to which he belongs (Islam), and in which efforts are done to provide him with concepts and special values present in religious legislations which enable him to interact with his community members in a healthy and purposeful manner.

All societies are quite keen about the social upbringing of individuals; and all human gatherings pursue the transference of concepts, values, systems, habits, traditions and all cultural frames, lifestyles and ways of living from the generation of parents and grandparents to the generation of children and grandchildren, and its embedment within their personalities. Moreover, social upbringing aims at achieving several goals, the most important of which are:

1. Reinforcing the child's primordial tendency to blend in with the community members and share their concerns and issues.

2. Introducing the child to the social heritage (concepts, values, manners, legislations, habits, traditions) of the social environment in which he lives and accustoming him to commit to the virtuous social values and manners.

3. Interacting positively with society and participating effectively in building it, and teaching him (the child) the art of dealing with others – individuals and institutions.

In pursuit of achieving these goals, there are several principles and methods that must be observed by the nurturer during the processes of social upbringing. And the most important of these principles are:

First: Upbringing on the Basis of Faithful Brotherhood

God ﷻ says: ﴾*The faithful are indeed brothers. Therefore make peace between your brothers and be wary of God, so that you may receive [His] mercy..*﴿[426]

The Noble Qur'ān emphasized on the principle of faith-based brotherhood, as it described the brotherhood between believers as one body, such that if one of them hurts the other aches for his pain. This is the peak of humanity in social upbringing. It is narrated that Imām al-Ṣādiq ؑ said: "A believer is the brother of another believer, (they are) like one body; it a part of him aches the rest of the body aches as well. And their souls are one; and a believer's soul is more connected to the soul of God than the sunray is to the sun."[427]

Second: Upbringing Upon the Principle of Human Equality

God ﷻ says: ﴾*O mankind! Be wary of your Lord who created you from a single soul*﴿[428]

---

[426] Sūrah al-Hujurāt, verse 10

[427] al-Kulaynī, Shaykh Muḥammad ibn Ya'qūb, Al-Kāfī, Vol. 2, p. 166. For capturing the meaning of these ḥadīth, review the lesson on Jihadi Upbringing.

[428] Sūrah al-Nisā', verse 1

Therefore, the child must be raised on the following perceptions:

a. The differences between people are a natural law; they also add beauty to the canvas of society thus manifesting the divine signs. God ﷻ said: ﴿*Among His signs is the creation of the heavens and the earth, and the difference of your languages and colors. There are indeed signs in that for those who know*﴾[429]

b. The criterion for superiority amongst mankind is – according to Islam – piety. It is narrated on behalf of Jaber ibn Abdillah al-Ansari (May God be pleased with him), that he said: "Halfway through the days of Tashriq, the Messenger of God ﷺ delivered for us the farewell speech, in which he said: O' people, your Lord is one and your father is one, therefore, there is no superiority for an Arab over a non-Arab, nor for a non-Arab over an Arab, nor for a red man over a black man nor for a black man over a red man, except in piety. Indeed, the noblest amongst you in the eyes of God is the most pious."[430]

Third: Upbringing on the Principle of Social Cohesion

The term cohere refers to something joining something else,[431] and cohesion from cohesiveness implies getting together and

---

429 Sūrah al-Rūm, verse 22

430 Al-Mundhirī, Abdul 'Azīm, al-Targhīb w al –Tarhīb min al-Hadīth al-Sharīf, commented on by Mustapha Muḥammad Amāra, Beirut, Dar al-Fikr, 1988 AD, L.T', Vol. 3, p. 613

431 Ibn Zakariyyah, Mu'jam Maqayīs al-Lugha, Vol. 1, p. 131

meeting. When people cohere, it means that they have gathered in love for one another. Cohesiveness is affability and love,[432] and affability is the tranquility of the heart which opposes the feeling of fearsome loneliness.

It is narrated that the Messenger of God ﷺ said: "A believer is familiar and affable, there is no goodness in a person who isn't affable. And the best of people is the most beneficial to them."[433]

Social cohesion is one of the most essential principle in a Muslim man's life; therefore, a child must be brought up in way that allows the members of his community to delight in his presence, such that he loves for them what he loves for himself and hates for them what he hates for himself.

Fourth: Accustoming the Child to General Social Values and Manner

There are several social values and manners on which the child must be brought up socially, such as:

a. Encouraging the child to participate in general social celebrations and activities and developing his spirit of social cooperation such as rushing to carry an old woman's bags who is burdened by holding them...

---

432 Al-Fayyoumi, Ahmad ibn Muḥammad, al-Misbāḥ al-Munīr fi Gharīb al-Sharḥ al-Kabīr, Beirut, Dar al-Kutub al-'Ilmiyya, 1398 AH, L.T', Vol. 1, p. 18

433 Al-Qada'i, Muḥammad ibn Salāma, Musnad al-Shihab, Beirut, al-Risāla Institute, 1985 AD, 1st edition, Vol. 1 , p. 108

b. Developing the spirit of preventing harm from approaching the community members by, for example, putting aside a glass bottle he finds in the street...

c. Accustoming the child to sympathize with others and give charity from his own money or property.

d. Accustoming the child to respect others, and especially honor the elderly. It is narrated that Abi Abdillah ﷺ said: “He is not one of us who doesn’t honor our elderly and have mercy on our young.”[434] He ﷺ also said: “Honor your elderly.”[435]

e. Accustoming the child to the manners of the tongue, such as: preventing the tongue from disclosing a secret of gossiping and accustoming him to good speech. It is narrated that when Imām al-Ṣādiq ﷺ was asked: What are the criteria of good morality? He said: “Lower your wings (in humility), speak kindly and meet your brother with gladness.”[436]

The Family’s Role in Social Upbringing

The family is considered the first social unit in which the child opens his eyes to life; in its arms, he gains the different relationship patterns with others and the methods of positive or negative interaction with them. The parents’ role is to build the child’s social personality starting from the family, by presenting

---

434 al-Kulaynī, Shaykh Muḥammad ibn Ya‘qūb, Al-Kāfī, Vol. 2, p. 165

435 Ibid.

436 Ibid., page 103

the familial community as a small example of the values, habits, manners and behaviors which he takes with him to society.

That's why Islam emphasized on building a good family relationship with children. For, although he stressed on honoring one's parents, as was mentioned in the book of God ﷻ *‹Your Lord has decreed that you shall not worship anyone except Him, and [He has enjoined] kindness to parents. Should they reach old age at your side —one of them or both— do not say to them, 'Fie!' And do not chide them, but speak to them noble words. Lower the wing of humility to them, out of mercy, and say, 'My Lord! Have mercy on them, just as they reared me when I was [a] small [child]!'›*[437] He also highlighted the importance of the parents' support of the child in honoring them, by carrying out their role in the good upbringing of the child by adopting all of its Islamic methods, values and manners.

The Etiquettes of Interacting with Parents

Islam stipulated a set of etiquettes and behaviors which contribute to supporting the child in honoring his parents, the most important of which are:

1. Accustoming the Child to Obeying his Parents:

Accustoming the child to obeying his parents' guidance, directions and orders, and to their dissatisfaction with him in case he repeatedly rejects their requests.

It is narrated that Imām ʿAlī ؑ said: "The child has a right upon his father, and the father a right upon his son. As for the father's

---

[437] Sūrah Isrāʾ, verses 23-24

right upon his son, it is that he obeys him in everything except in the disobedience of God ﷻ..."[438]

2. Accustoming the Child to Thanking his Parents:

Accustoming the child to constantly thank his parents for all that they surround him with such as care, attention and nurturing...

It is narrated that Imām al-Ṣādiq ﵇ said: "The child has three obligations towards his parents: thanking them in all circumstances, obeying their orders and prohibitions (except in the disobedience of God) and giving them advice privately and publicly."[439]

3. Accustoming the Child to Serve his Parents:

Accustoming the child to take the initiative in serving his parents whenever he feels that they need anything or service before they request it from him, nay even if they didn't request it, such as taking the initiative to bring them water whenever he feels that they are thirsty...

It is narrated that the Messenger of God ﷺ said: "The best gain is gaining the parents, and the best service is serving them, and the best charity is that which is spent on them, and the best sleep is next to them."[440]

---

[438] Nahj al-Balāghah, p. 546

[439] Ibn Shu'ba al-Harāni, Tuhaf al-'Uqūl 'an Al al-Rasoul, p. 322

[440] al-Mirzā al-Nūrī, Mustadrak al-Wasā'il, Vol. 15, p. 201

4. Accustoming the Child to the Etiquettes of Speaking with his Parents:

Accustoming the child to speaking in a mannerly way with his parents, and in a low voice; and parents must not approve – from early childhood – of the child raising his voice over theirs or screaming in their face or cursing them even if it was in a playful or joking manner.

5. Accustoming the Child to the Etiquettes of Body Language with his Parents:

Accustoming the child to never lay hands on his parents or hit them even if it was done as a joke.

Accustoming the child (in the negative way) to refrain from frowning in his parents' face; and parents must be dissatisfied with him giving them a look of resentment, anger and hatred. It is narrated that Imām al-Ṣādiq ؏ said: "...It is considered a form of dishonoring (the parents) for a man to look at his parents in a scowling manner."[441] In parallel, he must get accustomed to looking at them with love and mercy. It is narrated that the Messenger of God ﷺ said: "A child's loving gaze towards his parents is worship."[442]

---

[441] al-Kulaynī, Shaykh Muḥammad ibn Yaʿqūb, Al-Kāfī, Vol. 2, p. 349

[442] Ibn Shuʿba, Tuḥaf al-Uqūl, p. 46

6. Accustoming the Child to the Etiquettes of Walking, Sitting and Eating with his Parents:

Accustoming the child to refrain from sitting before his parents and walking past them; he must rather walk next to them if he was young – out of fear for him – or behind them if he was discerning. He must not start eating before his parents; he must rather wait for their attendance. It is narrated that Abi al-Ḥasan Mūsā ﷺ said: "A man asked the Messenger of God ﷺ what is the father's right upon his son? He ﷺ said: He mustn't call him by his first name, or walk in front of him, or sit before him, or do something which results in someone cursing him."[443]

7. Accustoming the Child to Bring Up his Parents during his Worship:

Accustoming the child to bring up his parents during his acts of worship such gifting them the reward of prayer, fasting, charity and reading the Qur'ān ... and prayer for their wellbeing, as the Qur'ān has disciplined us upon this in various places on behalf of the Prophets: Nūḥ, Ibrāhīm and Sulaymān ﷺ.[444]

It is narrated on behalf of Mu'ammar ibn Khallaf that he said: I said to Abi al-Ḥasan al-Riḍā ﷺ: "Do I pray for my parents if they don't know the truth? He said: Pray for them and perform charity on their behalf; and if they are alive and don't know the truth then treat them politely; for the Messenger of God ﷺ said:

---

[443] al-Kulaynī, Shaykh Muḥammad ibn Ya'qūb, Al-Kāfī, Vol. 2, p. 158

[444] Sūrah Ibrāhīm, verses 40-41, and Sūrah Nūḥ, verse 28, and Sūrah al-Naml, verse 19, and Sūrah al-Aḥqaf, verse 15

God sent me with mercy, not with dishonoring (one's parents)."[445]

8. Accustoming the Child to Refrain from Grieving his Parents:

Accustoming the child to refrain from any act that causes his parents sadness.

In the Messenger of God's ﷺ will to 'Alī ؑ: "O' 'Alī, he who grieves his parents has dishonored them."[446]

Accustoming the child to refrain from any act that results in people cursing his parents, and from cursing others so they don't curse his parents.[447]

9. Accustoming Children to a Relationship of Respect and Mercy amongst One Another at Home:

One of the manifestations of familial upbringing, which falls on the parents' shoulders, is accustoming their children to the general etiquettes in regards to their relationship amongst one another at home and to respecting and honoring the eldest brother. It is narrated that the Messenger of God ﷺ said: "The eldest sibling has the position of the father."[448]

---

[445] al-Kulaynī, Shaykh Muḥammad ibn Ya'qūb, Al-Kāfī, Vol. 2, p. 159

[446] al-Ṣadūq, Shaykh Muḥammad ibn 'Alī, Man Lā Yaḥḍuruh al-Faqīh, Vol. 4, p. 372

[447] Allāmah al-Majlisī, Rawdat al-Muṭṭaqin fi Sharḥ Man Lā Yaḥḍuruh al-Faqīh, Vol. 9, p. 419

[448] Ahmad ibn al-Ḥusayn al-Bayhaqi, Shu'ab al-Imān, Beirut-Lebanon, Dar al-Kutub al-'Ilmiyya, 1410 AH – 1990 AD, 1st edition, Vol. 6, p. 210

Accustoming the children to speaking to each other, delighting in each other's presence and advising and consulting each other.

10. Accustoming the Child to Respect Whoever has a Relationship with his Parents:

Accustoming the child to be kind to his parent's kin, friends and guests who enter the family home. For, narrations have encouraged honoring the parents' friends and relatives even after their death, let alone during their lifetime!

A man asked the Messenger of God ﷺ: "O' Messenger of God, I came to pay allegiance to you for the migration (*al-Hijra*), and I left my parents crying. So, he said: return to them and make them laugh. And another said: O' Messenger of God, is there anything left of honoring one's parents after their death? He ﷺ said: "yes, praying upon them, asking forgiveness for them, keeping their promise, honoring their friends and maintaining ties with their kin."[449]

Raising the Child on Maintaining Kinship Ties

The child must be raised upon building good relationships with the extended family like his grandfather, grandmother, paternal and maternal uncles and their children... and upon developing his sense of understanding the importance and necessity of having an emotional and social connection with one's relatives to kin, and introducing the child to all his relatives to kin, and teaching him – making him feel – the effects and blessings of maintaining kinship ties; for, it: prolongs one's life, repels

---

[449] Burūjirdī, Ayatullāh Sayyid Ḥusayn, Jāmiʿ Aḥādīth al-Shīʿa, Vol. 21, p. 426, and al-Sajistāni, Sunan Abi Dawoud, Vol. 2, p. 507

poverty, increases wealth, prevents affliction, populates the house, makes the spirit kinder, refines one's work and increases his sustenance ...etc. It is narrated that Imām al-Bāqir ﵇ said: "Maintaining kinship ties refines deeds, repels affliction, increases wealth, prolongs life, increases sustenance and brings love into one's household; therefore, let him be pious towards God and maintain his kinship ties."[450]

Raising (the Child) on Being a Good Neighbor

Narrations strongly emphasized on the neighbor's right, to the extent that the sanctity of the neighbor was given the same position as the mother's. It is narrated that the Messenger of God ﷺ said: "The neighbor's sanctity upon man is like that of his mother's."[451] Therefore, a child must be brought up in accordance with the values of being a good neighbor, such as:

Introducing the child to the neighbor's rights, accustoming him to treating him (the neighbor) beautifully and kindly, preventing harm from befalling the neighbor, refraining from harming him and being patient with harm caused by the neighbor. It is narrated that Imām al-Kāẓim ﵇ said: "Being a good neighbor doesn't lie in preventing harm (from befalling the neighbor); it is in being patient with harm (caused by him)."[452]

---

[450] al-Kulaynī, Shaykh Muḥammad ibn Ya'qūb, Al-Kāfī, Vol. 2, p. 152

[451] al-Ṭabrisī, Shaykh al-Faḍl ibn al-Ḥasan, Makārim al-Akhlāq, p. 126

[452] Ibn Shu'ba al-Harāni, Tuhaf al-Uqoul, p. 406

Raising (the Child) on Friendship

One of the most prominent manifestations of a social upbringing is raising the child on friendship, since it is an important stage in his life and, in its light, a set of perceptions, values and social etiquettes are formed, in addition to the modality of cooperating, interacting and participating with others... etc.

It is narrated that Imām ʿAlī ﷺ said: "A friend is the closest of the close ones."[453]

It is the child's right to have friends; however, parents must shoulder the responsibility of consciously monitoring the patterns of the child's relationship with his friends, especially since he doesn't have the required knowledge, experience and skills to assess his friends. Therefore, the parents must raise the child on some methods, skills, values and etiquettes in regards to his relationship with his friends, such as:

1. (On the positive side): Teaching the child and training him on choosing-well his friends, and on how to deal and interact with them, in light of specific criteria and within the list of good qualities and traits, which will be clarified shortly.

2. (On the negative side): Accustoming and training him on avoiding wicked friends in light of criteria that are mentioned later on as well.

---

[453] Al-Wāsiti, 'Uyūn al-Hikam wal-Mawā'iz, p. 50

3. Constant supervision, monitoring, guidance and direction of the child towards choosing his friends, especially that Islam considers that man takes the religion of his friend. It is narrated that the Messenger of God ﷺ said: "Man takes the religion of his friend; be aware then of whom you befriend."[454]

It is important to accustom the child to testing his friends before trusting them. It is narrated that Imām 'Alī ﵇ said: "Do not trust a friend before testing him."[455]

Raising the Child on the Values of Friendship

Parents must raise their child and train him on the values of friendship that are inspired from religious texts, the most important of which are:

1. Accustoming the child to get to know some details from his friend's life, such as asking him about the name of his father, his tribe, village, place of residence, hobbies... It is narrated that Abi Abdillah ﵇ said: the Messenger of God ﷺ said: "If any of you loves his Muslim brother, let him ask him about his name, his father's name and his tribe and clan's name. For, it is his dutiful right and of sincere brotherhood to ask him that; otherwise, it is an acquaintanceship of fools."[456]

---

[454] al-Mirzā al-Nūrī, Mustadrak al-Wasā'il, Vol. 8, p. 327

[455] Al-Wāsiti, 'Uyūn al-Hikam w al-Mawa'iz, p. 522

[456] al-Kulaynī, Shaykh Muḥammad ibn Ya'qūb, Al-Kāfī, Vol. 2, p. 671

2. Accustoming him to the fact that whenever feels love towards any of his friends or brothers, he should tell him that. It is narrated that Abi Abdillah ﷺ said: the Messenger of God ﷺ said: "If any of you loves his friend or brother, let him tell him that."[457]

3. Encouraging the child to be generous and kind hearted with friends; for, this brings love. It is narrated that Imām 'Alī ﷺ said: "The reason for love is generosity."[458]

4. Encouraging the child to visit his friends in situations of good health and disease, and to stand by his friend's side whenever an affliction befalls him. It is narrated that Imām 'Alī ﷺ said: "A friend isn't a true friend until he preserves his friend in three situations: in his affliction, his absence and his death."[459]

5. Accustoming him to forgive his friend when he wrongs him and to think well of him and give the benefit of the doubt. It is narrated that Imām 'Alī ﷺ said: "Do not be conquered by ill-thoughts; for, they don't leave room for pardon between you and a friend."[460]

6. To guide his friend towards his faults and weaknesses without sarcasm or ridicule. It is narrated that Imām 'Alī ﷺ

---

[457] Al-Barqi, al-Mahāsin, Vol. 1, p. 266

[458] Al-Wāsiti, 'Uyūn al-Hikam w al-Mawā'iz, p. 282

[459] Nahj al-Balāghah, p. 494

[460] Ibn Tawous, Radi al-Din Abi al-Qāssem 'Alī ibn Mūsā ibn Ja'far ibn Muḥammad al-Ḥasani al-Ḥusaynī, Kashf al-Maḥajja li Thamarāt al-Muhja, al-Najaf al-Ashraf, al-Haidariyyah press, 1370 AH – 1950 AD, L.T', p. 167

said: "A friend is but called a friend because he is honest with you in regards to yourself and faults. Whoever does that, listen to him; for, he is the friend."[461]

7. To advise his friends in a way that makes them feel that he has good and virtuous intentions towards them. It is narrated that Imām 'Alī ﷺ said: "Offer your advice to your friend."[462]

Main Concepts

Man is a social being by nature; and he cannot do without living with others and building different relationships with them. For, it is narrated that Imām al-Ṣādiq ﷺ said: "No one can do without people in his life; and people are in need of one another.

Society is a group of individuals who live in one geographical space and are connected to each other through private relationships in light of agreed-upon laws, values, customs, and traditions. Through their collaboration, they form and divide - amongst each other - roles and jobs as one interactive and organized entity which allows them to realize their goals, fulfill their needs and secure their requirements to a large extent.

Social upbringing is the process in which a child is transferred from an individual to a social life according to the religious system to which he belongs (Islam), and in which efforts are done to provide him with concepts and special values present in

---

461 Ibid., p. 178

462 Al-Tamīmī al-Amidī, Tasnīf Ghurar al-Hikam wa Durar al-Kalim, p. 421

religious legislations which enable him to interact with his community members in a healthy and purposeful manner.

The Noble Qur'ān emphasized on the principle of faith-based brotherhood, as it described the brotherhood between believers as one body, such that if one of them hurts the other aches for his pain. This is the peak of humanity in social upbringing. It is narrated that Imām al-Ṣādiq ﷺ said: "A believer is the brother of another believer, (they are) like one body; it a part of him aches the rest of the body aches as well. And their souls are one; and a believer's soul is more connected to the soul of God than the sunray is to the sun."

The family is considered the first social unit in which the child opens his eyes to life; in its arms, he gains the different relationship patterns with others and the methods of positive or negative interaction with them. The parents' role is to build the child's social personality starting from the family, by presenting the familial community as a small example of the values, habits, manners and behaviors which he takes with him to society.

The child must be raised upon building good relationships with the extended family like his grandfather, grandmother, paternal and maternal uncles and their children... and upon developing his sense of understanding the importance and necessity of having an emotional and social connection with one's relatives to kin, and teaching him the effects and blessings of maintaining kinship ties.

One of the most prominent manifestations of a social upbringing is raising the child on friendship, since it is an important stage in his life and, in its light, a set of perceptions, values and social etiquettes are formed, in addition to the modality of cooperating, interacting and participating with others...

Lesson Nineteen

A Worship-based Upbringing of a Child

Lesson Objectives

By the end of this lesson, the student should:

1. Understand the meaning of worship-based upbringing.
2. Mention the general educational principles of worship-based upbringing.
3. Determine the methods of a worship-based upbringing.

Raising the Child on Learning Jurisprudential Religious Matters

Raising a child – especially the discerning child – from a jurisprudential point of view requires teaching him the religious legislative rulings in way that suits his age stage, and accustoming him to what must be implemented from these rulings and averting him from what needs to be avoided - especially the great sins.

It is mentioned, in the exegesis that is attributed to Imām Ḥasan al-ʿAskarī, that God says: "... and I will adorn his parents with a garment that outweighs this world and everything it encompasses ... then it is said (to them): this is for teaching your child the Qur'ān, and for making him insightful in the religion of Islam, and training him on loving Muḥammad, the Messenger of God, and Imām ʿAlī, the vicegerent of God, and for teaching him their jurisprudential teachings..."[463]

Teaching the child the jurisprudential rulings of religion in a way that enables him to distinguish the permissible from the forbidden and the modality of purity and impurity... etc. has been emphasized by Islam; and the Messenger of God warned from parents who neglect the jurisprudential upbringing of their children. It is narrated that he looked at some children and said: "Woe to the children of the end of time for their parents. Someone said: O' Messenger of God, for their polytheist parents? He said: No, for their faithful parents; as they do not teach them any of the obligations, and if they (the

---

[463] The exegesis attributed to Imām al-ʿAskarī, the sacred city of Qom, verified and published by the school of Imām al-Mahdī, 1409 AH, 1st edition, p. 450, and al-Majlisī, al-ʿAllāma Muḥammad Bāqir, Biḥār al-Anwār, Vol. 7, p. 306

children) learned they would prevent them (from practicing), and they get contented with them for a trivial offering of this world. Thus, I disavow myself from them and they from me."[464]

In this lesson, we will exclusively cover worship-based upbringing, as one of the fields of jurisprudential upbringing.

Worship-based Upbringing

Worship-based upbringing requires, from the parents, accustoming the child to perform acts of worship as ordered by God ﷻ; in fact, one of the most important rights of the child upon his parents is supporting him in obeying God ﷻ and being submissive towards him.

It is narrated that Imām ʿAlī ibn al-Ḥusayn Zayn al-ʿĀbidīn ﵇ said: "As for your child's right, it is to know that he is from you, and an addition to you in this fleeting world with – both – his goodness and evil, and that you are responsible for what you have entrusted to him of good manners and indication towards God ﷻ and for your support in obeying Him..."[465]

And here, the nurturer encounters a set of questions: Isn't a child's mind incapable of comprehending the meaning of worship? Then, how can we order him to perform it? At what age do we start familiarizing a child to worship? And what are the acts of worship that we must accustom the child to performing?

---

464 al-Mirzā al-Nūrī, Mustadrak al-Wasāʾil, Vol. 15, p. 164, Burūjirdī, Ayatullāh Sayyid Ḥusayn, Jāmiʿ Aḥādīth al-Shīʿa, Vol. 21, p. 408

465 al-Ṣadūq, Shaykh Muḥammad ibn ʿAlī, Man Lā Yaḥḍuruh al-Faqīh, Vol. 2, p. 622

The answer to these questions will be clarified through raising several points:

The Recommendation of the Gradual Training of a Child on Worship

Man, naturally, moves from a state to another in a gradual manner. The process of change doesn't happen overnight; it rather needs time and to be provided to the child in stages. And since the mandatory duties and religious acts of worship are plentiful and various, and are abided by the child - all at once - when he reaches the religious age of puberty, the parents must – then – teach them to the child before this age so that we do not impose them on him all so suddenly and without any introduction – the thing that may create within him a sense of repulsion which will instill thereof feelings of loneliness, confinement and hardship.

For, prior training on acts of worship leads a person to delight in matters of worship with time. Islam has encouraged the practice of the child and his training on acts of worship such as prayer, fasting, charity and pilgrimage... so that he can benefit from them, when he reaches the religious age.

It is narrated that in his will to his son, the wise Luqman said: "O' son, if you are disciplined at a young age, it will benefit you in your old age."[466]

For, the fact that the mandatory duty isn't yet directed to the child doesn't necessarily coincide with the absence of

---

[466] Al-Qommi, 'Alī ibn Ibrahīm, Tafsīr al-Qommi, corrected by Tayyib al-Mūsāwi al-Jaza'erī, Qom, Dar al-Kitāb, 1404 AH, 3rd edition, Vol. 2, p. 164

accustoming him to the duties and training him on them; there, rather, is customary and rational accord in the opposite.

The judge Nu'man says: "Children are not under duty; however, the Imāms ﷺ were ordered in this regard as a matter of discipline in order to get accustomed to duty and for the child to grow upon it until he reaches the stage in which it becomes mandatory for him; thus, he will have been trained on it, delighted in it and familiarized himself with his obligations. This will be better for him so that he doesn't have to waste any time."[467]

That's why jurists have initiated a ruling that recommends the training of the child on worship.

Al-Mirza al-Qommi said: "It is recommended to train the boy or girl on acts of worship – as a recommended act. This aims at encouraging him to (perform acts of) worship before puberty so that he can familiarize himself with them and be able to perform them, which facilitates the process for him after puberty and allows him to grow upon these obligatory acts of worship. It (practice/*tamrin*) is derived from *marana*, i.e. habit, or from their saying: his hand got in the habit of working, thus it got tough. And the origin (in this ruling) is that it is recommended, which is not problematic."[468]

---

467 Al-Maghribi, al-Nu'mān ibn Muḥammad, Da'āem al-Islām, Vol. 1, p. 194

468 Al-Qommi, Abu al-Qāssem, Ghana'em al-Ayyām fi Masā'il al-Halāl w al-Harām, verified by Abbās Tabriziān, the publishing center related to the office of Islamic press, 1417 AH, 1st edition, p. 282

The Importance of Worship before the Age of Discernment

The child, in the stage of the second seven years, develops the ability to distinguish between the good and the bad. And jurists have agreed unanimously, based on religious texts, that a child cannot get accustomed to acts of worship before he enters into the age of discernment, which is seven. For at this age, the child develops the potential which allows him to gradually understand the meaning and objectives of worship and feel its sentimental value in his life in a way that suits his age stage. And practical experiences in the lives of religious children indicate this.

It is narrated that Imām Muḥammad ibn 'Alī al-Bāqir ﷺ said: "Boys are ordered to pray once they comprehend it (the prayer) and to fast once they endure it. Someone said to him: "And when is that?" He replied: "When they become six years of age.""[469]

The intended meaning behind intellect here is the capacity to distinguish the good from the bad, as clarified.

'Allāma al-Hilli says: "When a child reaches the age of seven, his father must teach him (the rulings of) purity and prayer, communal prayer and its attendance, so he gets accustomed to

---

[469] Al-Maghribi, al-Nu'mān ibn Muḥammad, Da'āe'm al-Islam, Vol. 1, p. 194

it; for, this is the age at which the child develops discernment in regards to worship..."[470]

Training the Child on Religious Acts of Worship

There are two perspectives in regards to training the child on religious worship before the age of puberty[471]:

1. The first perspective (apparent-practicing worship): Training a child on worship is quite important for familiarizing him with receiving the age of duty delightfully. This training is solely a process of practice, in the sense that the child doesn't receive any reward for performing an act of worship such as prayer, because the speech isn't addressed to the child but rather to his guardians in regards to ordering him to pray and fast before reaching puberty. And due to the fact that the Legislator ordered the guardians to train their children, the reward of this practice goes to the parents for carrying out a recommended act.

2. The second perspective (real-religious worship): It considers that in addition to the first aspect, the worship of a discerning child is also religious, in the sense that it is performed in obedience (to God),such that it deserves to be

---

[470] al-Ḥillī, al-'Allāma al-Ḥasan ibn Yūsuf, Tathkirat al-Fuqahā', Qom, Institute of Al al-Bayt li 'Ihya' al-Turāth, 1414 AH, 1st edition, Vol. 4, p. 335, and al-'Amili, Muḥammad ibn Jamāl al-Din Makki, al-Bayan, Qom, Majma' al-Thakhā'er al-Islāmiyya, L.T, stone edition, p. 153

[471] For details on this matter, review: al-Bujnuwardi, al-Qawā'id al-Fiqhiyya, Vol. 4, p. 109 and what follows.

rewarded for[472]. Therefore, directing an order (to someone) to order something is considered as an ordering of that thing itself, as proven by the science of the principles of jurisprudence. For, ordering the child's guardian to order the child to perform worship is an order of worship to the child; since the worship that is performed by the child is the subject of the legislator's order. The divine speech includes the discerning child; it's just that the absence of duty withholds the sense of obligation from it. Therefore, the thing that is withheld from the child is obligation and not the origin of legislation[473]; thus, for him, obligations will be recommendations and forbidden acts will be disapproved acts, in the sense that the dutiful rulings for a child are three: recommended, disapproved and permissible. Accordingly, a child performs an act of worship with the intention of performing a recommended act, and it is valid; and he is granted the reward of prayer or fasting or others. Narrative texts have encouraged the accustoming of the child to the worshipping acts of prayer and fasting, such as:

It is narrated that Abi Abdillah said, on behalf of his father al-Bāqir: "We order our sons to pray when they reach the age of five; therefore, order your sons to pray when they reach the age of five. And we order our boys to fast when they reach the age of seven as much as they endure to fast of the day - be it until mid-day or more or less – and if thirst and hunger[474] take over they break their fast, until they get accustomed to and

[472] al-Ḥillī, al-'Allāma al-Ḥasan ibn Yūsuf, Taḥrīr al-Aḥkām, Vol. 1, p. 485

[473] Review: al-Ghurawi, al-Tanqīḥ fi Sharḥ al-'Urwa al-Wuthqa, Chapter of al-Tahāra, Vol. 2, p. 153

[474] Al-Gharth means hunger.

endure fasting. Therefore, order your sons to fast when they reach the age of nine as much as they can fast during the day, and if thirst and hunger take over they break their fast."[475]

It is worthy to note that mentioning prayer and fasting serves as a list of examples rather than exclusivities. Therefore, the child must practice and be trained on other acts of worship as well. One of the testaments of the unexclusiveness of prayer and fasting is what was mentioned in narrations in regards to raising the child on giving charity with the intention of proximity from God ﷻ.

It is narrated on behalf of Muḥammad ibn Amr ibn Yazid, that Imām al-Riḍā ﵇ said: "... Order the boy to give charity of breadcrumbs, money and an object – even if it be little – with his hands; for, everything that is done for the sake of God – even in little amounts and as long as the intention in sincere – is great."[476]

The Principles of a Worship-based Upbringing

There are numerous general principles for upbringing that must be observed in the worship-based upbringing; they can be concluded from narrations:

First: Observing the principle of the gradual accustoming of the child to worship. For, when he is seven he gets accustomed to prayer. Then, when he is nine he gets accustomed to fasting.

[475] al-Kulaynī, Shaykh Muḥammad ibn Ya'qūb, Al-Kāfī, Vol. 3, p. 409

[476] Ibid., Vol. 4, p. 4. The context of the narration will be elaborated in the lesson of proper upbringing.

This applies to males; as for females, and due to the fact that her age of puberty is nine, it thus becomes obligatory for her.

Second: Observing the principle of capacity and refraining from burdening the child at this age what he cannot endure. He must rather be given the duty of performing worship according to his capacity. Imām al-Ṣādiq ﷺ was asked about the fasting of a child; Samā'a said: I asked him about the child, when does he fast? Imām al-Ṣādiq ﷺ said: "When he is strong enough to fast."[477]

Third: Observing the principle of sympathy and kindness so that the child doesn't repel against religion and hate worship and loathe it, especially that the nature of the child is inclined towards play, fun, luxury and comfort.

It is narrated that Abi Jā'far ﷺ said: "The Messenger of God ﷺ said: This religion is solid, so delve into it gently and do not make God's worship loathsome in the eyes of his servants, such that you become like a lonely rider who hasn't done any travel nor maintained any support."[478]

Fourth: Observing the principle of refraining from taking things lightly and indifferently, especially in prayer, such that he must order him to perform it. As for fasting, there's a margin for pardon in regards to the budding child, such that he can fast only half a day for example. Moreover, accustoming the child to prayer starts at the age of seven, which is, before accustoming him to fasting at the age of nine.

---

477 al-Kulaynī, Shaykh Muḥammad ibn Ya'qūb, Al-Kāfī, Vol. 4, p. 125

478 Ibid., Vol. 2, p. 86

The Methods of a Worship-based Upbringing

There are several methods that can be adopted by the nurturer in training the child and accustoming him to worship, such as:

First: the method of the behavioral example, whereby the nurturer carries out the acts of worship in front of the child to serve as an example, such as praying, fasting and performing supplication in front of the child. The Messenger of God ﷺ used this method with Imām al-Ḥusayn ؑ. It is narrated that Abi Abdillah ؑ said: "The Messenger of God ﷺ was praying, and next to him was Imām al-Ḥusayn ibn 'Alī ؑ. The Messenger of God ﷺ performed Takbir, yet Imām al-Ḥusayn ؑ didn't perform Takbir. Then the Messenger of God ﷺ performed Takbir, yet Imām al-Ḥusayn ؑ didn't. Then the Messenger of God ﷺ kept performing Takbir and Imām al-Ḥusayn ؑ kept working on his Takbir but he didn't perform it until the seventh Takbir. Then, Imām al-Ḥusayn ؑ performed the seventh Takbir. Then, Abu Abdillah ؑ said: Thus, it became a Sunnah."[479]

Second: The method of teaching through interactive participation, in the sense that the nurturer participates with the child in matters of worship; for example, he teaches him prayer and prays with him jointly...etc.

Third: The method of encouragement through peers, where he creates amongst them an environment of positive competition. This can happen by entering the child into an environment that takes care of worshipping acts in schools or scouts associations...

---

[479] al-Ṭūsī, Shaykh Muḥammad ibn al-Ḥasan, Tahdhīb al-Ahkām fī Sharh al-Muqni'ah, Vol. 2, p. 67

Fourth: Taking the discerning child to the mosque so he can participate in the communal prayer or supplication... whereby he gets encouraged to pray in front of a crowd.

Fifth: Adopting the method of the gift, attraction towards the reward in the Hereafter and to that prepared for him by God ﷻ.

Sixth: Adopting the method of the threat of punishment; for, upbringing requires sometimes the instillment of fear as it does of desire.

Main Concepts

Raising a child – especially the discerning child – from a jurisprudential point of view requires teaching him the religious legislative rulings in way that suits his age stage, and accustoming him to what must be implemented from these rulings and averting him from what needs to be avoided - especially the great sins.

Worship-based upbringing requires, from the parents, accustoming the child to perform acts of worship as ordered by God ﷻ; in fact, one of the most important rights of the child upon his parents is supporting him in obeying God ﷻ and being submissive towards him.

Man, naturally, moves from a state to another in a gradual manner. The process of change doesn't happen overnight; it rather needs time and to be provided to the child in stages. And since the mandatory duties and religious acts of worship are plentiful and various, and are abided by the child - all at once - when he reaches the religious age of puberty, the parents must – then – teach them to the child before this age so that we do not impose them on him all so suddenly and without any introduction – the thing that may create within him a sense of repulsion which will instill thereof feelings of loneliness, confinement and hardship.

The child, in the stage of the second seven years, develops the ability to distinguish between the good and the bad. And jurists have agreed unanimously, based on religious texts, that a child cannot get trained on acts of worship before he enters into the age of discernment. It can only be done afterwards.

The mentioning of prayer and fasting serves as a list of examples rather than exclusivities. Therefore, the child must practice and be trained on other acts of worship as well. One of the testaments of the unexclusiveness of prayer and fasting is what was mentioned in narrations in regards to raising the child on giving charity with the intention of proximity from God ﷻ.

There are numerous general principles for upbringing that must be observed in the worship-based upbringing; they can be concluded from narrations, such as: the behavioral method, the interactive participation, the method of the gift and the adoption of the method of instilling fear and desire.

Lesson Twenty

Raising Children through Play

Lesson Objectives

By the end of this lesson, the student should:

1. Define the concept of play and upbringing though play.
2. Realize the advantages and disadvantages of electronic games.
3. Get acquainted with the most important effects of upbringing through play.

Preamble

God ﷻ placed numerous primordial tendencies within the child, the most prominent of which is the intense desire for play and amusement. We find him, from childhood, inclined towards these primordial movements such as dancing, swaying and making funny moves. Some people may think that these moves lack importance and are purposeless; for, play is used in the sense of amusement, joking and absurdity. And it was used in this context in several verses[480], such as His ﷻ saying: ﴿*Those who took their religion for diversion and play*﴾[481], which is the opposite of seriousness; for, it is said: "Person X played, referring to the fact that he didn't have the right intention while doing so."[482]

Nonetheless, things are completely different in regards to children during the stage of their first seven years of age, where play has a fundamental role in shaping the child's identity in various physical, psychological and mental aspects – as will be clarified later.

The Terminological Meaning of Play

Play was given, by educational and psychological terminologies, several definitions, one of which is that it is "a guided activity carried out by children in order to develop their behavior and

---

[480] Sūrah al-Tawba, verse 65, Sūrah al-An'ām, verse 70, Sūrah al-Zukhruf, verse 83, Sūrah Muḥammad, verse 36, Sūrah al-Dukhān, verse 38, Sūrah al-Ankabout, verse 64

[481] Sūrah al-A'rāf, verse 51

[482] Al-Rāghib al-Asfahānī, al-Mufradāt fi Gharīb al-Qur'ān, p. 450

mental, physical and sentimental capacities, and it simultaneously achieves pleasure, amusement and a method of learning. It is the use of activities in pursuit of acquiring knowledge, familiarizing learning principles to children and expanding their cognitive horizons."[483]

Raising through Play

The process of upbringing through play demands that the nurturer prepares a supportive environment for the child to play in, prepares toys that are appropriate to his age stage and plays with him in a purposeful manner in which he invests his instincts to teach him and discipline him on some behaviors. Upbringing through play includes four aspects:

First: Preparing the environment that supports the child in carrying out his pleasurable activities freely and providing him with the necessary tools for playing.

Second: Investing game-based activities in teaching the child some concepts and principles, which is known as learning through play.

Third: Using play in giving the child a set of values and training him on some habits and good manners.

Fourth: Using play in the process of healing the child from some negative psychological reactions and behavioral disorders

[483] Al-Hila, Muḥammad Mahmoud, al-Al'āb al-Tarbawiyya wa Tatbiqāt Intājuha Psycholojiyyan wa Ta'limiyyan wa 'Amaliyyan, Amman, Dar al-Masīra, 2003 AD, 2nd edition, p. 225

such as fear and aggression, which is known as therapy through play.

The parents and nurturers must benefit from the method of playing in order to attract the child to perform some desired behaviors from early childhood[484], such as: using the game method to persuade him to eat, or get the treatment and take the medication. For example, if a child's body temperature rises and he doesn't want to put the piece of cloth that is soaked in cold water on his forehead, the father or mother can say to him: we will play the game of the doctor and the patient where we exchange roles. You will be the doctor and put the piece of cloth on me, then you will be the patient and I will put the piece of cloth on you...etc.

The same applies to any other activity from which the child is repelled. The nurturer will, thus, resort to attracting him towards it and eliminating repulsion thereof through play, especially if we realize the positive impact of play in shaping the child's identity and personality.

The Effects of Play on Building the Child's Identity

Psychologists and educators spoke of several effects for play on building the child's personality and shaping his identity. We cannot highlight them all; so, we will only mention a few effects:[485]

---

484 Review: al-Biblāwi, Viola, al-Usus al-Nafsiyya w al-Ijtimā'iyya li Binā' al-Manāhij fi Riyād al-Atfāl fi al-Watan al-Arabi, Tunis, The Arabian Organization for Education and Culture, 1986 AD, L.T', p. 128

485 For more details, review: al-'Anānī, Hanan Abdul Hamīd, al-La'b 'ind al-Atfāl, Amman, Dar al-Fikr, 2014 AD, 9th edition.

The Most Important Physical and Kinesthetic Effects:

Play contributes to the healthy physical and kinesthetic development of the child because it fulfills the following characteristics:

1. Strengthening the body muscles,
2. Learning kinesthetic skills such as jumping, climbing, running, hanging, and crawling...
3. The capacity of regulating and controlling the organs of the body and harmonizing its movements in a balanced way.
4. Progress in rhythmic movements and body language.

The Most Important Mental and Intellectual Effects:

1. Developing the faculty of sensory observation and gaining knowledge of the characteristics of things and their nature in terms of color, shape and size...
2. Developing intelligence, remembering, attention and focus... and the ability to compare between things.
3. Developing (the skill of) the search for solutions to the problems the child encounters during play, and developing mental flexibility by blending thoughts in a new way.
4. Developing the sense of innovation and creativity by having the child create his own toys and assemble them...

The Most Important Psychological and Sentimental Effects:

1. The feeling of pleasure, enjoyment, joy, liveliness, proficiency and self-esteem.
2. Self-reliance, self-confidence and managing his own affairs by himself.
3. Investing leisure without feeling annoyed, bored or worn out.
4. Balanced reactions, and reducing negative reactions such as nervousness, instability and anxiety.
5. Accepting defeat and failure with a good spirit.

The Most Important Social Effects:

1. Developing the skills of social communication, eliminating isolation and self-seclusion, and interacting positively with other children.
2. Organization, commitment to order and abiding by rules.
3. Competing and striving for success.
4. Developing the sense of possessiveness and learning how to preserve his things and property.
5. Strengthening friendship ties.

The Most Important Linguistic Effects:

1. Developing the ability to express visions and feelings and getting rid of speech defects.

2. Developing the ability of forming useful sentences and having a conversation.

3. Learning handwriting and writing.

Providing the Child with his Own Play-related Material

The parents must provide the gaming material that will be used (by the child) during his mobile activity. And they must be attentive to several points, the most important of which are:

1. Giving the child the toy as a gift, and making him feel that way; for, gifts increase affability, love and the emotional connection between the parents and child.[486]

2. Involving the child in the process of purchasing his own toys.[487]

3. Picking out attractive games that encourage the child and motivate him to be active and move, and which meet the conditions of safety and security.

4. Averting the child from games that are not in line with Islamic values, such as gambling games.

---

[486] Review the lesson: Raising by Love

[487] Review the lesson: Economic Upbringing

Is Play Specific to the First Seven Years?

The narrations of the Prophet ﷺ and Ahl al-Bayt عليهم السلام emphasized on the necessity of play during the first seven-year stage of a child's life. It is narrated that Abi Abdillah عليه السلام said: "Let your son play for seven years, get disciplined in seven years and accompany him for seven years. Thus he will succeed; otherwise, no good lies within him."[488]

The first seven years were specialized for play due to its prevalence at this stage; however, play doesn't end with closing this stage. It rather remains as a need for the child – while emphasizing still on the fact that the second seven-year stage is for scholastic education and training the child on worship-related matters such as prayer, fasting...etc., such that discipline prevails over this stage without having to deny the child's need for play in this position.

The Prophet Yūsuf عليه السلام, though he was nine years old when his brothers abandoned him in the depths of a well, the Qur'ān tells us a story – on behalf of his brothers when they spoke to their father: *﴾Let him go with us tomorrow so that he may eat lots of fruits and play, and we will indeed take [good] care of him﴿*[489] So, the Prophet Ya'qūb sent him with them to play. Moreover, he عليه السلام mentioned, in the letter he sent to the honored man of

---

[488] al-Ṣadūq, Shaykh Muḥammad ibn 'Alī, Man Lā Yaḥḍuruh al-Faqīh, Vol. 3, p. 492

[489] Sūrah Yūsuf, verse 12. Rat': to eat and drink luxuriously in springtime. Al-Farahd, al-'Ayn, Vol. 2, p. 67, the letters ra, ta and 'a are one word that implies vastness in food. Ibn Zakariyya, Mu'jam Maqāyīs al-Lugha, Vol. 2, p. 486. And it is said: We went out for indulgence and play, Ibn Manzour, Lisān al-'Arab, Vol. 8, p. 112.

Egypt, which was mentioned in a narration on behalf of Imām al-Bāqir ☙: "I had a child whom I named Yūsuf, and he was my joy amongst my children, the comfort of my eyes and the fruit of my heart; and his half-brothers asked me to send him with them for indulgence and play, so I sent him with them in the early morning..."[490]

The Parents' Responsibilities in Regards to Securing a Supportive Environment in which a Child Can Play

Parents must strive to secure a supportive environment for the child in which he can play freely and carry out his kinesthetic activity, especially the child who lives in the city and doesn't have a space to play in as opposed to the village where there is a more expansive room for that. Therefore, parents – who are financially comfortable – must provide the child with a specific room for play. And if there isn't enough space, then parents can arrange the living room in a special way that allows the child to play, which they can later rearrange whenever guests come to visit. Parents mustn't feel embarrassed and shy of the chaos in this or that room, they should rather feel proud of their conduct in front of people and clarify for them the fact that the healthy development of our child and yours is the fundamental element that should take precedence over any other concern.

Some parents may resort to prohibiting their children from playing due to their excessive worry about them; they must take into account that this inflicts psychological harm on the child. It is important to take precautions and be alert – it is required and it isn't excessive fear. Some parents may prohibit their children

---

490 al-ʿAyyāshī, Muḥammad ibn Masʿūd, Tafsīr al-ʿAyyāshī, Vol. 2, p. 190

from playing lest his body and clothes get dirty especially in villages; nonetheless, they overlook the fact that –by doing that – they have managed to suppress his talents, inhibit his tendencies from blooming and prospering, and deny him his right to play which has a negative impact on his identity and the shaping of his character.

It is worthy to note that giving a child a margin of freedom to move in play doesn't mean inattention to his activity and movement, and to monitoring the types of games he plays and its negative or positive impact on his behavior. However, this monitoring must be subtle so that we don't restrict his movement. Therefore, they should be attentive that playing doesn't lead to the negligence of other aspects such as food, for example, or that he doesn't eat his food quickly without chewing it well for instance, or that he doesn't take care of the sufficient hours of sleep. It is important that parents have their children at home by nightfall.

Moreover, playing must not be taken on the account of – the child – neglecting school assignments. And at the same time, he must not be deprived of playing due to exhausting him with studies, the thing that may gradually lead to his repulsion from knowledge which he finds to be the obstacle standing in between himself and his primordial inclination towards playing.

The Importance of Playing with the Child

Narrations emphasize on the importance of parents' participation in playing with their children due to its impact on satiating their emotional needs and making them feel the affability and delight in their relationship with their parents.

That's why playing with the child is considered a form of raising by love, because "when older people join the child in play and his love for it, they validate for him what he is doing and the meaning it carries."[491]

Parents must shrink themselves until they reach the position of a little kid when playing with him; and they must play with him according to his level – away from parental superiority. Narrations refer to this as 'being childish'. It is narrated that the Noble Prophet ﷺ said: "Let he who has a child act childishly with him."[492]

Furthermore, playing with the child has a fundamental role in discovering his character especially that the parental stature fades away during childish play with the child, which allows the latter to behave naturally and impulsively, and manifests his strong and weak points. Thus, parents will aim at strengthening the positive aspects and treating the disorders and negative aspects.

The Prophet's ﷺ Playfulness with al-Ḥasanein عليهما السلام

Islam doesn't give an order except that the Prophet ﷺ and his household عليهم السلام have embodied it in a practical way. For, it was of the Noble Prophet's ﷺ biography to play with his sons al-Ḥasan and al-Ḥusayn عليهما السلام, in pursuit of showing them his love for them and manifesting – to the nation – their great bountifulness and eminent position in the eye of God ﷻ. It is narrated that Jaber ibn Abdillah al-Ansari said: "I entered to see the Prophet ﷺ

---

491 Psychologia al-La'b, p. 267

492 Check out al-Tarīhī, Majma' al-Bahrain, Vol. 1, p. 260

walking on all four, and on his back were al-Ḥasan and al-Ḥusayn, and he was saying: the best of camels is yours, and the best of the righteous people are you two."[493]

There's a phenomenon that is recurrently carried out by children. It's that they ride and climb their parent's backs during prayer. Parents mustn't violate the child and push him strongly off their backs; they must rather allow him to do that and he will gradually abandon this habit with time. These were the manners of the Messenger of God ﷺ with al-Ḥasanein عليهما السلام.

It is narrated that Abi Sa'īd al-Khidrī said: "Imām al-Ḥasan عليه السلام approached the Messenger of God ﷺ as he was prostrating and climbed his back; so the Messenger of God held him by his hand until he stood up, then he performed Ruku so he got off his back; and when he got off he sent him away so he left."[494]

Main Concepts

God ﷻ placed numerous primordial tendencies within the child, the most prominent of which is the intense desire for play and amusement. We find him, from childhood, inclined towards these primordial movements such as dancing, swaying and making funny moves. Some people may think that these moves lack importance and are purposeless. Nonetheless, things

---

493 Al-Kūfi, Muḥammad ibn Sulaymān, Manāqib al-Imām 'Alī عليه السلام, verified by Muḥammad Bāqir al-Mahmoudi, the sacred Qom, Majma' Ihyā' al-Thaqāfa al-Islamiyya, 1412AH, 2st edition, Vol. 2, p. 247 and p. 269, and Ibn al-Maghazli, 'Alī ibn Muḥammad, 'Alī Abī Ṭālib, L.M, Intisharāt Sibt al-Nabi, 1426 AH, 1st edition, p. 304

494 Al-Haithamī, 'Alī ibn Abi Bakr, Majma' al-Zawā'id wa Manba' al-Fawā'id, Beirut, Dar al-Kutub al-Ilmiyya, 1408 AH – 1988 AD, Vol. 9, p. 175

are completely different in regards to children during the stage of their first seven years of age, where play has a fundamental role in shaping the child's identity in various physical, psychological and mental aspects.

Play was given, by educational and psychological terminologies, several definitions, one of which is that it is "a guided activity carried out by children in order to develop their behavior and mental, physical and sentimental capacities, and it simultaneously achieves pleasure, amusement and a method of learning. It is the use of activities in pursuit of acquiring knowledge, familiarizing learning principles to children and expanding their cognitive horizons."

Psychologists and educators spoke of the several effects play has on building the child's personality and shaping his identity, which include the physical, kinesthetic, mental, intellectual, psychological and sentimental... effects.

The first seven years were specialized for play due to its prevalence at this stage; however, play doesn't end with closing this stage. It rather remains as a need for the child – while emphasizing still on the fact that the second seven-year stage is for scholastic education and training the child on worship-related matters such as prayer, fasting...etc., such that discipline prevails over this stage without having to deny the child's need for play in this position.

Narrations emphasize on the importance of parents' participation in playing with their children due to its impact on satiating their emotional needs and making them feel the affability and delight in their relationship with their parents. That's why playing with the child is considered a form of raising by love, because "when older people join the child in play and his love for it, they validate for him what he is doing and the meaning it carries."

It was of the Noble Prophet's ﷺ biography to play with his sons al-Ḥasan and al-Ḥusayn ؏, in pursuit of showing them his love for them and manifesting – to the nation – their great bountifulness and eminent position in the eye of God ﷻ. It is narrated that Jāber ibn Abdillah al-Ansāri said: "I entered to see the Prophet ﷺ walking on all four, and on his back were al-Ḥasan and al-Ḥusayn, and he was saying: the best of camels is yours, and the best of the righteous people are you two."

www.ingramcontent.com/pod-product-compliance
Lightning Source LLC
Chambersburg PA
CBHW061136120626
46546CB00005B/1802
* 9 7 8 1 9 5 6 2 7 6 1 5 2 *